journeys in natural dyeing

TECHNIQUES FOR CREATING
COLOR AT HOME

KRISTINE VEJAR AND
ADRIENNE RODRIGUEZ

WITH SARAH OLLIKKALA JONES

PHOTOGRAPHY BY SARA REMINGTON
STYLING BY ALESSANDRA MORTOLA

abrams, new york

To Michelle Brauner, with
all the love in our hearts.

Editor: Meredith A. Clark
Designer: Brooke Reynolds
for inchmark
Production Manager:
Kathleen Gaffney

Library of Congress
Control Number:
2020931034

ISBN: 978-1-4197-4707-6
eISBN: 978-1-68335-989-0

Printed and bound in China

Permission was received
and compensation given to
individuals photographed
and included in this book
with the understanding of
the context in which they
are being published.

The material contained in
this book is presented only
for informational and
artistic purposes. If you use
plants or flowers you may
have found in the wild, for
any of the projects included
in this book, you are doing
so at your own risk. The
authors have made every
effort to provide well
researched, sufficient and
up-to-date information;
however, we also urge
caution in the use of this
information. The publisher
and authors accept no
responsibility or liability
for any errors, omissions,
or misrepresentations
expressed or implied,
contained herein, or for
any accidents, harmful
reactions or any other
specific reactions, injuries,
loss, legal consequences, or
incidental or consequential
damages suffered or
incurred by any reader of
this book. Readers should
seek health and safety
advice from physicians and
safety professionals.

Abrams books are available
at special discounts when
purchased in quantity for
premiums and promotions
as well as fundraising or
educational use. Special
editions can also be created
to specification. For details,
contact specialsales@
abramsbooks.com or the
address below.

Abrams® is a registered
trademark of Harry N.
Abrams, Inc.

ABRAMS The Art of Books
195 Broadway, New York, NY 10007
abramsbooks.com

10 9 8 7 6 5 4 3 2 1

A stack of naturally dyed batik fabrics created by the Java-based cooperative Batik Tulis Kebon Indah

contents

introduction

SIMILAR TO FOOD, COOKING, AND THE ACT of sharing a meal, our relationship to textiles, growing the materials used to make them, creating them, and using them, is a core tenet of our human experience. Like making and eating food, creating textiles cultivates connection, belonging, community, and friendships among people who might have never otherwise met. In the world of textiles, natural dyeing is the closest we come to the act of cooking. Natural dyers are the chefs of the textile world and can be found internationally.

For this book, we had the great privilege of visiting natural dyers from four countries—Iceland, Mexico, Indonesia, and Japan—who create textiles that are examples of where and when natural dyes, materials, and the resulting textiles evoke beauty, a connection to their local environment, and mastery of skill. Throughout this process, we gained insight as to how people living in four very different types of landscapes, create color from locally grown and foraged materials, and why this practice is meaningful to them. It became clear: Regardless of where one lives, as long as plants grow, creating color naturally is possible.

Inspired by what we witnessed, we furthered our commitment to understanding our natural dyes. We created an organized course of study to document the dyes and colors achieved using locally grown and foraged plants and mushrooms. And we began to analyze how they compare to one another in terms of hue and saturation, as well as how to widen this locally sourced palette through combining dyes, shifting pH, and adding iron, through textile design, and by adding patterns via wax and rice paste.

Using locally sourced dyes has become a way for us to honor nature on a daily basis and propels us to continually dive deeper into our natural-dyeing practice, learn more about our bioregion, and become better dyers and designers. Being in nature, and understanding it more, has greatly awakened our sense of gratitude for where we live and continues to enrich our care and respect for the earth.

Our goal in this book is to introduce you to those we met while traveling, honor their knowledge and practices, provide you with the results of our study, and teach you techniques to create a wide spectrum of color using your own locally sourced dyes. We hope that through reading this book you learn more about the legacy of natural dyeing around the world, gain a greater understanding of the natural world right outside your front door, embrace your local environment as a place to source color, meet others in your community who work with the environment, and celebrate and honor nature through the act of natural dyeing.

—KRISTINE AND ADRIENNE

Kristine and Adrienne working on their tiny indigo farm.

before you begin

STEPS IN THE DYEING PROCESS

Generally, this is the process one follows when using natural dyes. This will give you a sense of the overall stages and the timing. By following these steps, you will achieve the longest-lasting color possible for the dye you are using.

Stage 1: Weighing and Preparation. The goods to be dyed—fabric or yarn, for example—are weighed so the proper amount of dye, water, and associated substances are used during the dyeing process. Then the goods must be prepared and pre-wet before proceeding. Learn more about this stage starting on page 216.

Stage 2: Scouring. Scouring, or prewashing, removes any oil, starch, or other agents left in the goods from the manufacturing process. See pages 216–219 for more information.

Stage 3: Mordanting. Mordanting is the process of applying a naturally occurring, water-soluble metallic salt to create a bond between the fiber and the dye—it is a binder. This process helps you obtain more uniform results with greater color saturation and colorfastness. (If you're working with indigo, you won't need this step.) See pages 219–226 for more information.

Stage 4: Dyeing. The actual dyeing process will vary depending on which dye and technique you're using. Each technique will include specific dyeing instructions. The universal methods of dyeing used are One-Pot and Mason-Jar Dyeing (page 227).

Stage 5: Washing. After dyeing, textiles must be washed to remove any excess dye. See pages 236–237 for details.

PLANNING YOUR TIME

Since the entire dyeing process takes time, this chart should help you organize your workflow.

WEIGHING AND SCOURING:
Prep time = 30 minutes.
Cooking time = 1 hour + cooling time.

MORDANTING: Prep time = 30 minutes.
Cooking time = 1½ hours + cooling time.

DYEING: Prep time = 15 minutes.
Cooking time = 1½ hours. If you have more than one pot and burner, you can do multiple dye pots at once. Allow time for cooling.

WASHING: Time = 30 minutes.
Drying time = 24 hours from when hung to dry, at most.

USING PERCENTAGES IN DYEING

Note that in this book, all the amounts of scour, mordant, and dye are listed as percentages, making it easy to scale a recipe to suit any amount of goods. To do this, weigh your goods. This number is your weight of goods (WOG). Multiply by the percentage listed on the shade card. For example, let's say you have a skein of yarn weighing 50 g and you want to match a shade card listed at 100%. Here is your math:

$$\text{WOG} \times \text{dye\%} = \text{amount of dye needed}$$
$$\text{to reach a given shade}$$

$$50 \text{ g} \times 100\% = 50 \text{ g of dye needed}$$

GOLDEN RULES OF NATURAL DYEING

1. Keep notes. There is a direct correlation between the weight of what you are dyeing, the amount of dye, and the amount of water to the color you achieve. When you record your process, you will become a better dyer.

2. Be mindful of your fiber. There are two main types of fibers: protein-based, which come from animals and insects, and cellulose-based, which come from plants (page 214). The process of dyeing protein-based fibers is quite different from that for cellulose-based fibers, so take note as you work through the book.

3. For the best results, mordant. A mordant helps the dye bond with the fabric and provides longer lasting color.

4. Be careful with protein-based fibers. Do not allow the water to boil, as it will cause wool to felt and silk to become dull and brittle. And do not shock animal fibers by moving them from hot water to cold water, or vice versa, as this can also cause felting.

5. Water acts as the color white. If you add more water to your dyebath, you will get a lighter shade. We give a recommended ratio of water to goods for each shade card and project. When scaling up, you only need enough water to cover your goods. Before you start the dyeing process, you can place your dry goods in the pot you intend to use and gauge the amount of water needed. Once you start the dyeing process, you will be able to decide if you need to add additional water.

6. Your tap water's pH, mineral content, and any metals introduced from your pipes (like iron or copper) can affect the colors achieved with natural dyes. If you're having a hard time obtaining the same colors as displayed in this book and would like to get the colors shown, try using filtered or distilled water.

7. Certain natural dyes are especially responsive to pH. Throughout the book, you will learn about how the various shifts in pH will affect dye extraction, color, and texture—this is important information to use as you develop a repertoire of skills. Learning about pH, measuring pH through the use of strips or a meter (page 230) and recording the results in your dye journal (page 215) will help you understand your color results.

8. Metals, like iron, have an impact on color and texture (page 234). All colors in this book were created using stainless steel pots unless otherwise noted. Exercise caution when using iron. Use iron only with low heat, or it can make the texture of the fibers rough and brittle. Clean up well after using iron, because it can cause spots on future dyeing projects. If you are planning on using iron regularly, it is wise to have separate set of tools.

9. Use common-sense safety precautions, and take your time. Allow pots to cool before handling the goods, as it is safer to handle room-temperature water and fibers. Plus, allowing the goods to sit in the pot means better lightfastness and more saturated color.

before you begin: indigo

Indigo dyeing is different from other types of natural dyeing. Goods do not have to be mordanted before they are dyed, but they do need to be scoured. The term *vat* is used for a dyebath made using indigo and includes all agents added, as well as the vessel.

As the focus of this book is on growing and using locally sourced dyes, most of the indigo recipes use *Persicaria tinctoria*, a plant containing the precursors of indigo pigment that grows well in a wide variety of climates. Instructions for growing *Persicaria tinctoria* can be found on pages 114–116.

RECIPES

Dyeing with Fresh *Persicaria tinctoria* Using a Blender and Ice (page 119): This is the simplest, fastest recipe, requiring just a couple of handfuls of fresh leaves. Harvest the leaves and dye with them immediately. This dyebath is highly perishable; after an hour it can no longer reliably dye goods. The color created is a gorgeous turquoise. If you want that inky blue indigo is known for, create one of the other indigo recipes explained in this book. This recipe works only with protein-based fibers, such as wool and silk.

Extracting Indigo Pigment from Fresh *Persicaria tinctoria* to Dry or Dye (page 190): Either indigo can be extracted from fresh leaves to be dried and used at a later date, or a vat can be made that is long-lasting and makes the classic blues indigo is known for. This process takes about two days and requires about 1,000 leaves. To get the deepest blues from the least amount of pigment, instructions for making a vat using ferrous sulfate are included in this recipe.

Creating a Fermented Indigo Vat Using Composted *Persicaria tinctoria* (page 120): In this process, the leaves are harvested, dried, composted, and made into dye using a fermentation process (pages. Either 40 pounds of fresh leaves or 20 pounds of dried leaves are required to complete this recipe. This is the most labor- and time-intensive process in the book, taking the better part of a year to create, though in our opinion well worth it. The blues from this vat are outstanding.

Making an Indigo-Fructose-Limestone Vat (page 196): If you are not growing *Persicaria tinctoria* and you are using purchased natural indigo pigment instead, that's OK! You can jump directly to the recipe for creating the Indigo-Fructose-Limestone Vat. This recipe works best if allowed to rest for twenty-four hours before using.

CROCKING

Because indigo is not attached to the fibers with a chemical bond, any sort of repeated pressure can cause the indigo to be pushed out of the fiber, resulting in crocking. Crocking is the release of excess indigo that was not removed during the washing process and occurs with goods that are freshly dyed. To help prevent crocking, apply dye gradually through successive dips and make sure the vat is created properly. After you apply pressure to the goods, the excess indigo will wear off and it will stop transferring.

INDIGO-BASED SHADE CARDS

The following shade cards include indigo and demonstrate the relationship between indigo and fiber type, as well as how much indigo and how many dips are needed to obtain a spectrum of blue.

- Base Palette on Wool (page 79)
- Natural Dyes on Silk (page 87)
- Dyeing with Fresh *Persicaria tinctoria* (page 117)
- Indigo-Fructose-Limestone Vat on Cotton and Linen (page 195)
- Blues Made Using a Fermented Indigo Vat (page 132)

DYEING WITH INDIGO

Though indigo vats can be made a variety of ways, the process of dyeing with indigo remains generally the same. Use the instructions below to guide you. Refer to each recipe before dyeing for any necessary details particular to the style of vat you are using. The more you observe and record the characteristics of your indigo vat and how your goods are taking the dye, the better you will understand the indigo dyeing process.

When dyeing with indigo pigment, whether it is purchased natural indigo pigment, that which you have extracted, or composted, the following criteria must be met and is discussed in each recipe:

- The vat must be alkaline, with a pH between 10 and 11.
- Oxygen must be removed from the vat.

INSTRUCTIONS

1. Pre-wet your goods in an alkaline bath until thoroughly wet.

2. If a cluster of bubbles has formed on the surface of the vat, called a flower and made of unreduced indigo pigment, take a spoon and remove the flower from the vat and dispose of it.

3. Remove the pre-wet goods from the alkaline bath and squeeze gently to remove excess water.

4. Slowly lower the pre-wet goods into the vat.

5. Hold the goods under the surface of the vat for 5 minutes. If dyeing fabric or clothing, massage the liquid into the fabric under the surface. If dyeing yarn, drape it over a dowel, rotate once or twice, so all parts spend time submerged in the vat. Rotating the goods in the vat to avoid uneven application of color is most important during the first dip. Use slow, careful movements to avoid stirring up the sediment or introducing air to the vat. Avoid rapid up and down movements, as this will introduce oxygen into the vat and will stir up the sediment along the bottom of the vat.

6. After 5 minutes, gently lift the goods out of the vat, squeezing them as you remove them, allowing the excess liquid to drip back into the vat.

7. Hang the goods on the drying rack or clothesline, if working with fabric, flatten, and allow them to rest for 10 minutes before dipping again. Repeat steps 5 and 6 to make a darker color. It is recommended you dip goods at least 3 times for maximum colorfastness. After every 3 dips into the indigo vat, rinse the goods in the alkaline bath. Squeeze gently to remove excess water. If the alkaline bath is becoming saturated with dye and turning blue, make a fresh bath.

8. Once you are done dyeing your goods, proceed to the neutralizing and washing instructions on page 236.

CHAPTER ONE

ICELAND

the cold, the wind, and the comfort of natural color //
letters from the ring road

AS WOOL- AND NATURE-LOVING PEOPLE, it seemed inevitable that we would one day make it to Iceland—a place rumored to have sheep roaming freely across the country, where hand-knitting has been embedded in the culture to the extent that they have a national sweater—the *lopapeysa*—and yarn is widely available in grocery stores. Given that, coupled with Iceland's incredible, varied, natural beauty, how could we not go?

Plants cover only 23 percent of Iceland. Snow can be expected from October to May, creating a very short growing season. While the sun in Iceland barely sets during the summer, in the winter, there can be as little as four to five hours of sunlight. We came to Iceland with the hope of learning more about how people who live within this extreme climate create color naturally. And how textiles and natural color aid in their existence and add to their happiness. We had also been studying lichen dyeing and wanted to learn more. Iceland is home to a vast array of lichen, and dyeing with lichen is said to have been practiced by Vikings, the earliest inhabitants of Iceland, and is still practiced by some today.

We arrived in June, when the sun nearly stops setting, instead hovering right above the horizon. We rented a tiny car to set off on Iceland's Ring Road, a two-lane highway that travels the circumference of the island. Our first stop was Reykjavík, to visit the Icelandic Handknitting Shop, and where we picked up a couple of iconic Icelandic sweaters to keep us warm during our stay. The shop was filled to the brim with hand-knit sweaters in endless colors, made out of Lopi, the iconic yarn found all over Iceland that is made of Icelandic wool.

By afternoon, we had reached the beginning of the southern edge of the country and were excited to visit Þingborg Wool Center, a co-op run by the local fiber community. The shop features their own line of Icelandic wool yarn. Icelandic sheep, a rare breed adapted to Iceland's arctic climate, are unique in that they grow two coats: a soft, short, fluffy inner layer called *thel* to keep them warm and a coarse, longer outer layer called *tog* to keep them dry. Lopi, which is what most Icelandic knitting patterns are designed for, is made of both *thel* and *tog*. But at Þingborg, once their sheep are shorn, the community gathers the wool and separates the locks to be spun into two different yarns. The softer *thel* is used for next-to-skin garments, and the coarser tog is used for outerwear, rugs, and ropes.

As we toured around Iceland, we took in its incredible, vast landscape, visited many small shops offering handknits, and saw lots of sheep.

HAND MADE
GARMENTS
FROM ICELANDIC
WOOL
AND OTHER THINGS
FOR SALE.

We quickly found the display of naturally dyed yarn and collected samples of those created by local plants and lichen, including birch, crowberry, lady's mantle, meadowsweet, grainless water dock, and rhubarb root. Some of the colors had been altered by the addition of iron, and there was a wide array of undyed colors. Also available in the shop were buttons and toggles made of sheep's horn and sheepskins. All parts of the sheep are used; nothing is left to waste. We got into the car to continue our day's journey. After a few hours, we pulled over to eat dinner. The windows of the restaurant faced the ocean, the water was a deep, dark gray. In between the ocean and the restaurant, there was a stunning field of purple lupine, illuminated by the crisp, golden light of the barely setting sun. It was the perfect end to a perfect day.

The next morning, we rose early and continued around the Ring Road. For the next seven days, we saw basalt rock formations, waterfalls, moss, lichen, lava rock, reindeer, puffins, birds, horses, very few people, and lots and lots of lupine and sheep. As the wind swept off the ocean, so fast and brisk that it pierced through our many layers of clothing, we pondered what it would have been like to live here hundreds of years ago through the cold, dark winters. What would one have worn for warmth? What would one have eaten? And how would one stay hopeful through all the dark winters? With family in Minnesota, and having visited them in the middle of winter, we had an idea of what it would be like to be surrounded by snow for long amounts of time. But Minnesota is still farther south, so we had not experienced the very short days that they have in Iceland.

One afternoon, after spending the morning looping back and forth around tiny bays created by the peninsular fingers of the fjords, we pulled over to take a break. We walked down a hillside overlooking a babbling brook and lay on the grass. Upon closer inspection, we noticed tiny forests of lichen. There were so many varieties we lost count. We marveled at the amazing diversity in shape, size, and color. Only a small percentage of lichen have been identified in Iceland. So we often wondered if maybe we were looking at a yet-to-be-named variety. Lichens are a combination of fungi and algae and are commonly found on rocks and trees. They cover 6 percent of the earth, and sometimes live for thousands of years and on average only grow less than an inch a year. According to fossil records, they have been on Earth for four hundred million years and can be used by scientists to date a location by their size—just like counting the rings of a tree to find its age. They are the first organisms to inhabit newly exposed rock, therefore creating a fertile environment that eventually leads to plant growth, are indicators of air quality, and provide nutrients and sustenance to wildlife, so they are very important to the ecosystem. They also have the potential to dye fibers an array of colors, which, of course, is highly intriguing. Taking all of the above into consideration, and the potential negative impact we could have on the environment by using lichen as a dye, we asked ourselves—under what circumstances would we use lichen as a dye, and to what extent?

In the middle of one of our long days of driving, we noticed a sign for a turf house museum. A turf house is built into the earth and is the style of housing many Icelanders lived in from the time the country was first settled in the ninth century through the middle of the twentieth century. We immediately pulled over. The walls and ceilings of the living rooms and bedrooms were wood-paneled, much as you would expect from the interior of any house; however, the homes were connected via earthen corridors, in which the ceilings were made of branches and the walls were made of layers of turf and lava rock. The kitchen was also constructed in this manner. Tools used to create textiles—a spinning wheel, lazy kate, loom, sock and glove blockers—were sprinkled throughout the rooms. Our guide taught us

Touring the turf house museum, we saw the ways in which textiles softened and warmed the home.

that making textiles gave people something to do during the long winters. The results provided warmth, comfort, and protection from the elements. Handwoven blankets covered the beds. Many of them were brown and gray, the natural colors of the sheep's fleece, but on one piece, a bright red embroidered initial grabbed our attention. In that moment, it was evident the powerful, positive impact even a small bit of red or pink would have had on one's mental health in the dead of winter, and how one would have felt the necessity to create that dyed pop of color. We could now understand the importance of lichen, which is plentiful in Iceland, as a source of color, especially when there might not be a plant able to produce hues such as red and pink.

More than halfway through our trip, our next major textile stop was Blönduós, a small oceanside town located in northwestern Iceland and home to the Icelandic Textile Center and Textile Museum. It just so happened that on the day of our arrival, it was also the location of the inaugural Iceland Knit Fest, where we attended a natural dyeing lecture by Guðrún Bjarnadóttir, a local natural dyer whose studio we were planning to visit later.

The Icelandic Textile Center was founded in 2005, with the goal of promoting and developing Icelandic textiles. It is housed in the Kvennaskólinn, a one-hundred-year-old building—once a women's college and now a thriving multiple story series of textile studios, including weaving and natural dyeing. Students, artists, and scholars come from all over the world to participate in its textile residency program, to use the studios to create Icelandic-inspired art, and to work on the Vatnsdæla Tapestry Project. Adjacent to the Icelandic Textile Center is the Textile Museum, which houses a vast collection of Icelandic textiles, including a display of historical garments, such as shoes made from fish skins with incredible attention to detail and hand-knit intarsia cushions to protect one's feet from the hard ground.

After visiting the Icelandic Textile Center and stitching on the Vatnsdæla Tapestry, we traveled a few hours to Borgarnes. Located in the middle of verdant green pastures speckled with gorgeous galloping horses and surrounded by mountains is the studio of natural dyer and botanist Guðrún Bjarnadóttir. As we walked up, Guðrún's dog Triggur bounded toward us and throughout our time stayed by our side. Guðrún's warm studio was steamy with bubbling pots. She lifted the lids to give us a peek inside. We were excited to see her dyeing with the local lichen *Parmelia saxatilis*. The smell was divine—slightly spicy and a little like freshly laundered clothes. Over lunch, Guðrún explained to us that lichen has been used as a dye in Iceland for centuries. Because Guðrún studies the ways that lichens and plants have been used in Iceland historically and considers their use as part of her heritage, she is drawn to continue this tradition. That said, she acknowledges that if lichen dyeing were to become popular and many others began to dye with this practice, it could have a detrimental impact on the environment.

Other locally grown dyes with a long history in Iceland that Guðrún uses include birch leaves, which she prefers to gather in early spring, and the leaves of the yarrow plant. One of Guðrún's favorite dyes is made with rhubarb leaves and roots. Rhubarb became a common plant in Iceland in the nineteenth century. Many people have it in their yards and often give it to Guðrún to dye with. She also uses indigo and madder; though they have to be imported, they have been used for a very long time in Iceland and aid in creating a full spectrum of color.

A newer dye Guðrún finds important to use is lupine, because it is incredibly invasive in Iceland. Guðrún said, "I am always telling people to respect nature, to never take too much of the plant, but that does not apply to the lupine . . . we have enough." All along our travels we had been admiring the beauty of lupine and were

Guðrún uses a wide variety of dyes to add color to her yarn, such as lichen, lupine, and rhubarb.

now learning about the incredibly devastating impact it is having on their environment, crowding out native plants and lichen. This really drove home the necessity of looking more closely at the plants one associates with a place, to identify invasive plants and use them as dyes.

For mordanting, Guðrún currently uses imported aluminum potassium sulfate, but once long ago club moss (*Diphasiastrum alpinum*) was used in Iceland. We noticed a sample sitting on her studio shelf. Club moss has the ability to absorb aluminum from the soil, making it useful as a mordant. We were aware of *Symplocos*, a plant used in Indonesia for mordant, but were unaware of club moss, so this was exciting to learn.

Guðrún began using natural dyes in 2009. She had been reading about natural dyes, and after seeing a woman at a farmers market using them, she felt inspired to finally try the process herself. When asked what advice she would give to new natural dyers, Guðrún advised, "The only way you can be good at something is to practice and read a lot. You can never become a good dyer only by reading about dyeing, but it will definitely help you understand your mistakes and learn from them." Over the years, Guðrún did just that—she continued to practice and read about natural dyeing. And soon she had created a natural dyeing studio and small shop where people from around the world visit her to purchase her naturally dyed Icelandic-wool yarn and to learn about her process.

"It is the surprise of the color that keeps me going. I can never control the color perfectly and every once in a while I am pleasantly surprised with the outcome and learn something new. If the same color always came out of the dyepot, I would soon be bored. And the possibilities are endless to try new plants, fungus, or lichens and experience something new."

As we left Guðrún's studio, knowing that we may never use lichen to dye, we picked up a few skeins of her rust-colored lichen-dyed yarn for our collection. If anything, to just give it a sniff and to remember our amazing afternoon with Guðrún. Driving back into Reykjavík that evening approaching Summer Solstice, the sun sat on the horizon for hours, never leaving Iceland, its rays covering everything within its reach with the most glorious rose-colored light, giving us ideas for new colorways. It was the perfect ending to an incredible trip.

If people in Iceland, a country with such sharp fluctuations in weather and light, can use plants for dyeing, it is possible to use locally sourced dyes nearly everywhere. After our visit with Guðrún, we made a stronger commitment to making the most of our local plant dyes. We were inspired by Guðrún's practice of combining local plants with imported dyes, like madder and cochineal. This is a wonderful compromise and a viable option for anyone who would like to use natural dyes to create a full spectrum of color but feel limited by what is available locally. Guðrún also opened our eyes to identifying and using invasive plants. Upon returning home, we began to identify the invasive plants in our area, and we try to use those plants first whenever possible. And finally, because of its slow growth, coupled with the increase in poor air quality, thus endangering some lichens, we concluded that for the time being we would forgo dyeing with lichen or using it in our workshops. Instead, we're focused on learning more about lichen's close relative, an organism very close to our hearts that grows quickly in comparison: fungi! Keep reading to learn more.

Þingborg Wool Center
Road 1, 8 km East from Selfoss
gamlathingborg@gmail.com
thingborg.net

Guðrún Bjarnadóttir of Hespa, Selfoss
hespa@hespa.is
www.hespa.is

Naturally dyed yarn we collected on our trip around Iceland.

iceland-inspired palette

Leaving Iceland, we challenged ourselves to create the widest range of colors using locally sourced plants and mushrooms. We found the dyes featured in this chapter in our neighborhood, our local forest, and our pantry. See the shade cards on the following pages to view the colors made from these dyes.

1 Avocado pits

2 Hibiscus flowers

3 Birch bark and leaves

4 Redwood cones

5 Chestnuts

6 Dock root

7 Rhubarb root

8 Yellow and red onion skins

9 Juniper berries

10 Acorns

11 Lavender leaves and flowers

12 Lupine flowers

13 Purple plum leaves

14 Iron

15 Yarn—undyed white, light gray, and dark gray Lopi

shade card: locally sourced plant dyes

GOODS: Léttlopi (100% Icelandic wool) yarn, #0051 white, #0054 light ash heather (light gray), #0056 ash heather (dark gray)

SCOUR: Scouring Wool (page 217)

MORDANT: Mordanting Protein-Based Fibers with Aluminum Potassium Sulfate (page 219)

DYE: One-pot (page 227); all colors were created using 100 g goods and 8–9 cups (1.9–2 L) water in a 3-quart (2.8-L) pot.

NOTES: The table on the right shows the yarn dipped into a solution of light iron water (page 234) once the dyeing was complete.

To learn how to use percentages in the dyeing process, see page 10.

	WITHOUT IRON			WITH IRON		
	WHITE	**LIGHT GREY**	**DARK GREY**	**WHITE**	**LIGHT GREY**	**DARK GREY**
AVOCADO PITS, FRESH*	200%	200%	200%	200%	200%	200%
HIBISCUS, DRIED	200%	200%	200%	200%	200%	200%
BIRCH BARK, FRESH*	400%	400%	400%	400%	400%	400%
REDWOOD CONES, FRESH	100%	100%	100%	100%	100%	100%
CHESTNUTS, FRESH	100%	100%	100%	100%	100%	100%
DOCK ROOT, FRESH**	100%	100%	100%	100%	100%	100%
RHUBARB ROOT, FRESH**	100%	100%	100%	100%	100%	100%
YELLOW ONION SKINS, DRIED	30%	30%	30%	30%	30%	30%
JUNIPER BERRIES, DRIED	100%	100%	100%	100%	100%	100%

*Used baking soda pH modifier during the dyeing process to raise the pH; lowered the pH with lemon juice before dyeing (page 231).

**Used limestone pH modifier to raise the pH after the dyeing process (page 232).

shade card:
locally sourced plant dyes—continued

	WITHOUT IRON			WITH IRON		
	WHITE	**LIGHT GREY**	**DARK GREY**	**WHITE**	**LIGHT GREY**	**DARK GREY**
DOCK ROOT, FRESH	100%	100%	100%	100%	100%	100%
RHUBARB ROOT, FRESH	100%	100%	100%	100%	100%	100%
ACORNS, FRESH	100%	100%	100%	100%	100%	100%
DOCK LEAVES, FRESH	100%	100%	100%	100%	100%	100%
BIRCH LEAVES, FRESH	100%	100%	100%	100%	100%	100%
LAVENDER LEAVES AND FLOWERS, FRESH	100%	100%	100%	100%	100%	100%
LUPINE FLOWERS, FRESH	100%	100%	100%	100%	100%	100%
PURPLE PLUM LEAVES, FRESH	100%	100%	100%	100%	100%	100%
RED ONION SKINS, DRIED	30%	30%	30%	30%	30%	30%

shade card: locally sourced mushroom dyes

GOODS: Léttlopi (100% Icelandic wool) yarn, #0051 white, #0054 light ash heather (light gray), #0056 ash heather (dark gray)

SCOUR: Scouring Wool (page 217)

MORDANT: Mordanting Protein-Based Fibers with Aluminum Potassium Sulfate (page 219)

DYE: One-pot (page 227); all colors were created using 100 g goods and 8–9 cups (1.9–2 L) water in a 3-quart (2.8-L) pot.

NOTES: The right half of the table shows the yarn dipped into a solution of light iron water (page 234) once the dyeing was complete.

To learn how to use percentages in the dyeing process, see page 10.

	WITHOUT IRON			WITH IRON		
	WHITE	LIGHT GREY	DARK GREY	WHITE	LIGHT GREY	DARK GREY
LOBSTER *(HYPOMYCES LACTIFLUORUM)*	400%	400%	400%	400%	400%	400%
DYER'S RED CORT *(CORTINARIUS SEMISANGUINEUS)*	200%	200%	200%	200%	200%	200%
DYER'S POLYPHORE *(PHAEOLUS SCHWEINITZII)*	100%	100%	100%	100%	100%	100%
JUMBO GYM *(GYMNOPILUS VENTRICOSUS)*	100%	100%	100%	100%	100%	100%
SULPHUR TUFT *(HYPHOLOMA FASCICULARE)*	200%	200%	200%	200%	200%	200%
WESTERN JACK-O'-LANTERN *(OMPHALOTUS OLIVASCENS)*	200%	200%	200%	200%	200%	200%
DYER'S PUFFBALL *(PISOLITHUS ARHIZUS)*	400%	400%	400%	400%	400%	400%

locally sourced mushroom dyes

1. LOBSTER MUSHROOM,
HYPOMYCES LACTIFLUORUM

The orange-red color and texture of this mushroom's skin are reminiscent of a lobster; hence its common name. It is typically found near its host mushrooms, *Lactarius* and *Russula*. Using a knife, gently trim off the red skin of the mushroom and add the peels to the dyepot. Create orange with neutral-pH water and pink/red with alkaline water.

2. DYER'S RED CORT,
CORTINARIUS SEMISANGUINEUS

The stem, cap, and gills are unmistakable because of the deep bloodred color. Look for it at the base of conifer and birch trees. This is one of the most prized dye mushrooms to find, because it produces amazing reds, pinks, and oranges.

3. DYER'S POLYPORE,
PHAEOLUS SCHWEINITZII

An orange shelf mushroom that grows concentrically from a single stem, this mushroom is tough and dense and has a fuzzy texture. As it ages, it turns more brown and wood-like and can grow to the size of a dinner plate. It thrives on decomposing conifer trees, specifically pine and Douglas fir, can be found growing on the base of the tree trunk.

4. JUMBO GYM,
GYMNOPILUS VENTRICOSUS

A large yellow-orange gilled mushroom with a defined cap and stem, jumbo gym grows in groups on the decomposing logs and stumps of conifers and hardwood trees. Gives a warm yellow color that shifts to green if dipped in an iron solution.

5. SULPHUR TUFT,
HYPHOLOMA FASCICULARE

This small yellow gilled mushroom grows in clusters on rotting conifer and hardwood stumps. These are the first mushrooms Miriam Rice, one of the first people to write about dyeing with mushrooms, tried.

6. WESTERN JACK-O'-LANTERN,
OMPHALOTUS OLIVASCENS

A gilled mushroom. Its yellow-orange cap has olive tones and grows in clusters on hard-wood trunks, stumps, and wood buried in leaf litter. It likes oaks and eucalyptus. The gills follow the length of the stem. Though this mushroom makes a great source for dye, the color can be a bit hard to predict. It is possible to get grays with lavender undertones, beige, and brown.

7. DYER'S PUFFBALL,
PISOLITHUS ARHIZUS

This mushroom can be found growing in the ground in both city and country, singularly and in patches. You may think this brown, bulbous protrusion, often referred to as a Dead Man's Foot, is a dirt clod. Use gloves and a dust mask while adding it to the dyepot; the powdery spores are easily airborne. Due to its water-resistant nature, add a drop of dish soap to the dyepot to help combine the spores with water. Crumble the mushroom into the pot and slowly stir to submerge.

using locally available dyes

Given the short growing season and the plethora of sheep that range freely and nibble on what might have been a tree, Iceland has a limited number of plants and trees from which to choose for dyeing—and yet the country has a vibrant natural-dyeing culture. This was very inspiring and led us to look more closely at the plants in our neighborhood, garden, and grocer, as well as to wonder if and how we could make a full palette of color from such plants. While the Iceland-inspired shade card gives you examples of what you can use, ultimately we hope that you look to your local land to provide dyes. Here are some helpful guidelines when cultivating your own local palette.

Gathering Dyes

Your pantry and grocery store are other places where you can source dyes. Save the edible part of the plant for eating and use the inedible parts, such as onion skins, to make a great, easily accessible dye.

Growing a dye garden is a wonderful way to source dyestuffs. There are plenty of plants that are very easy to grow and where a little bit of dye goes a long way, such as marigolds—as you can see on the Mexico-inspired shade card (page 71). If you don't have access to your own yard, community gardens are a great way to meet others excited about gardening and to grow dye plants.

Foraging for plants and mushrooms around your neighborhood and in your local forest is another way to find dye. When our sky fills with rain clouds, we get excited. Two days after the rain stops, we head into the forest to look for mushrooms. Start at the base of a tree and walk around slowly, looking at the ground. If there are a lot of leaves, look for tiny bumps where a mushroom may be hiding.

Forming Community

A big part of transitioning our dyeing practice from using mainly imported natural-dyeing extracts to incorporating more locally sourced dyestuffs has been connecting with our local community—meeting our neighbors, gardeners, those who prune trees, farmers, and chefs.

The types of mushrooms listed in this book are those that are relatively easy to find in and around the Bay Area and are rather common in other parts of the United States. That being said, it is really helpful to join your local mycological society, read online forums based nearby, or pick up a mushroom guide focused on your area, to understand if the mushrooms listed here are available near you, what time of year they are available, and where they are commonly found. Most local mycological societies have forays to forage with the group. This is a lot of fun, and you can meet others who are knowledgeable and enthusiastic about mushrooms.

Many of the dyestuffs we are looking for are being discarded or composted, like onion skins or the branches leftover from pruning. So whenever we can, we join the cycle, inherit the plants, extract the color, and then compost the spent dyestuffs. Knowing more people in our community and getting a glimpse into their plant- and mushroom-based practices has been an added bonus to our natural-dyeing practice!

Learning How to Identify Plants and Mushrooms

To identify plants and mushrooms takes time, though with perseverance, as you strengthen your skills and begin to recognize leaves, roots, and petals that can make dye, the natural world will soon come alive and be much more meaningful. Start with those things you see most.

Flowers are one way plants are classified, so this is a good place to start. Look closely at the parts of the

---

Dyer's Polypore, Jumbo Gym, Sulphur Tuft, and Dyer's Puffball are all mushrooms that can be used to dye. See page 33 for more information.

FORAGING TOOLS

In addition to the things you would bring on a hike in the woods, here are some recommended tools for foraging:

- Mushroom knife: a pocketknife with a small brush at the end opposite the blade
- Basket with paper bags to wrap mushrooms, leaves, and bark
- Notepad and pen
- Camera for documenting
- Field guides to help with identification of mushrooms and plants
- Water-resistant pants
- Flashlight and whistle
- Tecnu soap for poison oak/poison ivy exposure
- Hand sanitizer or gloves

SAFETY PRECAUTIONS:

When you're learning to identify mushrooms, it is as important to learn to identify any plants that may grow nearby that can be hazardous to your health, like poison oak and poison ivy. Avoid touching these plants. When you are done foraging, make sure to wash your hands. In this book, we are only addressing mushrooms as a dye: Please do not eat any of them. Keep mushrooms away from children and animals.

flower—the petals, stamens, sepal, and all the parts in between. What are the colors and shapes you see? Notice the stem, the height of the plant, and the leaves. Are the leaves round, pointed, oval, or needles like a pine tree? When you look at a tree, is the texture of the trunk's bark smooth, rough, peeling? What color is it? All these details, when they come together as a collection, as found on the plant, will lead to its identification. You will start to learn how plants are classified and grouped into species and families and what this may mean as a natural dyer.

Mushrooms are the fruiting body of an underground network of individual branching filaments called *hyphae*. As a group they are called *mycelium*, and they work similarly to the way roots do for plants and trees. The mushrooms burst to the surface to disperse microscopic spores (seeds) for more mycelium to grow and spread. Mushrooms and their growing patterns are highly interdependent on rainfall and types of trees in the area. One of the best times to see mushrooms is a few days to a few weeks after a good rain; at this time many will begin to fruit with the boost of moisture. To identify mushrooms correctly and understand when and where they grow in your area, look at the color and shape of the mushroom, and learn to identify the types of trees mushrooms like to live alongside.

The mushrooms featured in this book represent three mycological types: gilled, shelf, and puffball. Gilled mushrooms, those that are shaped like a little umbrella, are most recognizable based on those found in the grocery store. The top of the mushroom is called the cap. Under the cap there are radiating blades called gills, where the spores are produced and released. The handle of the umbrella is called the stem or stipe. Dye mushrooms in this shape include *Cortinarius semisanguineus*, *Cortinarius cinnamomeum*, *Hypholoma fasciculare*, *Omphalotus olivascens*, and *Gymnopilus ventricosus*.

Shelf mushrooms are called such because they look like a shelf hanging on the side of a living or dead tree. An example of this type of mushroom is *Phaeolus schweinitzii* (Dyer's Polypore). Instead of gills, it has a spongy layer of tubes under its cap to release its spores.

Puffballs are bulbous, do not have a visible stalk or stem, and typically grow on the ground. Their spores are produced internally, and eventually as the mushroom ages it cracks or develops an opening for the spores to escape. The spores are so plentiful and small the dispersal appears as a brown puff of smoke! *Pisolithus arhizus* (Dyer's Puffball) is an example of a puffball and is one of our absolute favorite mushrooms to dye with, because it is so potent and easy to find in our neighborhood and it grows all year long.

Unlike plants, fungi do not have chlorophyll to create energy; they survive by producing enzymes to digest plant and animal tissues for their nutrients. Some mushrooms gather nutrients from decomposing trees and leaves, while others are parasitic and take over other mushrooms. Then there are those who live symbiotically with a given tree or plant. It is important to know how the specific mushroom you are looking for receives nutrients, because it is a clue to finding them while foraging. For example, *Hypomyces lactifluorum* (Lobster mushrooms) are parasitic mushrooms that take over *Lactarius* and *Russula* mushrooms. The *Pisolithus arhizus* (Dyer's Puffball) lives symbiotically with conifers, such as pine, and hardwood trees, such as birch, oak, and maple. Refer to page 33 for specific characteristics of the mushrooms featured in this book.

Photographing plants and mushrooms and researching them later by referring to plant and mushroom identification books, or by visiting your local nursery and botanical garden, is a great way to hone your skills at identification.

Understanding Native and Invasive Plants

In every wool store we visited while in Iceland, we sought naturally dyed yarn, specifically those dyed with locally foraged plants, and purchased skeins as samples and inspiration. While visiting natural dyer and botanist Guðrún Bjarnadottir, she taught us about the history of lupine in Iceland as an invasive species. Our conversation with Guðrún reinforced a concept we were already working with: When gathering plants in the wild, always gather invasive plants first.

When visiting your local plant nursery, you may have noticed a section called Native Plants. These are plants that botanists have determined have been growing naturally in your region for a very long time. This means the climate is suitable for them to thrive, and it typically means that they will thrive with very little care by humans. This most likely also means that the insects and birds in the area will also live harmoniously among such plants, and the plants will be of benefit to them. In California, many of the plants that fall into this category take little water to grow—a huge plus!

As populations of people have grown and shifted, trade increased, and plants imported, some have taken root and taken over. In California, this is the case with eucalyptus, dock, and fennel. Invasive plants crowd out native plants. When hiking through the California countryside, we often imagine what it might have looked like one hundred or five hundred years ago, when there were more native plant populations.

So when it comes to gathering plants, gather invasive plants first and foremost. Learn which are native and invasive by researching online (see page 37 for helpful resources). When it comes to gathering native plants for dyeing, proceed with caution: Gather only 10 percent or less of a single plant's foliage. Better yet, if you can grow it, do so, to add to the native plant population.

Extracting Dye

To extract dye from plants, mushrooms, and insects, you can either extract the color first and then add the goods to be dyed, or extract the color at the same time as dyeing the goods.

Extracting the color at the same time as dyeing is the fastest method and conserves the most energy. Because the goods are sharing a vessel with the whole dyestuffs, the dye matter can embed itself into the goods, especially yarn. Sometimes having the dyestuff in the pot with the goods may result in little saturated bits of color. We rather like both of these effects—coming across a small stem or a small marigold petal when knitting is a sweet reminder of what the yarn was dyed with, and having a smudge of more saturated color because a plant or mushroom rested closely to the fabric during the dyeing process captures a unique moment within the dyeing process. To remove excess dyestuff: Once you are done dyeing and the goods have cooled, squeeze out as much moisture as possible, work over a sink or go outside, and shake the goods so the dyestuff falls off. Give the goods a rinse in clean water, squeeze out as much water as possible, and shake the goods again. When working with yarn, more dyestuff will be released when turning the skeins into balls.

If you would prefer your yarn to be free of dye material, desire your goods to have a uniform color, or are raising the pH to extract color, extract the color first: Heat the dyestuff with water for one hour. Then pour the dyebath through a strainer or cheesecloth. Discard the dyestuff, add the dyebath back to the pot, and add the goods you wish to dye. Heat for one hour.

Different parts of the plants can take longer to break down in the dyeing process. Flowers release their color fastest in about one hour of heating, whereas leaves from trees, which can be more leathery and waxy, bark, and acorns can take a bit longer, taking at least two hours of heating. Chopping the dyestuff as finely as possible will give the best color; exposing more surface area allows more of the dye to be extracted.

MINDFUL GATHERING

When gathering, remember these safety and etiquette guidelines:

- If you decide to experiment with foraged plants not listed in this book, be sure to identify the plant before working with it. Some plants and mushrooms are dangerous and are better left in the wild.
- If a plant has *tinctoria* in its name, it is likely to be a good dye plant. A single common name such as *coreopsis* can be misleading, as there are nuances within the family that affect the dyeing process: *Coreopsis tinctoria* produces a rich orange and mahogany color, while *Coreopsis grandiflora* produces yellow.
- Learn your local laws about gathering on private or public land; it may be against the law to gather on public land without permission from the agency in charge. Even with permission, be considerate of the many creatures large and small that may be living in the place where you are gathering and who depend on plants and mushrooms for food and shelter.
- Gathering windfall—what has already fallen to the ground—is a kind way to interact with nature.
- Learn which plants are considered invasive species and gather those first.
- Collect only what is necessary to complete your project.
- When harvesting mushrooms, use your knife to cut the stem near the ground. Avoid pulling the mushroom out of the ground, which disturbs its mycelium. If you move leaves to harvest mushrooms, move them back.

Testing Plants and Mushrooms for Dye Viability

If you have gathered plants and mushrooms that are not in this book and you are curious to see whether they contain dye, take 10 g of fresh dye and dye a 10 g skein of yarn. Remember that water acts as the color white when dyeing, so use only enough water to cover the goods to get the most saturated colors. Record the amount of water used. As you repeat these tests with different plants and mushrooms, use the same amounts of dye, fiber, and water so you can compare results. You can test multiple dyes at once using the Mason Jar Dyeing method (page 227). This method is great when using small quantities of yarn and dye. If the shade of color you have achieved is light, try increasing the amount of dyestuff. As you can see on the shade cards we created, in some cases we increased the dyestuff to 400 percent. If the shade of color you have achieved is very dark, and there is still dye left in the dyepot, try lowering the amount of dyestuff the next time you try this dye.

NOTE: We suggest using a small amount of yarn, because you then need only a small amount of dyestuff—and, in case the plant or mushroom does not yield any color or you do not like the color, to conserve yarn. Also, this is a nice quantity of yarn to place within one's dye journal as a sample. That being said, this is only a suggestion. If you would like to use a larger skein of yarn, go ahead; just make sure to use the same amount of dyestuff to achieve the best color.

If you would like to learn more about the lightfastness of the dye, take a portion of the sample you have dyed and set it in a well-lit space. Look at it from time to time, and compare it with the original sample in your dye journal to see if and how the color changes. If you would like to learn more about its colorfastness, wash it multiple times and observe the results.

By testing dyes in this way, using the same amounts of dye, fiber, and water, you can compare the saturations of the dyes with one another so you can estimate the amount you would increase or decrease the dye to achieve different shades. If the color is very saturated, this means the dyestuff will provide a range of shades, making it a great dye to explore further. See page 72 to read more about making multiple shades.

Comparing Fresh Dyestuffs with Dried Dyestuffs

If you are trying to re-create colors on the shade cards, make sure to note whether fresh or dried dyestuffs were used—as the difference in weight between fresh and dried dyestuffs can impact the color. By and large, plants, mushrooms, and insects give the same color whether fresh or dry. That being said, if you are looking to reproduce a color, and you would like to gather and store plants to be used at a later date, it is important to understand how much water the dyestuff loses when it is dried. Being able to store dyestuffs allows you to use natural dyes throughout the year, beyond when they are in season. On average, dyestuffs lose about 70 percent of their weight when dried. It is best to run your own tests, though. Here's how:

Take 10 g of fresh dye and dye a 10 g skein of yarn. Remember to record the amount of water used. Then take another 10 g of fresh dye, set it aside, allow it to dry, weigh it, and record the weight. Multiply this weight by 10 to get the percentage of dye needed to accomplish the same color when working with dry plant material. Use this percentage to dye another 10 g skein of yarn, making sure to use the same amount of water you used with the fresh dyestuff, and compare the results. The two skeins should be very close in color, if not exact.

For example: 10 g of fresh marigold flower heads weighs 2.5 g when dried. The percentage of dye needed to achieve the same color using dried marigold flower heads is 25. To dye 10 g of yarn, you need 2.5 g dry marigold flower heads. To dye 100 g of yarn, you need 25 g dry marigold flower heads.

Drying and Storing Dye Plants and Mushrooms

Once plants and mushrooms are harvested, brush off any excess dirt. Set in a well-ventilated area out of direct sunlight. Old window screens set on bricks make a great tool for drying plants. Once thoroughly dry, place in an airtight container such as a mason jar.

Setting Expectations: Colorfastness and Lightfastness

Several terms are used to describe the various properties of a dyed textile: *lightfastness*, *washfastness*, and *colorfastness*. Lightfastness refers to what happens to a color over time as it is exposed to light, while washfastness refers to how a color is affected by laundering. The overall measurement of both of these qualities is referred to as colorfastness. The choice of dyes and dyeing techniques used have a direct effect on colorfastness. All dyed color fades, no matter whether it is natural or synthetic. To help naturally dyed goods achieve and retain their desired color, the processes of scouring and mordanting are encouraged. Once a fiber has been mordanted, it can be re-dyed without having to re-mordant.

When experimenting with the plants in your neighborhood, you will find some plants will give you color and others will not. And then, though you have scoured and mordanted your goods, you will still find that some of the colors you have made fade . . . quickly. Though what does quickly mean? For some, quickly is fifty years, and for others it is one week. When setting out to dye and experimenting with local dyes, it is important to understand your expectations around how long you would like a color to last, as it may impact which plants you choose to use.

Every person is going to have a different opinion on how long they would like dyed color to last, and it is likely their expectation is going to be interwoven with the project they intend to make. For example, if you are making a quilt or doing colorwork knitting and the color

fades, it would be nearly impossible to re-dye the project and capture the multitude of colors used originally. For these projects, it may be best to use dyes that have a proven record of colorfastness and have commonly been used in production dye studios. These dyes include madder, cochineal, logwood, weld, plants and trees bearing high tannic properties such as oak, maple, and acacia (cutch), and indigo. While all are considered very colorfast, even within this group some last longer than others. If you are especially concerned with colorfastness, it is wise to take the time to test the colorfastness of the dyes you plan to use.

If you are curious about your garden and the plants in your neighborhood, time is free-flowing, and you are either OK with fading or with re-dyeing, the world is your oyster. It is really exciting to use the plants immediately available to you. It brings a whole new life and meaning to the plants around you. In terms of sustainability, it could be better to use a plant that can be found locally or one you can grow, even if some of the dye sourced may fade in the next few years and the textile may need to be re-dyed, than to use plants that may give color for fifty years but have to be imported.

WIDENING THE SPECTRUM

As you test the plants in your neighborhood, you will most likely end up with a lot of yellow goods. This isn't surprising, as yellow is the most common color created by plants. Though isn't it nice to discover other colors? Here are the methods we used when making the shade cards to move beyond yellow and create a wider spectrum of color:

Keep Experimenting and Keep Good Notes

When running these tests, even though we did have a lot of yellow, we had a few surprises—like the lupine flowers imparting a light tourmaline green (whereas lupine leaves yield yellow). Don't give up hope. Keep trying!

Record the details of your dyeing experiments so you can remember them. Understanding the relationship between the plant and the amount used, the type and amount of fiber used, and the amount of water will make you a better dyer. Read more about the note-taking process on page 215.

Use Naturally Colored Fibers to Create a Larger Palette

Sheep and cotton grow in a range of natural colors. White wool and cotton may be the most commonly found, but with a bit of persistence it is possible to find an incredible range of naturally colored wool, such as silver, gray, black, taupe, and brown, and cotton in shades of umber, brown, and green. Using these naturally colored fibers makes an incredible difference when working with locally sourced dyes. As you can see from the swatches on the shade cards in this and the following chapter, naturally colored wools play an important role in widening the spectrum.

Use Different Parts of the Plants at Different Times of the Year

You don't necessarily need a lot of plants to work with—sometimes simply using different parts of the plant at different times of the year can yield a variety of colors. Test the leaves, flowers, bark, and roots. Look to the shade card for examples of how we used dock root to get a warm, rusty orange and the same plant's leaves to get a clear, vibrant yellow. The season can impact the color a plant imparts, too, because the water in the plant fluctuates and affects its composition. Choose your favorite tree and try using its bark and leaves in the spring, summer, fall, and winter. Compare your results.

Shifting pH

Some dyestuffs are particularly sensitive to shifts in pH. Raising and lowering the pH in the dyeing process can lead to creating more colors. For example, to get the soft petal pinks as seen on the shade cards from avocado pits and birch bark, the pH was raised when extracting the dye, and then lowered when used as a dye to protect the hand of the wool. When trying to extract the color without raising the pH, the resulting color was often brown and the process took longer. Swatches made of rhubarb and dock root shifted from golden yellow to a deep terra-cotta by submerging the goods in a basic solution of water and limestone. To learn how to raise and lower pH when using natural dyes, see page 230.

Use Iron

Iron adds a gray tone to the colors, shifting them to a darker, moodier shade; oranges shift to brown, yellows shift to green. This is an easy way to widen your palette using local plants. Both of the Iceland-inspired shade cards include a panel where we shifted the color of the dyed samples using the light iron water solution below. Take care: Protein-based fibers are especially prone to damage during the iron application process. Iron can make the texture feel rough and the fibers brittle. Submerge the goods in the iron solution only as long as to achieve the desired color, and keep the heat low. To learn how to use iron to shift colors, see page 234.

eco-printed table linens

MATERIALS

1 place mat and napkin, 100% linen, scoured (page 220) and mordanted with soy milk (page 227)

Yellow onion skins

Strong cotton string, like kitchen twine, or button and craft thread

TOOLS

Scissors

Wooden dowel, PVC pipe, or branch, approximately 1 to 2 inches (2.5 to 5 cm) in diameter, 7 inches (17 cm) long

3- to 5-quart (2.8- to 4.7-L) stainless steel pot with lid

Tongs

Timer

Thermometer

ECO-PRINTING, THE PROCESS of taking a plant or mushroom and printing with it on fabric or yarn, is another great way to test if a plant or mushroom contains dye. In the eco-printing process, you are applying pressure, pushing the plant or mushroom into the fabric rather than dissolving the plant in water, so you are starting with the most concentrated application of the plant's dye. It will be easy to see from the print whether or not the plant gives dye easily. If you are testing plants and mushrooms and they do not yield any color or you do not like the results, always remember that once a fabric or yarn is mordanted, you can always re-dye it.

This project features easily available items from your grocery store and pantry that can be used to create beautiful textiles. Soybeans are used as a mordant. Onion skins, a phenomenal and easily accessible dyestuff giving saturated warm shades of gold and orange, are used to create patterns evocative of geological formations. Red onion skins can also be used.

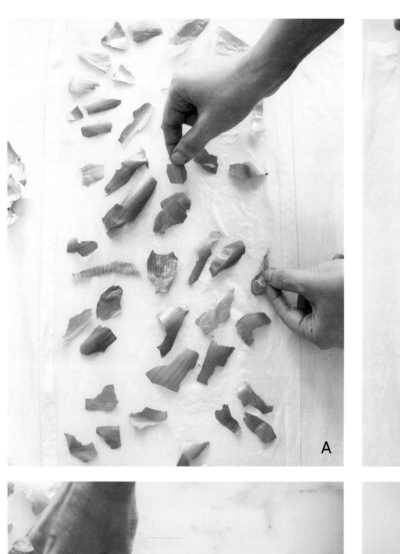

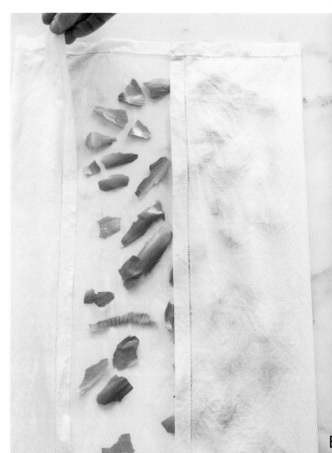

INSTRUCTIONS

1. Soak the place mat in warm water until fully saturated. Lay the place mat flat on your work surface. Place the onion skins along the middle of the place mat. In order to capture the shape of the onion skins, place them in a single layer. (A) Fold the bottom quarter of the place mat up to cover, the edge of the place mat meeting its center, then fold the top quarter down to enclose the onion skins, meeting the center of the place mat. Fold once more, along the center of the place mat. Make sure that the folded width of the fabric fits onto the dowel; refold if necessary. (B)

2. To form the bundle, starting at one end, roll the place mat tightly around the dowel.

3. Repeat step 1 with the napkin, then roll the napkin tightly over the place mat around the same dowel. (C)

4. Wrap the rolled bundle tightly with the string. (D) Place the bundle in the pot.

5. Add enough water to the pot to completely submerge the bundle.

6. Heat, covered, to 190°F (88°C), turning the bundle every 15 minutes. Adjust the heat to hold at this temperature and simmer for an additional 60 minutes, continuing to turn the bundle every 15 minutes. (E)

7. Turn off the heat. Allow the bundle to cool in the water.

8. Snip off the threads and unroll the bundle. Remove the onion skins and admire the results! (F)

9. Wash the goods (page 236) and allow to dry.

basalt knit hat

SIZE
One size fits most

FINISHED MEASUREMENTS
20-inch (50-cm) circumference × 8 inches (20 cm) tall

NOTE: This hat will stretch to fit up to a 22-inch (55-cm) head circumference.

GAUGE
18 stitches and 20 rows over 4 inches (10 cm) in colorwork, blocked

MATERIALS
Lopi Lettlopi (100% Icelandic wool; 109 yards [100 m]/50 g), 1 skein each:
Color A: #0054 light ash heather
Color B: Plum leaves on #0056 ash heather
Color C: #0051 white
Color D: Chestnut on #0051 white
Color E: Plum leaves on #0051 white

ONE OF THE HIGHLIGHTS of visiting Iceland is the number of shops featuring hand-knits. You will see mitts, hats, and scarves, but the most ubiquitous knitwear in the country is the iconic *lopapeysa*, a wool sweater made out of Icelandic wool. There are stacks of sweaters, both pullovers and cardigans, in a variety of sizes, all designed to keep the wearer warm in Iceland's cold, damp climate. In some shops, you will also find large cakes of yarn, many in the natural colors of the sheep, as well as kits so you can knit your own *lopapeysa*. Lopi, the iconic yarn found across Iceland, even in its grocery stores. We chose the three undyed colors offered in this yarn, to overdye with locally foraged dyestuffs, to create this hat.

The most striking feature of a *lopapeysa* is the colorwork yoke. Colorwork knitting provides extra warmth and is fun and engaging to knit. It is also a great way to make use of small skeins of color. Through the process of testing the plants in our neighborhood, we amassed quite a collection of small hanks of naturally dyed yarn. With this in mind, we designed a hat that would use a small amount of several colors, making the most of our small batches of yarn. Colorwork knitting is an ingenious way to make a little naturally dyed yarn go a long way, and it allows the small amount of dye you have gathered to create maximum impact. For those who love neutrals but would like to incorporate a little color into their wardrobe, these small pops of dyed yarn are a great way to celebrate local color.

To complete the colorwork, you will need about 5 yards (5 m) for each of the two larger motifs and 3 yards (3 m) for each color on the accent band.

TOOLS

One US 5 (3.75 mm) circular needle (for cast-on and ribbing)

One US 6 (4 mm) circular needle or size needed to obtain gauge

One set of four double-pointed needles size US 6 (4 mm) or size needed to obtain gauge

Stitch markers

Tapestry needle

STITCH PATTERN

3 × 3 Rib
All rounds: *K3, p3; repeat from * to end.

HAT

Using smaller circular needle, cast on 90 stitches with color A. Join for working in the round, being careful not to twist stitches; place marker for beginning of round.

Begin 3 × 3 Rib; work even until piece measures 1 inch (2.5 cm) from the cast-on. Knit 3 rounds.
Work rows 1–19 of the chart.
Knit 9 rounds.

SHAPE CROWN

NOTE: Change to double-pointed needles when necessary for the number of stitches on the needle.

Next Row (begin decreases): *K3, sl 1, k2tog, psso, k4; repeat from * to end.
Next Row: *K2, sl 1, k2tog, psso, k3; repeat from * to end.
Next Row: *K1, sl 1, k2tog, psso, k2; repeat from * to end.
Next Row: *Sl 1, k2tog, psso, k1; repeat from * to end.
Next Row: *K2tog; repeat from * to end.

Cut yarn, leaving a 12-inch (30.5-cm) tail; thread tail through remaining stitches, pull tight, and fasten off. Weave in ends and block as desired.

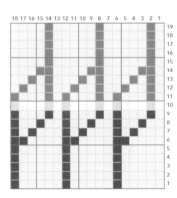

CHART COLOR KEY

Color A:
Color B:
Color C:
Color D:
Color E:

HAT COLORWAYS (COLOR A AND COLOR C ARE UNDYED)

HAT	COLOR B	COLOR D	COLOR E
1	Plum leaves on dark gray	Chestnut on white	Plum leaves on white
2	Rhubarb root on dark gray	Birch leaves on white	Rhubarb root on white
3	Lavender on dark gray	Lavender on white	Lupine on white
4	Cort on dark gray	Dock leaves on white	Cort on white
5	Redwood cones on dark gray	Yellow onion skins on white	Redwood cones on white

blönduós-inspired mending

MATERIALS

Lopi Lettlopi (100% Icelandic wool; 109 yards [100 m]/50 g), naturally dyed, 1–5 yards depending on the size of the mending project in desired color(s)

TOOLS

Scissors or snips

Tapestry needle

Erasable fabric pen

Rectangles on front of the sweater:
• Pink-colored rectangle: #0051 white yarn dyed with avocado pits
• Orange-colored rectangle: #0051 white yarn dyed with juniper berries
Circle on the collar:
• outline: #0056 ash heather yarn dyed with hibiscus
• fill: #0056 ash heather yarn, undyed

NOTE: For best results, use a yarn the same gauge as the yarn used to knit the sweater.

WHEN WE WERE INTRODUCED TO THIS style of stitching through the Vatnsdæla Tapestry Project in Blönduós, it immediately became apparent that it would be a great way to mend sweaters. You can choose to outline your design using a backstitch to provide extra stability or go straight to the fill stitch to mend the fabric.

INSTRUCTIONS

1. Looking closely at the hole in your knit piece, carefully remove any frayed or cut yarn, exposing any live stitches.

2. Thread your tapestry needle with the color you have chosen for the fill. Use a length of yarn three times the circumference of the hole you are mending. Insert the tapestry needle through all the live stitches. Catch the stitches alongside the live stitches for extra stability. Ignore the frayed yarn ends. Taking these steps will stop the hole from growing any larger. Weave in the ends.

3. Using the air-erasable pen, draw a shape at least ½ inch (12 mm) larger than the hole you are covering.

4. Thread your tapestry needle with your fill-in color. Using the guidelines you have drawn, start stitching all the way to the left of the shape you are filling, and work across the shape toward the opposite edge. Make vertical stitches ¼ inch (6 mm) apart; work only along the right side of the fabric. There will be gaps between the lines of stitching. Work back in the direction you came in the same way, closing any gaps. You may need to repeat this a couple of times to completely fill in the shape.

5. Once the vertical fill is complete, make horizontal stitches over them. Anchor any long horizontal stitches with small stitches. (This is called couching and adds durability to the stitches.) When complete, weave in the ends.

6. If you would like to add an outline, rethread your needle with your desired color. Using a ½-inch (12 mm) backstitch, stitch along the outline. To avoid creating and accentuating any gap between the rows of knit stitches on your sweater, intentionally sew through the sweater's stitches, splitting them, when possible.

7. Once complete, cut the yarn, weave in your ends, and happily wear your newly repaired sweater!

CHAPTER TWO

MEXICO

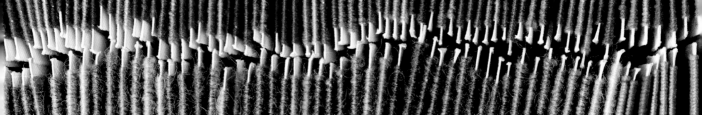

a rainbow of natural color //
letters from teotitlán del valle

WE FIRST MET DEMETRIO BAUTISTA LAZO at a fiber spinning conference in Lake Tahoe in 2012. He was offering his naturally dyed, handwoven rugs for sale. Nature informed Demetrio's dyeing and weaving via motifs and locally sourced color; there was a distinct impression of place upon his textiles. We were completely captivated by his work and the range of naturally dyed colors he was achieving. Over the years, friends of ours traveled to Oaxaca to dye and weave with Demetrio and always came back beaming, telling us we had to go. So finally, the day came when we decided it had been long enough—it was time to head to Oaxaca, an epicenter of handmade textiles and natural dyeing, to visit Demetrio.

Dyeing with cochineal, the scale insect that grows upon the nopal cactus, is said to have originated in Oaxaca. Though we had been dyeing with imported cochineal for many years, in our desire to learn more about the source of our dyes, as we have been doing with the wool we use in our line of yarns, we wanted to travel to Oaxaca to see where and how cochineal was grown, and how dyers like Demetrio use it in their work. What we thought would be a rather straightforward trip blossomed into an incredible journey. With Demetrio as our guide, we met many artisans and craftspeople, all of whom have contributed to Oaxaca's incredible textile legacy.

We flew into Oaxaca City, Demetrio picked us up, and away we went! We drove out of the bustling city center and into the country. The winding two-lane road took us through small villages and past rows and rows of large agave used to make mezcal. After an hour or so, we reached the small village of Chichicapám. There we met Cristina and Agustina, cousins who enjoy each other's company while creating handspun yarn from local sheep's wool in a range of natural colors. Using a pair of brushes called *handcards*, Cristina takes washed sheep's fleece and brushes the wool to open it, creating a small cylinder of wool called a *rolag*. Agustina takes the wool Cristina has prepared and, one rolag at a time, carefully and precisely using her spindle, adds twist to the wool, creating yarn, wrapping it inch by inch around the bottom of her spindle. Eventually, once the spindle is full of yarn, Agustina wraps it into a ball. Demetrio particularly enjoys dyeing and weaving with their handspun yarn because of the wide range of natural colors available; the handspun texture adds body and life to his rugs, and he enjoys supporting the two cousins. Using naturally colored wools greatly enhances the naturally dyed spectrum of color, making it possible to achieve colors otherwise impossible to get. Weaving the naturally colored wools alongside naturally dyed wools is an apt way to create contrast and a beautiful way to incorporate another aspect of nature and beauty into any piece. We selected a range of natural colors of their handspun yarn to be used during our week of dyeing. We completed

---

Cristina and Agustina handspin wool that is later dyed at Demetrio's courtyard studio. In the hills above Teotitlán del Valle, we gather wild *pericón*.

the day's journey in Teotitlán del Valle, the village where Demetrio is from and where his guesthouse, natural dyeing and weaving workshop, and shop are located.

Nestled in the foothills of the Sierra Juárez mountains, the Zapotec village Teotitlán del Valle is the Oaxacan epicenter for weaving rugs. Demetrio uses elements from existing rug motifs that are part of the lexicon of Teotitlán del Valle, including designs that represent the natural elements, such as stars, agave plants, and butterflies. He also uses designs that are derived from his Zapotec history, like the geometric carvings on the walls of Mitla and Monte Albán. Mitla, located about 12 miles (20 km) from Teotitlán, was inhabited from 100–650 AD. It was the religious center for the Zapotecs and holds the tombs of Zapotec kings. It is unique in that the designs on the walls are made of individually carved stones that fit together without mortar, creating a relief mosaic unlike any other site in Mexico. Monte Albán, a bit farther away, was built by the Zapotecs 2,500 years ago and was the first large urban complex in Mesoamerica. At first it was a ceremonial center, and then became the Zapotec sociopolitical and economic center. At Monte Albán, the artwork is expressed through murals, sculptures, carvings, pottery, and many other ornaments. Both places are important archaeological sites relating to the Zapotec political and religious history. By using elements from these two places in his rugs, Demetrio honors his heritage and maintains the legacy of this important history.

The next day at the break of dawn, the air chilly, we drove into the hills above Teotitlán del Valle to gather dyes. The arid plains quickly gave way to steep green hills of oak and agave. Oaxaca has an incredible amount of biodiversity—at least eight of the fourteen vegetation zones present in Mexico can be found in Oaxaca. There are more than 8,400 registered plant species, including pines, oaks, giant philodendrons, bromeliads, orchids, agave, cactus—such as the nopal, the preferred abode of cochineal—coffee, and cacao tree. First, we went to a field filled with *pericón* (*Tagetes lucida*), its

tiny golden flowers glowing with the rising sun, and we harvested an armful. We returned to the car and continued driving up the steep hill. We stopped, parked on the side of the road, and pulled electric orange dodder (*Cuscuta sp.*), a parasitic plant resembling plastic netting, off its unsuspecting victim. We drove deeper into the hills, to a stand of grand oak trees, their branches intertwined with one another, blocking out the light, with pale grayish-green lichen (*Usnea sp.*) cascading from the lowest branches. Demetrio gathered a bagful. Upon returning to the studio, there were whole pomegranates, dried by the sun and cracked, as well as pecan leaves and hulls, dried cochineal, chunks of indigo, and a green plant unrecognizable to us, which Demetrio referred to as *muicle* (*Justicia spicigera*), all waiting to be used as dyes.

We started by breaking down the balls of yarn into small skeins with the plan of making as many colors possible in a week's time. We began preparing the yarn for scouring and mordanting, and though these steps may be a bit on the boring side, as playing with color is always more fun and rewarding, they are absolutely necessary in creating long-lasting color. Demetrio pulled out a yucca root and, using a cheese grater, shredded it into a large pot of water, to be used as the soap to prewash the wool. Sure enough, as he began to take the skeins of yarn and agitate the water, soap suds began to form. After all the skeins had been washed, it was time to mordant the yarn.

In the mid-1990s, Demetrio was working with his father, weaving and using aniline dyes to create rugs. They had many wholesale clients in the United States and business was good. There were a few people in Demetrio's village using natural dyes, and tourists were expressing interest in natural dyeing, so he decided to learn more. Motivated to produce a different type of product for the industry that had a richer context, he wanted to continue this family legacy of weaving with the addition of natural dyeing as a value-added element.

Things were a bit touch and go at first. He knew people were combining cochineal with baking soda to get

Demetrio weaves a naturally dyed rug. He often creates complicated geometric patterns and employs many colors, such as in the example shown.

purple but couldn't understand exactly how to get there. "I used one kilo baking soda, boiling hot water, and a lot of my wool, and I completely ruined it. My dad was so mad at me; he said, 'See, I told you, you can't do that. Why can't you be normal? You know, everybody's doing this [using aniline dyes]. Why do you want to use natural dyes? You're just wasting our wool, our money, and our time.' But I didn't give up and found the way to do it." Learning by trial and error meant a lot of time and materials lost but offered invaluable lessons, too. Demetrio told us a real turning point in his practice was learning about and understanding how pH impacts fibers and various dyes. From ruining that batch of wool by using baking soda and cochineal, Demetrio then proceeded with caution when it came to raising the pH to create an alkaline environment. He enjoyed learning about natural dyes because they challenged him. Demetrio continued to practice and experiment, and soon enough, he expanded his approach to using other dyes.

Now that the scouring and mordanting was complete, it was time to start the fun part—dyeing. The first day, we started with cochineal. We learned how to grind cochineal using the metate y mano. Demetrio set his dad up with a bucket of limes and a juicer, and his dad began to make lime juice. Then Demetrio took out two pots and placed the same amount of cochineal and water in each, though to one of the pots he added the lime juice, and began to heat them. Once the two pots came up to temperature, we began to add yarn. The yarn in the pot with only water and cochineal made pink. The yarn in the pot with the added lime juice—red! To make purple, we dipped cochineal-dyed yarn into baths of baking soda and limestone.

Using the collected and foraged dyes, over the next few days, we ran multiple dyepots, some made of singular dyes, some made of multiple dyes. We added many shades of naturally colored yarn: white, light brown, dark brown, and gray, and sometimes added skeins of yarn that

had been dyed with cochineal and *pericón*, layering colors. We were tossing in yarn here and there. Finally, once we had built up hundreds of colors, we made an indigo vat and dipped the array of naturally colored wool yarn and some of the naturally dyed mini skeins of yarn in indigo, completing our full spectrum of color.

In the afternoons, after lunch, Demetrio would weave. Throughout the courtyard, the sound of his weaving reverberated—pressing the pedal on the loom, causing one heddle to lower and another to raise, throwing the shuttle, packing the newly passed, naturally dyed strand of wool with the beater. Repeat. Each time this motion happened, it sounded like one beat on a drum, an incredibly happy noise. Every so often there was a pause, as Demetrio reached a motif requiring an extra bobbin of thread to be wound through the warp, and then to pack down the yarn, he would pull the beater toward him—*boom!*

Once Demetrio got the hang of natural dyeing, he switched completely from aniline dyes to natural dyes. "I started liking it and discovering how natural dyes, like cochineal and indigo and plants and lichen, work and got so excited to see all these colors coming from nature. Plus, I wanted to leave these skills to my kids." Though Demetrio was really excited about naturally dyed rugs, his clients weren't. When he used chemical dyes, his wholesale rate was lower, and those selling his rugs could mark the rugs up three or four times. When he shifted to natural dyes, due to the higher labor and material costs involved, the prices he needed to charge increased. So those retailing the rugs could not make as much of a profit. He sold very few rugs for the first year, and then slowly things began to turn around. People who were looking for naturally dyed rugs began to seek him out. After three years, his mom and dad became interested in natural dyeing and he began to

teach them. Demetrio's three sisters also practice natural dyeing, and his son Victor, a recent high school graduate, practices natural dyeing and weaving and is beginning to work alongside Demetrio.

Honoring the richness of the visual language imbued within Demetrio's rugs and reflective of this heritage left us thinking about what shapes and forms may come to enrich our own textile designs, and about how Demetrio makes the most out of yarn dyed using materials that are hard to source or that he wants to use sparingly in order to protect the local habitat, such as *Usnea*. For example, the rug he was weaving while we were visiting was made mainly from naturally colored wool, with periodic highlights in the shape of diamonds formed by yarn dyed with *Usnea*. This is a beautiful example of the balance that can be achieved between natural color and observance and conservation of the plant's habitat.

When you're working with Demetrio, it feels like absolutely every shade of color is possible when using natural dyes. Similar to the feeling we had when we left Iceland, we left Oaxaca with a strengthened commitment to working with dyes made from our local dyestuffs, and to look more closely at pH to understand the nuances between the various agents that can raise and lower pH, as well as how those agents impact the shade of color according to when they are introduced in the natural dyeing process. Hearing Demetrio's story of switching from aniline to natural dyes, something he and his family were successful at, encouraged us to be brave and to continue taking risks for this process we love.

Demetrio Bautista Lazo
Demetrio.bautista.lazo@gmail.com
demetrio@teotitlan.com
www.teotitlan.com
To meet Agustina and Cristina, please contact Demetrio.

To create a rainbow of natural colors, a yucca root is used to scour the goods, Demetrio gathers dodder, and Adrienne grinds indigo. A pot nearby simmers with lichen and pomegranate.

hot pink //
letters from tlapanochestli

TLAPANOCHESTLI, MEANING "COLORS OF the cochineal," is located ten miles south of Oaxaca City in the town of San Bartolo Coyotepec. It is a farm, museum, research center, and teaching space dedicated to raising cochineal and the preservation of the use of cochineal by the Oaxacan people. Large banners flying near the entrance of the ranch announced the presence of cochineal through large images of stylistic red bugs. Driving through and walking to the main facility, we are surrounded by eight-foot-tall cacti, *Opuntia*. Their common English name is prickly pear, though you may also hear them referred to as *nopal*, their common Spanish name, derived from the Nahuatl word *nohpalli*. There are more than one hundred known species, the majority of which reside in Mexico. *Opuntia* are endemic to the Americas; in Mexico, they grow wild and are also cultivated for food. The nopal de castilla (*Opuntia ficus indica*) and the nopal de San Gabriel (*Opuntia tomentosa*) are the species grown at Tlapanochestli, because they are particularly nutritious for the cochineal diet. They have dense, oblong fleshy paddles, bigger than our heads, and they are some of the largest *Opuntia* cactus we have ever seen. Growing in neat rows, they vary in age and size.

We were greeted and welcomed to Tlapanochestli by the director, Manuel Loera Fernández, a researcher, teacher, and advocate for cochineal. He teaches people from around the world about the many facets of the little bug, its importance as a pigment to dye textiles, food, and makeup, as well as how to cultivate cochineal. He also hosts workshops in natural dyeing at the farm. Manuel maintains the legacy of Tlapanochestli's founder, Ignacio del Río y Dueñas, who started the farm more than thirty years ago.

To start our tour, we watched a short film about the history and life of cochineal. Native to Oaxaca, Mexico, cochineal was one of the main exports of Mexico to Europe in the sixteenth and seventeenth centuries. It is a small scale insect that feeds on *Opuntia* and protects itself with a white fuzz. When used in natural dyeing, it gives a spectrum of pinks, reds, and purples depending on pH level. After the film, we entered a small museum dedicated to the history, art, and textiles connected to cochineal. There are various food products that contain the red dye, and numerous artworks are created with cochineal-tinted paint. Whether we know it or not, cochineal has had a great impact on all our lives.

Then we visited a greenhouse where there were numerous cactus paddles standing up in trays of sand. We used magnifying glasses to inspect the tiny insects living on the paddles. Since these were cultivated cochineal, there were some as big as a coffee bean, much larger than their wild counterparts. Only the female cochineal is harvested for dye. Its life cycle is a total of three months. The adult male is a winged insect and only lives three to five days. This is just enough time to mate with a female, who will bear 150 to 200 eggs. The small baskets hanging on the top of the nopal paddle act as a

---

Rows of *Opuntia* are grown to feed the hungry cochineal. Tiny baskets hung on the cactus provide protection for the insects' eggs. Dried cochineal are ground into dye so they can make dozens of shades of pink, red, orange, and purple.

The white waxy filament is a sign that cochineal are present. The cochineal have hatched and moved from the basket, and are now maturing while they extract nutrients from the *Opuntia*.

nursery. About twenty female cochineal are placed inside the small basket to lay eggs, which will hatch in only two days. The mother is covered with white waxy filament, which protects her from the sun. The tiny nymphs crawl out of the basket over their mother to pick up some of the white waxy filament and onto the paddle to choose a spot to suck the juice from the cactus to grow. Carminic acid, the active ingredient of the dye, is present in the cochineal to protect them from microorganisms. After ninety days, all female cochineal, who are at least 2 millimeters long, are brushed off, sorted by size, and then dried for sale, production is limited at Tlapanochestli, so the facility focuses on supplying local artisans with cochineal. As we were about to leave, we saw a small store with various products for sale that contain cochineal and couldn't resist purchasing a tube of red lipstick, one of the original uses of the pigment.

Manuel's role is much greater than simply creating dye for people to make pink colored items—he is protecting and preserving a cultural heritage and history that is intertwined with this dye. We thanked Manuel and returned to the car. Reflecting on our time with Manuel reminded us of the importance of knowing where our dyes come from and of meeting those who have dedicated their lives to the production and processing of the dye. Seeing the dye growing, and learning about the time, labor, education, and resources it takes to create this dye (and others), we are reminded to take great care when using natural dyes, and to use every last drop.

Manuel Loera Fernández
Tlapanochestli Grana Cochinilla
Matamoros #100
San Bartolo Coyotepec, Oaxaca, Mexico
Telephone: +52 951 204 7433
Facebook: @Tlapanochestli

silk clouds //
letters from san pedro cajonos

ONE MORNING, WE PILED INTO DEMETRIO'S car and headed for the remote mountainside village of San Pedro Cajonos. This village specializes in the cultivation, spinning, weaving, and dyeing of silk. Demetrio parked the car, and we walked along a narrow, steep road through the village that leads to the studio of Moisés Martínez Velasco and Gladys Garcia Flores. It didn't take long to spot silkworms. Only a few steps into the village, perched on a low wall, we saw a Styrofoam container holding a pair of silk moths, mating and laying eggs. Next to them were silkworms eating mulberry leaves, who would soon start spinning silk cocoons and begin their transition into moths.

Silk that is processed on an industrial scale is typically classified into two categories: cultivated and wild. Cultivated silk is created from the cocoons of *Bombyx mori*, the most common silkworm. While in their larval stage, silkworms are given only leaves from the mulberry tree to eat. When the fattened caterpillars spin their cocoons, their specialized diet results in a very fine, soft white fiber with a consistent texture. Wild silk is produced by hundreds of different types of silkworms that eat a wide variety of leaves. Unlike the cultivated silkworm, wild silkworms complete their metamorphosis and emerge from the cocoons as moths. Their silk is naturally brown or beige from their varied diet, and their fiber tends to be coarser with more textural nuances.

Silk fiber, yarn, and fabric are not only impacted by how the moths are raised and by what they are fed but also by how the fiber is extracted from the cocoon. With cultivated silk, the filament is typically extracted from the unbroken cocoon, reeled onto a bobbin, and twisted with other filaments for strength. The core of the cocoon, and any other bits not part of that single filament wrapped around the cocoon, is either discarded or made into a special fiber called *noil*. Then the silk thread is treated to remove the sericin that lubricated the filament as it was spun by the silkworm, creating an extremely lustrous, soft, supple white thread that can then be woven or knit into fabric. Whereas with wild silk, the moth hatches from the cocoon and breaks the filament, so it cannot be reeled like cultivated silk. Instead, it is treated like wool, and multiple strands are carded and combed. This becomes silk top, which is then spun into yarn. This yarn, while still shiny and beautiful, is not as lustrous as that made from reeled, cultivated silk.

All this being said, as with many things covered in this book, there are many more nuances with locally grown materials and process than with large-scale production. The silk in Oaxaca is interesting because it is a combination of cultivated and wild silk. The silkworms eat mainly if not entirely a diet of mulberry leaves, so white silk is produced. Except for the very few moths that are allowed to hatch and mate in order to make more silkworms, most cocoons are taken whole. However, instead of reeling silk from the whole cocoons, the entire cocoon is spun into silk thread. To prepare the cocoon for spinning, a pot is filled with warm water and a pinch of either soda ash or baking soda to raise the pH of the water, causing the cocoons to soften when added to the pot. The silk thread

made from this type of preparation is matte, more similar to wild silk or silk noil, but stronger than noil from spinning the longer silk filaments.

Moisés and Gladys's studio consists of a single room, providing a space for Moisés's loom and a table and chair for Gladys to use as a surface to finish his weavings. The studio opens out to a large patio overlooking a deep valley and miles of rolling hills. This is where their dye studio is. Moisés and Gladys work together to create handspun, handwoven, naturally dyed shawls (*rebozos*) and tunics (*huipiles*). Her baby strapped to her back, Gladys places a painted bowl made from the fruit of the calabash tree on a chair. She rests her spindle in the bowl. As she takes a handful of softened silk cocoons, she sends her spindle twirling with the flick of her fingers, and as the twist travels into the silk fibers she holds, she pulls the fibers away from the spindle, creating a thin strand of silk thread. She stops and winds the thread onto the spindle and repeats the process over and over again. Over the course of many days, she will have spun enough silk to weave a piece of fabric for either a shawl, a tunic, or a dress.

Moisés picks up the warped backstrap loom, attached to a sturdy beam integral to the foundation of the studio, and walks about six feet from the beam. He places the loom over his head, the strap resting along the center of his back, and as he leans back, the weight of his body is the counterbalance to tighten the warp. He begins to weave a piece of silk fabric made from Gladys's spindle-spun silk thread. Moisés uses natural dyes, such as cochineal, indigo, and brazilwood, to add color to their pieces. Sometimes he dyes the silk thread before it is woven. Other times he dyes the piece afterward. Gladys, her baby at her side, completes their pieces by adding decorative knotting and tassels. Moisés and Gladys's process of spinning, weaving, and naturally dyeing locally grown silk provides an inspirational model for a very approachable, sustainable way to create a low-impact, local fiber practice requiring only a few tools.

Contact Information:
Moisés Martínez Velasco
mtzvmoises@gmail.com
moisesmtzv@hotmail.com

Gladys and Moisés work as a team to create hand-spun, hand-woven, naturally dyed silk textiles, such as the stack of scarves pictured. Gladys spins the silk and finishes the pieces; Moisés weaves and dyes them.

dyeing with tixinda //
letters from huatulco

WHEN WE STARTED PRACTICING THE ART of natural dyeing, we would hear stories of people using a rare crustacean called *Plicopurpura pansa,* known as *Caracol purpura* in Spanish and *tixinda* (pronounced "tishinda") in Mixtec, to dye yarn purple. This type of dyeing is still practiced in Oaxaca, one of the last places to still do so, by Don Habacuc Avendaño Luis. For hundreds of years, his community and family have been growing their own cotton, spinning it, making the long journey to the coast to dye it with *tixinda,* and returning to the village to weave the dyed purple threads on a backstrap loom into cloth for ceremonial and everyday clothing. As Habacuc says, "This is an ancient practice that defines our culture."

Tixinda is the only dye in the world that works similarly to indigo. The main dye molecule in *tixinda* (6,6'-dibromoindigotin) is closely related to indigotin (the main dye molecule in indigo). The differences in the molecule are what cause the dye to be purple rather than blue. In both situations, the dyer applies a colorless form of the dye to the goods. After being exposed to air, the dye changes to its true color: blue in the case of indigo, purple in the case of *tixinda.*

To meet Habacuc, we traveled with Demetrio from Teotitlán del Valle in central Oaxaca to the coastal city of Huatulco. Our trip took about six hours and exemplified the distinctly different bioregions within Oaxaca. In the crisp, cool air of Teotitlán, we had become accustomed to starting our day wearing layers and began this day like all the others. However, as we transversed the Sierra Madre del Sur mountains, riding along hairpin curves as we headed south to Huatulco, the oak and pine trees gave way to bromeliads and large-leafed banana trees and a wave of humidity sat heavy on our shoulders. Upon our arrival, we quickly changed into shorts and headed to the beach with Demetrio to swim and watch the sunset. We went to bed early, excited for the next day's dyeing adventure, where the ocean would be our dye studio.

The next morning, we drove out to a secluded cove following an unmarked dirt road that dropped us at the edge of the sea. Small huts lined the shore; tables and chairs all facing the lapping waves were set up along the

Habacuc and Rafael scale rocks to find the unassuming snail *Plicopurpura.* The sea snail secretes a milky liquid that makes a purple dye. After the yarn has been dyed, it is woven into traditional textiles, such as the *posahuanco* pictured.

beach, serving a variety of seafood and drinks. When dyeing with *tixinda*, you have to wait for low tide to be able to reach under the rocks to find the *Plicopurpura pansa*. While we waited for low tide, we sat with Habacuc, his son Rafael Avendaño Lopez, and Demetrio to learn more about Habacuc's history as a dyer.

Habacuc has been dyeing with *tixinda* for more than sixty years. In 1956, when Habacuc was fifteen years old, he asked his uncle if he could accompany him to the coast and learn to dye. His uncle said Habacuc could come as long as he could walk two hundred kilometers from his village, Pinotepa de Don Luis in Western Oaxaca to the coastal town of Puerto Ángel, over eight days. There, at the time, *tixinda* could be found living on the rocks near the beach. Habacuc felt that he could make the journey, so he set off with his uncle and other dyers in the community.

Once they reached the beach, his uncle taught Habacuc to take the snail from the rock, to gently touch the snail, causing the snail to secrete the dye, and to pour this secretion onto the cotton yarn Habacuc had brought with him. Then, to preserve the snail, his uncle taught him to place the snail back under the rock and to never place the snail on the rock in the hot sun. Habacuc was taught to take great care of the snail, to not harm it in the dyeing process, and to preserve it for the future so their dyeing tradition could continue.

Unlike his uncle and the other dyers, who had brought many skeins of yarn to dye and would spend multiple days dyeing, Habacuc had brought only a couple of skeins of yarn made of cotton grown and spun by those in his community, and was done dyeing within the first day or so. Since Habacuc was out of cotton yarn to dye and he had eaten all his food and would need to buy more for his trip home, he went to work in the port. Once his uncle was done dyeing, they returned to the village together. From then on, Habacuc returned with his uncle to the coast about every three months to continue dyeing. Visiting the coast with his uncle was an opportunity

for Habacuc to contribute to the long-standing heritage of his community and to experience life outside the village—for example, he remembers quite clearly the day he first saw an automobile. Today Habacuc is one of fifteen dyers left in his village. The youth of the village aren't as interested in the dyeing process as young Habacuc was. The dyers and the weavers of his village created a cooperative named Tixinda. Habacuc is the head of the dyeing part of the cooperative. They have a special permit granted by the government to use the snail, a protected species, for dyeing. Dyeing happens October through May, once the snails are done breeding. The population of this species of snail has reduced drastically as a result of people poaching it for food and to the increasing development along the coast. Habacuc now has to travel further, as he had done when we met him, to Huatulco because *tixinda* can no longer be found in Puerto Ángel. In the past, three skeins of yarn could be dyed in a day, whereas now they are lucky to get one-third of a skein of yarn dyed in a day.

Once dyed, the purple threads are brought back to the village and woven into cloth. Items woven include *posahuanco*, a piece of cloth worn as a sarong by the women of the village to celebrations like the town fiesta, parties celebrating saints, and weddings. This piece of cloth is so integral to their custom that a bride will weave one to wear on her wedding day. It is composed of bands of purple, pink, and blue stripes. The purple is made from *tixinda*. Historically, the pink was made from cochineal, and the blue was made from indigo, though now both of these colors are made using synthetic dyes. Also woven is cloth for *huipiles*, featuring motifs of scorpions, turkey, mountain corn, women holding hands, and stars made using *tixinda* dyed yarn. Sometimes naturally colored brown cotton, called *coyuchi*, is also used. Once the weaving of the cloth is completed, the *huipil* is seamed using crochet. At this time, the garments are made first for the community, and some are sold for sale to help sustain their way of life.

Alongside Habacuc, Rafael, and Demetrio, we boarded a small turquoise motorboat. The sun was beaming down, and waves lapped alongside the boat as we headed out into the ocean. Our seats were simple wooden boards, and every time we crashed through a wave we bounced in the air and back down again. Having only seen a few photos of the process, we were so excited to see *tixinda* dyeing in real life. After a ten-minute ride, we arrived at a secluded cove within the Huatulco National Park, the place where Habacuc has been given permission to dye with *tixinda*.

The captain of the boat took us in as far as he could, but due to the crashing waves and the rocky shore, he had to drop us about fifteen feet from the beach. Holding our bags above our heads, we hesitantly lowered ourselves into the warm water and, finding our footing, carefully walked to the shore. We looked around us in awe of the beauty: the arid terra-cotta desert meeting the aquamarine sea. We spent the afternoon in sweltering humid heat on a cliff over the ocean, dodging waves, listening to Habacuc describe how he dyes with the snail, and watching him. In one hand, he held his only tool, a two-foot-long narrow wooden stick. On one end it is sharpened into a point, and on the other it is shaped flat. He explains that these two sides help with the gentle care needed to remove the snails from the rocks without harming them. He also uses this tool to help stabilize himself as he climbs up, over, and around large rocks along the coast. Around his other hand, he wrapped the cotton yarn he is dyeing, making it possible for him to continue using his hands as he climbs rocks, and to dye as he goes. With one eye on the waves as they crash up over the rocks, he bends to inspect underneath the rocks, looking for the snails. Once he finds a snail, he gently removes it and tickles its belly, causing the snail to secrete the dye, and then pours the dye on the cotton thread wrapped around his hand. The color of the dye is first yellow-green, then turns to blue, and finally to purple. He quickly places the snail back to the underside of the rock and continues his journey along the rocks.

After three hours of working, as he told us on the beach, only one-third of the small skein of cotton yarn wrapped around Habacuc's hand is dyed. As the tide is coming in, we must stop for the day. We waded back out to the boat, bobbing in the ocean, where the captain helped pull us back into the boat. We enjoyed the cool breeze as we made our way back to the beach. We finished our day sharing lunch—a freshly caught grilled snapper—while Habacuc pondered whether he will return the next day to continue dyeing or to head home.

While any natural dyeing requires a deep commitment, witnessing Habacuc dyeing, learning that *Plicopurpura pansa* is becoming increasingly difficult to find, and hearing that the youth in Habacuc's village prefer to engage in activities other than dyeing heightens our concern and adds an urgency to support this rare form of dyeing before it disappears. It is possible to do so by purchasing handwoven, hand-dyed goods created by Habacuc and the Tixinda cooperative.

Rafael Avendaño Lopez
Telephone / WA: +52 954 544 8648
rafaavenlop@gmail.com

mexico-inspired palette

After visiting Mexico, we chose four dyes that represent the primary colors and created an incredible range of shades by altering pH and combining them in different ways. The cochineal was sourced from Tlapanochestli in Oaxaca; all other dyes were grown locally. See the shade cards on the following pages to view the colors made from these dyes.

1 Cochineal
  (fresh, dried, and powdered)

2 Marigolds

3 Pomegranates

4 Indigo

5 Limes

6 Limestone
  (represented as shells)

7 Cream of tartar

8 Yarn—undyed yarn used in the
  shade cards: AVFKW Flock,
  lighthouse, granite

9 Yarn—undyed white silk yarn
  and silk cocoons

widen your palette through dyeing techniques

The textiles created in Oaxaca are an incredible testimony to how locally sourced dyes can be altered and combined to create an incredible array of colors. Furthermore, they are an example of how to use one's locally sourced dyes to create textiles that are indicative and reflective of one's heritage and life experiences. Whereas in the last chapter the focus was on how to find dye within your local environment, this chapter is focused on how to take such dyes and widen your palette by honing in upon those dyes that are most potent and getting to know them better—their strength and if and how they respond to shifts in pH—and then, how to use dyeing techniques such as combining dyes, creating an ombré effect, and gradient dyeing to widen the spectrum and make the most of your locally sourced dyes. This chapter also touches upon how textiles can be a medium to express and remember experiences that are meaningful to you, as well as yet another way to widen your palette through design and placement of color.

The first step to gaining a deeper understanding of how to create a wider palette using your locally sourced dyes is to create a base palette (pages 72–76) in which you change the concentration of a particular dye and make multiple shades, and then, once you have this understanding, combine dyes. The shade cards (pages 78–87) indicate the amount of dye used and demonstrate how to create colors where both dyes shine. They also demonstrate how the order in which you apply the dyes will impact the final color; by switching which dye is applied first, you can create a very nuanced and full palette. Even more colors can be made by adding multiple dyes to one pot and then adding your goods to the dye.

The colors created in this chapter are only a small glimpse of what can be achieved using the techniques discussed. Use the shade cards as a guideline when combining dyes found in your area. Through combining dyes and the other dyeing techniques discussed in this chapter, there really are endless possibillites of shades, hues, and patterns of color to be made.

NOTE: Though the focus of this chapter is on wool and silk yarn, you can use the concepts and techniques discussed on fabric and cellulose-based fibers. Simply use the scouring and mordanting recipes created for those fibers, and be aware that due to the differences in composition, the colors may show up differently—offering even more possibilities.

CREATE A BASE PALETTE

If you are finding it difficult to create orange, green, or purple using only one dyestuff, combining dyes can be the key to creating those colors in a multitude of shades. You can, of course, simply combine dyes together in a pot and see what comes of it. Though to create the largest range of hues and shades, it is helpful to take the time to really study how each dye works before beginning to combine them. This can be accomplished through studying the strength of dye given by a particular plant, mushroom, or insect.

Just as with vegetables and spices, each dye has its own characteristics and flavor. When cooking to create a tasty dish, the flavors must be in balance—the same concept applies with color. Some dyes, like cochineal, are very potent, and only a small amount is needed to achieve a strong color. But with pomegranates, much more is needed to create the same saturation. There is a fine balance in honoring the strength of both dyes so one does not completely overpower the other, which easily happens with particularly strong dyes like cochineal and indigo.

The first step when approaching combining dyes is to create a base palette:

• Choose dyes that represent the primary colors of red, yellow, and blue. In this case, we have chosen cochineal to represent red, marigolds and pomegranates for yellow, and indigo as blue. Though the focus in this chapter is on the colors that can be created by combining these dyes, which are local to us, feel free to substitute with those that are local to you. For example, madder could be used as red; and sprigs of lavender, birch leaves, or yellow onion skins for yellow. Indigo provides the most colorfast blue, so there really isn't a substitute for it. Also, please note, though marigolds and pomegranates are somewhat similar in color, from the shade cards you can see they are different enough to create two sets of colors. Make sure to use the plethora of yellows nature provides to expand your palette.

• Focus on dyestuffs that are strong enough to make 3–5 shades of color; such dyes include those that create a medium or darker shade of color at 1–100% on the WOG. To create multiple shades of color, use either one of the Two Basic Methods of Dyeing (pages 227–229), and create a series of dyebaths with higher and lower amounts of dyestuff. The Base Palette shade card (page 79) gives you an example of increments and percentages to try.

• Test the dyes you have chosen to see if they are impacted by shifts in pH, as this will allow you to create even more colors from a single dye (page 230). You can use the colors made by shifting the pH as base colors in your palette, to be combined with other colors, as we have done with cochineal and as demonstrated on the Base Palette shade card. You can re-create similar effects using madder, dock, and rhubarb root, all dyes sensitive to shifts in pH.

Once you have completed the above steps, have made a series of colors and shades, and understand the strength of each dye, you now have a solid base palette from which to work and to create a spectrum of color with infinite possibilities.

The Dyes Used on the Base Palette Shade Card

COCHINEAL

Wild cochineal can be found growing in California and in the southwestern United States. If you live in these areas, keep an eye out for nopal cacti, and check to see if you can spot the fuzzy white layer indicating their presence. Cochineal will kill the cactus and are seen as a pest, so most people tend to remove them by spraying them off using water. If you would like to use wild cochineal as dye, carefully scrape it off the cactus using a spoon. You can use the cochineal fresh or dried to dye. If you would like to dry them, place the cochineal in the sun.

If you have access to fresh cochineal, you can start your own miniature cochineal farm. If you have the space, plant a nopal cactus in your yard, or grow one in a pot. Or you can create a smaller, more temporary version by placing nopal paddles in a container filled with sand or gravel. Instead of using the freshly harvested cochineal as dye, move them to your nopal paddles. Harvest the cochineal regularly, and make sure to add new, fresh nopal paddles to the container, for the health and longevity of your cochineal farm.

If you do not have access to cochineal locally, dried cochineal are widely available for sale. To dye with cochineal, grind cochineal bugs finely using an electric spice grinder or a mortar and pestle. Some people like to extract the color first (page 38), as ground bits of cochineal can leave dark spots. Strain cochineal using a fine mesh sieve lined with a coffee filter.

There are dyes, such as cochineal, whose color is easily impacted by shifts in pH in the mordanting and dyeing processes, as well as through baths following the dyeing process. Furthermore, the agent used to shift the pH matters. For example, if you dye with cochineal without affecting the pH, it is likely you will get a sallow purple. By lowering the pH when working with cochineal, you can get a vibrant pink. This can be accomplished by lowering the pH in the mordanting process or in the dyeing process, each of which will provide a different pink. By lowering the pH in the mordanting *and* dyeing process, as long as the pH is lower than a 3, requiring the addition of lime juice, lemon juice, or citric acid to the dyebath, you can achieve red. Once the goods have been dyed, by placing the goods into high pH baths, the color of the goods will shift to an array of purples.

For more information on how pH works and methods of shifting pH, see the Shifting pH section (page 230). You can apply these same principles and recipes to any dye sensitive to shifts in pH, such as dock root, rhubarb root, and madder root.

NOTE: Though cream of tartar is used in the mordanting process for wool to be dyed with cochineal, when mordanting silk, omit cream of tartar to protect the luster and to obtain the deepest color.

MARIGOLDS

Marigolds are incredibly easy to grow and use. The plant's leaves can be used, but the flowers create the big, bold shades of yellow reminiscent of the pure gold rays of sunshine. When using dried marigolds, focus on the petals rather than the stems to get clear shades of gold.

POMEGRANATES

Whole, dried pomegranates give gold and tobacco colors and were used for the shade cards in this section. Fresh pomegranate skins give light tan. If pomegranates grow in your area, ask your local farmer if there are any that cannot be sold at the market. Those who make juice are another possibility. You can also crack a pomegranate open slightly and either leave it out in the sun to bake or bake it on your lowest setting in the oven. When the pomegranate gets very dry, shrinks in size, and is a bit dusty, it's ready to use. Use a mortar and pestle to break the pomegranate into smaller pieces for use as dye.

INDIGO

Indigo is the key component to making vivid jewel tones when overdyeing reds, pinks, yellows, and golds. While there are a variety of indigo recipes in this book, in this chapter we focused on the indigo-fructose-limestone vat, as it is the most accessible indigo vat and easy to create at home. In looking closely at this vat, we noticed that less indigo is needed to dye wool, compared to indigo dyeing silk and cellulose, so we created a separate recipe for wool. Here are the recipes for the indigo vats used to create the samples on the shade card:

	#1	#2	#3	#4	#5
INDIGO	3.25g	13g	19.5g	26g	32.5g
LIMESTONE	6.5g	26g	39g	52g	65g
FRUCTOSE	9.75g	39g	58.5g	78g	97.5g

The samples on the shade card represent five different strengths of vats and what each of those strengths looks like when dipped three times or six times on white and gray yarn. When combining indigo with other dyes through layering, it can easily overpower the other color being used. These different strengths of vats will make it easier to create harmonious color combinations, where both dyes shine.

You will make the indigo-fructose-limestone vat as you would for the other fibers, following the instructions on page 196. However, due to the characteristics of wool, when dyeing with this type of vat, there are a couple of special considerations. To dye with indigo, the indigo vat must be alkaline (pH 10). Since wool is especially sensitive to alkaline environments, the high alkalinity of the vat can damage the fiber, making the texture brittle and easy to break. When indigo-dyeing wool, keep your indigo-fructose-limestone vat at 95–100°F (35–38°C).

Adrienne holds chunks of indigo dye. A dye pot with whole pomegranates slowly cooks, extracting the dye.

Avoid letting wool goods touch the bottom of the vat, and make sure to follow all instructions regarding washing and neutralization (pages 236–237).

DYEING TECHNIQUES USED TO WIDEN THE SPECTRUM

When applying the dyeing techniques discussed in this section, use whichever of the Two Basic Methods of Dyeing (pages 227–229) suits the size of project you are completing, unless otherwise noted. All the techniques discussed below can be either used on their own or combined to create your own unique colorways. For example, combine dyes and use this dyebath to create an ombré-dyed yarn. Apply a layer of eco-printing over the ombré-dyed yarn; the possibilities are endless.

Combining Dyes

LAYERING COLORS USING MULTIPLE DYEBATHS

Apply the first layer of dye. Once cooled, squeeze as much dye from the goods as possible. You do not need to wash the goods before proceeding to the second application of dye. Create a new dyebath as you did for the first layer of color with the next dye. See the shade cards on pages 80–87 for a selection of results from layering cochineal, marigold, and pomegranate dyes.

LAYERING COLORS USING INDIGO

If you choose to apply indigo first, do so, rinse the fibers, then mordant using aluminum potassium sulfate and cream of tartar, and then dye using cochineal, marigold, or pomegranate. The mordanting process is acidic and helps to bring down the pH of the indigo-dyeing process.

If you choose to apply cochineal, marigold, or pomegranate first, mordant using aluminum potassium sulfate and cream of tartar, then dye, and then dip into the indigo vat. Follow the instructions on page 237 to wash and neutralize your indigo-dyed yarn. See the shade cards on pages 82–87 to view the incredible jewel tones created by layering indigo with other dyes.

COMBINING COLORS IN ONE DYEPOT

Instead of adding only one dye, add two (or more) dyes.

Ombré Dyeing

Another way to achieve more interesting colors with few ingredients is to slowly add a skein of yarn to the dyepot, inch by inch. This will create a gradual range of color along the skein; the portion of the skein placed first in the dyebath will be darkest in color, and the last portion to enter the dyepot will be the lightest in color. If you wish, you can leave the top portion of the skein out of the pot to keep it white. To keep the skein out of the dyebath, place a pair of chopsticks or wooden skewer along the top of the pot and drape the yarn over it. Don't drape your goods over the side of the pot: The heat will singe them. For a gentle gradation, slowly lower the skein into the pot over the course of 45 minutes. For a sharper contrast, lower a portion of the skein of yarn into the dyepot when first starting to dye, and after 45 minutes, add the rest of the skein to the dyebath. After the last portion of yarn is added to the pot, continue to heat for another 30 minutes to set the dye. To calculate the amount of dye needed, roughly calculate the weight of the yarn that will first go into the dyepot, and base your math on this amount. If you calculate the amount of dye on the whole skein of yarn, you will have too much dye, and the skein will end up being nearly all the same color.

Eco-Printing Yarn

To eco-print on yarn, pre-wet a skein of yarn, squeeze out excess water, and lay it open on a flat surface. Sprinkle petals onto the yarn and push the petals into the strands of yarn. Twist the yarn back into a skein so the petals are wedged inside. Follow the instructions for Eco-Printed Table Linens (page 42) to set the color. Keep the yarn twisted into a skein while heating.

Gradient Dyeing

The goal of this method of dyeing is to create as many shades as possible by slowly adding multiple skeins of yarn into the dyepot over the course of at least an hour. The first skeins added to the dyepot will absorb the most dye and will be the most saturated in color; as more skeins are added and there is less dye in the pot, they will be increasingly lighter in color. This can be a little tricky—it is going to call upon your intuition—but the spontaneous results, which will be nearly impossible to reproduce, are worth it. We love these special one-of-a-kind colors!

Gather all the skeins of yarn you would like to dye using this method. It's nice to have a range of naturally colored wool on hand, to really pull some darker shades and push that palette to the limit! Choose the color you want the first skein of yarn to be. Calculate the amount of dye needed to make that color on only the weight of the first skein of yarn. Add enough water to cover one skein of yarn. Follow the instructions for One-Pot Dyeing (page 227). Once the dyebath has reached 190°F (88°C), gently push the first skein of yarn aside and pour enough warm water into the pot to cover the soon-to-be-added second skein of yarn. Do not pour this water onto the skein of yarn already in the pot; try to pour the water along the inside of the pot.

Add your next skein of yarn. Maintain the temperature for about 20 to 30 minutes, then add more water, as described above, and the next skein of yarn. Repeat this until you have added all your skeins of yarn and achieved a range of color across the skeins.

Once you are done dyeing, wash the skeins and analyze your results. If there are any repetitive colors that you would like to shift into a new color, set them aside to overdye using either indigo or multiple dyebaths (page 76) to continue pushing the spectrum.

Using Exhaust Baths

At the end of a dyeing session using medium and dark shades, most likely there will be dye left in the pot. This leftover dyebath is referred to as an exhaust bath; it can be a great way to make unique colors and use every last drop of dye.

To see an example of the colors that can be achieved using this method, refer to the silk shade card (page 87). To create the shades seen on this shade card, scour and mordant three skeins of yarn, each weighing the same amount. Take one skein of yarn and create a dyebath using the WOG of only this skein of yarn, using the percentage listed to calculate the amount of dye. Once the skein is done dyeing, and cool to touch, squeeze as much dye from the goods as possible back into the pot. Wash and hang the skein to dry (page 236). Take the second skein of yarn and dye it in the same dyebath, without adding any more dye. The colors achieved from this step are referred to as Exhaust Bath 1 on the shade card. After removing the second skein the same way as the first skein, dye the third skein in the same dyebath. The colors achieved from this step are referred to as Exhaust Bath 2 on the shade card. At this point, the dyebath is either completely exhausted or close to being exhausted with very little to no dye left in it.

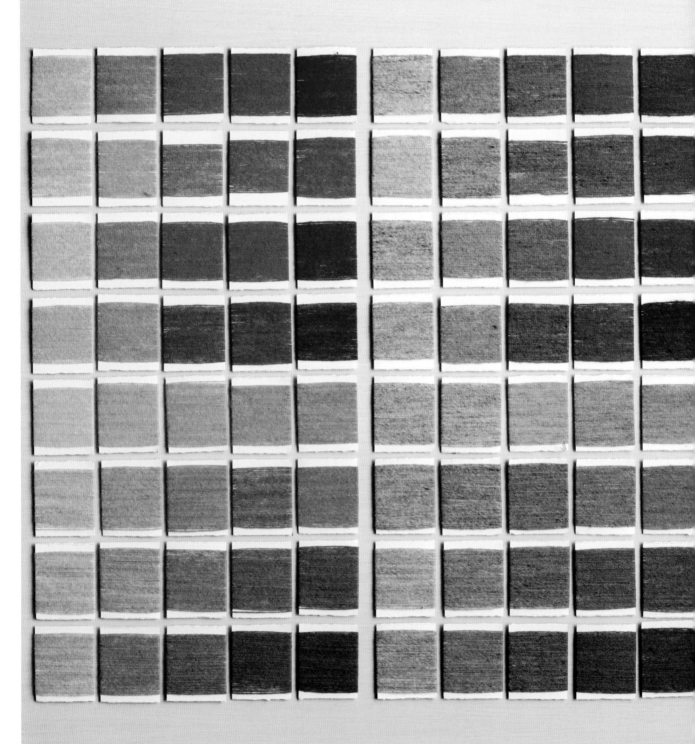

shade card: base palette on wool

GOODS: A Verb for Keeping Warm Flock (100% US wool) yarn, lighthouse (white), granite (gray)

SCOUR: Scouring Wool (page 217)

MORDANT: Mordanting Wool with Aluminum Potassium Sulfate and Cream of Tartar (page 220)

DYE: Colors made with cochineal, marigold, and pomegranates were created by using 100 g of goods and 8–9 cups (1.9–2 L) water in a 3-quart (2.8-L) pot. Follow the instructions on page 12 for colors made with indigo.

To learn how to use percentages in the dyeing process, see page 10.

DYE	WHITE YARN					GRAY YARN				
COCHINEAL	0.1%	0.5%	2%	4%	8%	0.1%	0.5%	2%	4%	8%
COCHINEAL WITH LIME JUICE*	0.1%	0.5%	2%	4%	8%	0.1%	0.5%	2%	4%	8%
COCHINEAL + LIMESTONE**	0.1%	0.5%	2%	4%	8%	0.1%	0.5%	2%	4%	8%
COCHINEAL WITH LIME JUICE* + LIMESTONE**	0.1%	0.5%	2%	4%	8%	0.1%	0.5%	2%	4%	8%
MARIGOLD	2%	4%	12%	16%	24%	2%	4%	12%	16%	24%
POMEGRANATE	10%	25%	50%	100%	150%	10%	25%	50%	100%	150%
INDIGO— 3 DIPS	#1	#2	#3	#4	#5	#1	#2	#3	#4	#5
INDIGO— 6 DIPS	#1	#2	#3	#4	#5	#1	#2	#3	#4	#5

*Added lime juice to the dyebath (page 231).

**Dipped into limestone solution after dyeing (page 232).

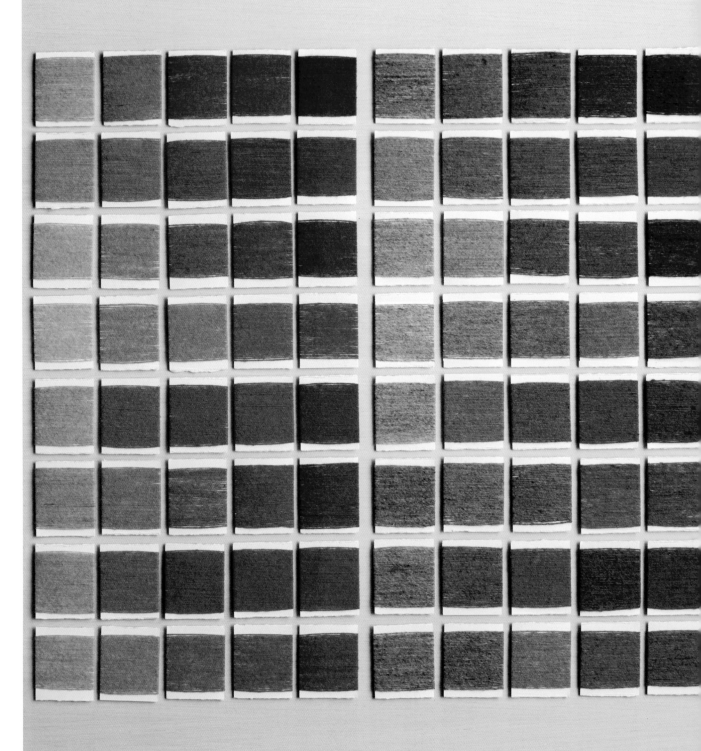

shade card: cochineal, marigold, and pomegranate overdyes

GOODS: A Verb for Keeping Warm Flock (100% US wool) yarn, lighthouse (white), granite (gray)

SCOUR: Scouring Wool (page 217)

MORDANT: Mordanting Wool with Aluminum Potassium Sulfate and Cream of Tartar (page 220)

DYE: All colors created by using 100 g of goods and 8–9 cups (1.9–2 L) water in a 3-quart (2.8-L) pot.

NOTES: The dyes in each row are listed according to order of application; for example, in the row Cochineal + Marigold, the yarn was first dyed with cochineal and then dyed with marigolds. The first percentage listed corresponds to the amount of cochineal used, and the second percentage listed corresponds to the amount of marigolds used. See Layering Colors Using Multiple Dyebaths (page 76) to learn more. To learn how to use percentages in the dyeing process, see page 10.

DYE	WHITE YARN					GRAY YARN				
COCHINEAL + MARIGOLD	0.1% + 4%	0.5% + 6%	2% + 16%	4% + 24%	8% + 32%	0.1% + 4%	0.5% + 6%	2% + 16%	4% + 24%	8% + 32%
MARIGOLD + COCHINEAL	2% + 0.1%	4% + 0.25%	12% + 0.5%	16% + 2%	24% + 3%	2% + 0.1%	4% + 0.25%	12% + 0.5%	16% + 2%	24% + 3%
COCHINEAL WITH LIME JUICE* + MARIGOLD	0.1% + 4%	0.5% + 6%	2% + 16%	4% + 24%	8% + 32%	0.1% + 4%	0.5% + 6%	2% + 16%	4% + 24%	8% + 32%
MARIGOLD + COCHINEAL WITH LIME JUICE*	2% + 0.1%	4% + 0.25%	12% + 0.5%	16% + 2%	24% + 3%	2% + 0.1%	4% + 0.25%	12% + 0.5%	16% + 2%	24% + 3%
COCHINEAL + POMEGRANATE	0.1% + 1%	0.5% + 50%	2% + 100%	4% + 150%	8% + 200%	0.1% + 1%	0.5% + 50%	2% + 100%	4% + 150%	8% + 200%
POMEGRANATE + COCHINEAL	10% + 0.1%	25% + 0.25%	50% + 0.5%	100% + 2%	150% + 3%	10% + 0.1%	25% + 0.25%	50% + 0.5%	100% + 2%	150% + 3%
COCHINEAL WITH LIME JUICE* + POMEGRANATE	0.1% + 1%	0.5% + 50%	2% + 100%	4% + 150%	8% + 200%	0.1% + 1%	0.5% + 50%	2% + 100%	4% + 150%	8% + 200%
POMEGRANATE + COCHINEAL WITH LIME JUICE*	10% + 0.1%	25% + 0.25%	50% + 0.5%	100% + 2%	150% + 3%	10% + 0.1%	25% + 0.25%	50% + 0.5%	100% + 2%	150% + 3%

*Added lime juice to the dyebath (page 231).

shade card: cochineal, marigold, and pomegranate overdyed with indigo

GOODS: A Verb for Keeping Warm Flock (100% US wool) yarn, lighthouse (white), granite (gray)

SCOUR: Scouring Wool (page 217)

MORDANT: Mordanting Wool with Aluminum Potassium Sulfate and Cream of Tartar (page 220)

DYE: Colors made with cochineal, marigold, and pomegranate were created using 100 g of goods and 8–9 cups (1.9–2 L) water in a 3-quart (2.8-L) pot. Follow instructions on page 12 for colors made with indigo.

NOTES: The dyes in each row are listed according to order of application; for example, in the row Cochineal + Indigo, the yarn was first dyed with cochineal, then dipped into the indigo vat. The percentage listed corresponds to the amount of cochineal used and the number listed corresponds to the indigo vat used. See Layering Colors Using Multiple Dyebaths (page 76) to learn more. To learn how to use percentages in the dyeing process, see page 10.

DYE	WHITE YARN					GRAY YARN				
COCHINEAL + INDIGO—3 DIPS	0.1% + #1	0.5% + #2	2% + #3	4% + #4	8% + #5	0.1% + #1	0.5% + #2	2% + #3	4% + #4	8% + #5
COCHINEAL + INDIGO—6 DIPS	0.1% + #1	0.5% + #2	2% + #3	4% + #4	8% + #5	0.1% + #1	0.5% + #2	2% + #3	4% + #4	8% + #5
COCHINEAL/ LIME JUICE* + INDIGO—3 DIPS	0.1% + #1	0.5% + #2	2% + #3	4% + #4	8% + #5	0.1% + #1	0.5% + #2	2% + #3	4% + #4	8% + #5
COCHINEAL/ LIME JUICE* + INDIGO—6 DIPS	0.1% + #1	0.5% + #2	2% + #3	4% + #4	8% + #5	0.1% + #1	0.5% + #2	2% + #3	4% + #4	8% + #5
MARIGOLDS + INDIGO—3 DIPS	0.1% + #1	0.5% + #2	2% + #3	4% + #4	8% + #5	0.1% + #1	0.5% + #2	2% + #3	4% + #4	8% + #5
MARIGOLDS + INDIGO—6 DIPS	0.1% + #1	0.5% + #2	2% + #3	4% + #4	8% + #5	0.1% + #1	0.5% + #2	2% + #3	4% + #4	8% + #5
POMEGRANATE + INDIGO—3 DIPS	0.1% + #1	0.5% + #2	2% + #3	4% + #4	8% + #5	0.1% + #1	0.5% + #2	2% + #3	4% + #4	8% + #5
POMEGRANATE + INDIGO—6 DIPS	0.1% + #1	0.5% + #2	2% + #3	4% + #4	8% + #5	0.1% + #1	0.5% + #2	2% + #3	4% + #4	8% + #5

*Added lime juice to the dyebath (page 231).

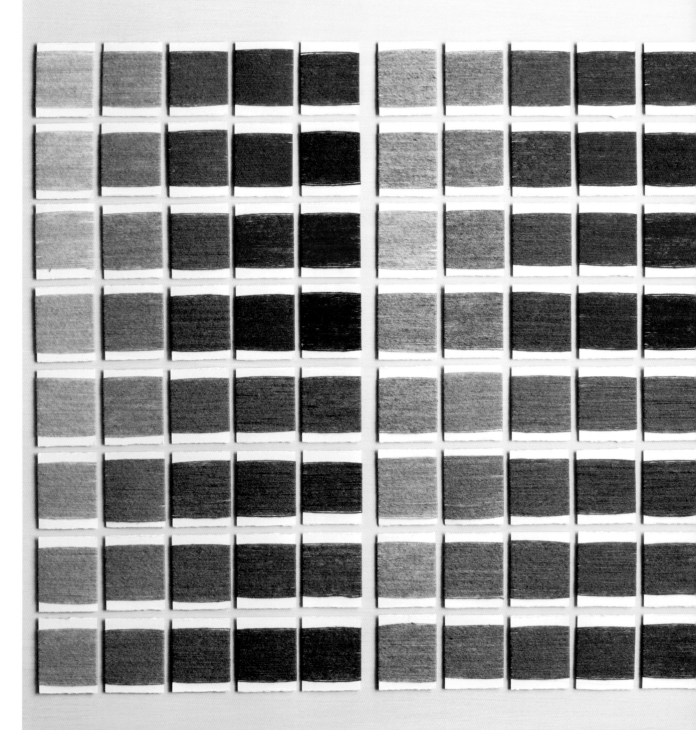

shade card: indigo overdyed with cochineal, marigold, and pomegranate

GOODS: A Verb for Keeping Warm Flock (100% US wool) yarn, lighthouse (white), granite (gray)

SCOUR: Scouring Wool (page 217)

MORDANT: Mordanting Wool with Aluminum Potassium Sulfate and Cream of Tartar (page 220)

DYE: Follow instructions on page 12 for colors made with indigo. Colors made with cochineal, marigold, and pomegranate were created using 100 g of goods and 8–9 cups (1.9–2 L) water in a 3-quart (2.8-L) pot.

NOTES: The dyes in each row are listed according to order of application; for example, in the row Indigo + Cochineal, the yarn was first dipped into the indigo vat and then dyed with cochineal. The number listed corresponds to the indigo vat used, and the percentage listed corresponds to the amount of cochineal used. See Layering Colors Using Multiple Dyebaths (page 76) to learn more. To learn how to use percentages in the dyeing process, see page 10.

DYE	WHITE YARN					GRAY YARN				
INDIGO—3 DIPS + COCHINEAL	#1 + 0.1%	#2 + 0.5%	#3 + 2%	#4 + 4%	#5 + 8%	#1 + 0.1%	#2 + 0.5%	#3 + 2%	#4 + 4%	#5 + 8%
INDIGO—6 DIPS + COCHINEAL	#1 + 0.1%	#2 + 0.5%	#3 + 2%	#4 + 4%	#5 + 8%	#1 + 0.1%	#2 + 0.5%	#3 + 2%	#4 + 4%	#5 + 8%
INDIGO—3 DIPS + COCHINEAL/ LIME JUICE*	#1 + 0.1%	#2 + 0.5%	#3 + 2%	#4 + 4%	#5 + 8%	0.1% + #1	0.5% + #2	2% + #3	4% + #4	8% + #5
INDIGO—6 DIPS + COCHINEAL/ LIME JUICE*	#1 + 0.1%	#2 + 0.5%	#3 + 2%	#4 + 4%	#5 + 8%	0.1% + #1	0.5% + #2	2% + #3	4% + #4	8% + #5
INDIGO—3 DIPS + MARIGOLD	#1 + 0.1%	#2 + 0.5%	#3 + 2%	#4 + 4%	#5 + 8%	0.1% + #1	0.5% + #2	2% + #3	4% + #4	8% + #5
INDIGO—6 DIPS + MARIGOLDS	#1 + 0.1%	#2 + 0.5%	#3 + 2%	#4 + 4%	#5 + 8%	0.1% + #1	0.5% + #2	2% + #3	4% + #4	8% + #5
INDIGO—3 DIPS + POMEGRANATE	#1 + 0.1%	#2 + 0.5%	#3 + 2%	#4 + 4%	#5 + 8%	0.1% + #1	0.5% + #2	2% + #3	4% + #4	8% + #5
INDIGO—6 DIPS + POMEGRANATE	#1 + 0.1%	#2 + 0.5%	#3 + 2%	#4 + 4%	#5 + 8%	0.1% + #1	0.5% + #2	2% + #3	4% + #4	8% + #5

*Added lime juice to the dyebath (page 231).

shade card: natural dyes on silk, including indigo overdyes

GOODS: A Verb for Keeping Warm Lumen (100% silk noil) yarn, lighthouse (white)

SCOUR: Scouring Silk (page 218)

MORDANT: Mordanting Protein-Based Fibers with Aluminum Potassium Sulfate (page 219)

DYE: Colors made with cochineal and marigold were created using 100 g of goods and 4½ cups (1 L) water in a 3-quart (2.8-L) pot.

NOTES: The section titled White Yarn was made by scouring and mordanting the yarn, and then, using the WOG of only the first skein of yarn and the percentage listed in the far left column, dyeing it. Subsequent skeins of yarn were dyed in the leftover dyebath. Follow the instructions on page 77 to learn more.

The section titled Indigo-Dyed Yarn was made by scouring the yarn and dyeing with indigo. The yarn was then mordanted, and overdyed using the same dyes, percentages, and method of using exhaust baths as the left side of the shade card. Follow the instructions, using vat #3, on page 195 for colors made with indigo.

	WHITE YARN			INDIGO-DYED YARN		
INDIGO	n/a	n/a	n/a	9 dips	6 dips	3 dips
COCHINEAL	20%	Exhaust Bath 1	Exhaust Bath 2	9 dips + 20%	6 dips + Exhaust Bath 1	3 dips + Exhaust Bath 2
COCHINEAL WITH CREAM OF TARTAR*	20%	Exhaust Bath 1	Exhaust Bath 2	9 dips + 20%	6 dips + Exhaust Bath 1	3 dips + Exhaust Bath 2
COCHINEAL WITH LIME JUICE**	20%	Exhaust Bath 1	Exhaust Bath 2	9 dips + 20%	6 dips + Exhaust Bath 1	3 dips + Exhaust Bath 2
MARIGOLD	40%	Exhaust Bath 1	Exhaust Bath 2	9 dips + 20%	6 dips + Exhaust Bath 1	3 dips + Exhaust Bath 2

*Added cream of tartar at 10% on the WOG to the dyebath (page 231).

**Added lime juice to the dyebath (page 231).

depth of field cowl

ONE OF THE MOST COMMONLY asked questions at A Verb for Keeping Warm is how to choose colors when planning a project. This simple cowl pattern is the perfect canvas to study color, use your naturally dyed yarn, and learn about color combinations that make your heart sing. Let's approach this topic head-on and break it down so working with color can be fun. And remember, the more you work with color, the easier the process becomes.

FIND INSPIRATION

First, find a point of inspiration, such as a favorite photo. When planning this cowl, we chose a photo taken during one of our fondest memories of Oaxaca. On our way to the village of San Pedro Cajonos, we stopped for breakfast at a quaint café. The morning was foggy and cool, and the inside of the café was warm from the curling flames of fire in the hearth used to cook our food and redolent of the scent of freshly brewed coffee intermingled with a slight hint of woodsmoke. The colors of the interior were particularly pleasing—the jade color of the walls juxtaposed with the terra-cotta earthenware, the cerulean blue and ivory of the enamelware pots used to cook the food. The palette found in this photo, and which the cowl features, are embedded with fond memories—from visiting this café to the day ahead meeting dyers and weavers and talking about textiles. Wearing the cowl is like being transported back to that day and is a reminder of the happiness and gratitude we felt when in Oaxaca.

DESIGN A PALETTE

Choose a photo to guide your selection of colors. Make a list of the colors you see, particularly those that stand out or hold particular meaning to you. Compare the photo and your list with the colors on the shade card, noting those that match, and dye them. Or you may have already created a variety of naturally dyed hues and shades to choose from.

DECIDE HOW TO USE YOUR CHOSEN PALETTE

Use watercolors or colored pencils to decide how to use the colors in your cowl. In the cowl pictured, we decided to use dyed color for only one-third of the cowl. The rest of the cowl was knit using naturally colored light-brown and white marled wool yarn. The order of the colors found in the photo is the same order used when knit. Though we only used dyed color for a portion of our cowl and went for a more literal emulation of the photo, you can knit your cowl entirely out of dyed yarn and pattern your chosen colors any way you like.

One size fits most

**7½ inches (19 cm) wide
× 44 inches (112 cm)
circumference**

GAUGE

**30 stitches and 30
rows over 4 inches
(10 cm), blocked**

MATERIALS

**A Verb for Keeping
Warm Flock (100%
California wool; 290
yards [265 m]/50 g]):
1 skein granite, total
weight 50 g; plus
various colors from dyed
samples, total weight
40 g (232 yd [212 m])**

TOOLS

**One US 1 (2.25 mm)
24-inch (61-cm) circular
needle**

**Crochet hook, in simi-
lar size to the knitting
needle (for provisional
cast-on)**

**Waste yarn, in similar
size to the yarn used for
the cowl (for provisional
cast-on)**

Tapestry needle

DYEING

You will need about 90 g of yarn to knit this cowl. Although approximately 40 g is made up of dyed yarn and 50 g of undyed yarn, we recommend dyeing at least 50–100 g of yarn, so you will have enough to choose from when knitting the cowl. To create the cowl pictured, we dyed collections of pinks, corals, and reds, terra-cotta, blue, and sea green. We created mini-skeins of yarn, each weighing about 5 g, and used the Mason Jar Dyeing (page 227) method with 8-ounce jam jars instead of quart-size jars, as well as gradient dyeing (page 77) to create the widest array of color.

BLENDING COLOR THROUGH KNITTING

The way color is used in this cowl is evocative of painting—one color blends into the next, and sometimes a wisp of color makes an appearance within long blocks of color. This was done by using colors that are incredibly close to one another in hue and by creating gradients via the technique of spit-splicing (an easy way to splice and make joins while knitting). When you want to change colors, break the yarn. Fray the end of the yarn you just broke and the new yarn you would like to join. Wet both ends, using spit or water, then roll them together vigorously using the palms of your hands. Another way to blend color while knitting is to create stripes, as shown in the swatch on page 89.

COWL

1. Use a provisional cast-on to cast on 56 stitches.

2. Knit until the piece measures 44 inches (112 cm), or until desired length. While knitting, refer to your inspirational photo and the illustration you have created to guide when you will change colors. If you have designed your cowl to be one-third dyed, as we have, this means about 14 inches (34 cm) of your cowl will use dyed yarn. As you knit, be aware of this length as well as the colors and amount of naturally dyed yarn available, and roughly gauge when to change colors. Keep your entire palette close at hand, be open to making changes to your design (if you feel like changing the amount of color used in the cowl, please do), tune in to your innate sense of color, and you will have a piece that is uniquely yours.

3. Use a three-needle bind-off to connect the two ends of the cowl.

4. Cut yarn, leaving a 6-inch (15-cm) tail. Weave in ends and block as desired.

panorama woven silk bookmark

DIMENSIONS

Ranging in size from
1½ to 2 inches (4–5 cm)
wide × 5¾ to 6 inches
(14.5–15 cm) long
(8 inches/20 cm long
with tassels)

TOOLS

Schacht Easel Weaver
6 EPI (any width),
Schacht Lilli Loom,
or comparable
tapestry loom

6-inch (15-cm) weaving
needle (recommended)

Small tapestry needle
(for weaving in ends)

Scissors

MATERIALS

3-4 colors of A Verb for
Keeping Warm Lumen
(100% silk, 300 yards
[274 m]/50 g): each
finished bookmark
weighs about 3 grams,
have 60 yards [55 m]/
10 grams of yarn per
color on hand.

IN ADDITION TO USING dyeing techniques to widen your palette, the form and design of the textile itself can expand the possibilities of your locally sourced dyes. For example, in knitted and woven fabrics, the choice of stitch or pattern can change how the colors in the textile appear.

The small shape of this woven bookmark, only requiring a few yards of yarn, provides the perfect place to explore using colors together in new ways. Where warp (the yarns running vertically on the loom) and weft (the horizontal yarns) meet, new colors can be created. Where a light and dark color meet, you see a blending of the two shades, creating a third color. Two tonal colors may blend together and look solid, but when you look closely you can see their separate hues, offering subtle nuances depending on what angle you are viewing the woven fabric. Allow the chains at the beginning and end to blend into your weaving by using the same colors or cap your piece by making the chains in a contrasting color.

The plain weave pattern is simple and straightforward, making this a good beginner weaving project. We chose to use a very thin silk yarn, reminiscent of the yarn we saw being spun and woven in Oaxaca. Feel free to use a thicker yarn if it is easier for you to warp and weave (depending on the thickness of your yarn, warp at 6 EPI [ends per inch] or 12 EPI). Though our bookmarks are made from one type of yarn; consider using other yarns that you have dyed (such as from other sections of this book) to add accents and texture. This is a great project to use up small ends of naturally dyed yarn. To move beyond a bookmark, consider making a larger piece of fabric, which could become an accessory, wall hanging, panel on a garment, or small bag.

NOTE: We are using an inexpensive and easily accessible tapestry loom, with teeth set at 6 EPI. Using the instructions and illustrations included with the loom is helpful when warping. In order to create a more densely woven fabric, triple your set and warp the loom at 18 EPI by winding three strands of yarn onto your loom at once.

INSTRUCTIONS

WARP LOOM AT 18 EPI

1. Determine the width of your weaving and center it on the loom.

2. Cut three lengths of warp yarn. At the left side of your weaving, where you would like your weaving to begin, tie the ends of your warp yarn onto a tooth on the bottom beam.

3. Carry the yarns to the tooth on the top beam that is directly opposite where you tied your ends, and wrap the yarn over the tooth. Carry the yarns back to the bottom beam, go around the next tooth, and back up to the top. Repeat until you have warped the width of your planned weaving. If you would like to change colors, pull up the slack in your weaving (see step 5), tie off your yarns to a warp tooth, and tie the new ones onto the same tooth.

4. After you have finished winding all of the warp yarn onto your loom, wrap the warp yarns around a beam tooth to secure it temporarily while you tighten the warp yarns.

5. Starting at the first three warp yarns, pull up on each one to tighten the tension. Continue taking up slack from one warp yarn to the next all the way across the loom. Take out this extra length of yarn and tie the ends securely to a warp tooth to fasten.

TIE CHAIN TO SPACE WARP YARNS

1. Cut a length of yarn that is 6 times the width of the warp.

2. Fold the yarn in half and insert both ends into the tapestry needle.

3. From left to right, pass the needle under the leftmost warp yarn, about 2 inches (5 cm) above the bottom warp teeth. Pass the needle through the loop at the end of the weft yarn. Pull the loop snugly around the warp yarn. The two strands in your tapestry needle are now attached to your warp yarn. (A)

4. Pass the needle over the next warp yarn, then under the yarn and between the two threads attached to the warp yarn. Pull the loop snugly around the warp yarn so that it is evenly spaced with the first warp yarn. (B)

5. Repeat step 4 for the rest of your warp yarns. Keep your tension and spacing as even as possible. Keep the chain parallel with the beam. (C)

6. When you reach the last warp yarn, remove your tapestry needle. You will weave in the ends of the yarn used to create the chain when finishing your weaving. This chain will be a decorative element in your finished weaving.

7. Repeat these steps to create a chain 2 inches (5 cm) from the top of the loom (just under the warp beam). Take care that you keep the warp yarns in the same order as you did at the bottom. This chain is purely functional and will not be on your finished weaving.

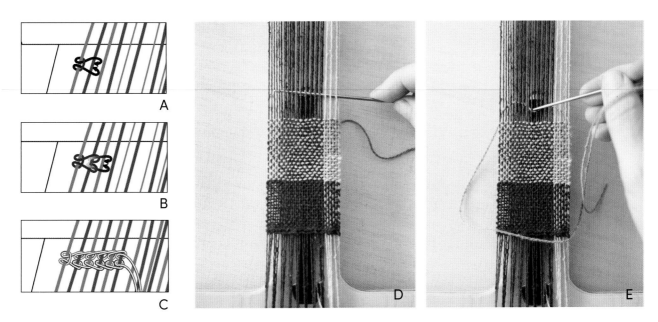

Images from Schacht Lilli Loom manual

BEGIN WEAVING

1. (First Row) Thread the weaving needle with the first weft yarn. Depending on the amount of color you would like to weave, your weft yarn can be anywhere from 6 inches (15 cm) to 36 (90 cm) long. Starting at the right side of your warp, begin weaving plain weave by passing the weaving needle under the first warp yarn, over the second, under the third, etc., until you reach the end. **(D)** Leaving a 2-inch (5-cm) tail at the start, pull the weft yarn through at a 45-degree angle. Beat your weft gently with your weaving needle, first in the center, and then from the direction the weft yarn is traveling to the end of the weaving. **(E)** Make sure it rests snugly against the chain stitch.

2. (Second Row) On the left side of your warp, pass your tapestry needle under the first warp yarn, over the second, under the third, etc., and weave a second row. Pull the weft yarn through at a 45-degree angle and beat as in step 1.

3. Continue weaving in this manner. You can weave a plain weave fabric, or pack weft yarns a little more closely for a slightly denser fabric. Change colors when desired. To change to a new color, cut your working yarn leaving a 1-inch (2.5-cm) tail, and place this tail into the next shed alongside your new color to secure it.

4. Once your weaving is your desired length, follow steps 1–6 of "Tie Chain to Space Warp Yarns" to create a chain across the top of your weaving, directly against the last weft yarn.

FINISHING

1. Cut through the warp threads, just below the top beam and above the bottom beam to remove the weaving from the loom. (Because you have created a chain across the top of your weaving, you no longer need the chain created just below the top beam.)

2. Weave in all unsecured ends on the back side of the fabric, including chain stitch ends, and trim.

3. Trim warp threads to 1 inch (2.5 cm) or desired length to create tassels.

CHAPTER THREE

JAPAN

when the earth makes the color of the sky //
letters from tokushima

BUAISOU ARE A GROUP OF YOUNG INDIGO farmers and dyers who grow *Persicaria tinctoria*, a variety of buckwheat containing indigotin. They harvest and dry the leaves (like tea or tobacco), compost them for about 120 days, and then use this compost to create fermented indigo dye vats. Their ability to create each nuanced shade of indigo is remarkable, from the very lightest shade, with the slightest hint of blue, to the darkest shade that's nearly black, like the color a moonless midnight sky. This process is passed down primarily through an oral tradition of training and study over the course of multiple years.

Starting in 2012, we began participating in the efforts going on in California to grow, compost, and create fermented indigo vats modeled after the style used by BUAISOU. We were initially drawn to this process because it enabled us to be self-sufficient, to cultivate our own indigo dye instead of being dependent upon importing the pigment. We are fascinated by the use of fermentation in the dyeing process, and the ability to use ambient bacteria to replace materials that are normally required to make indigo work, which would most likely need to be imported or purchased from sources outside our area. Though we had documented every detail over the past few years trying to understand the process, and had success at creating this kind of vat, our dream was to see this process in Japan, so we were incredibly excited to travel to Tokushima, to see up close and in person this incredible process.

We started our day in Arimatsu, the historical center of *shibori* resist-dyeing, and prepared ourselves for a very long day of travel. We boarded our first of five trains and watched the countryside change, making our way through Nagoya, Kyoto, Osaka, Kobe, Okayama, and Takamatsu, finally reaching our destination, Tokushima Prefecture, located on the island of Shikoku and home to the historical commercial center of growing and composting indigo in Japan.

Our friend Kyoko, the manager of BUAISOU, greeted us at the train station. We zoomed through the town, up hills, down hills, past little houses and soba noodle shops in her tiny car; we could not have been happier. The land we drove through was mostly agricultural, with lots of rice fields and other vegetables growing. We arrived in the late afternoon, when the sun was low in the sky, and many birds were flying over the fields.

The BUAISOU studio is a large, rustic building on the corner of two small converging country roads. The

---

A field of flowering *Persicaria tinctoria* will provide the seeds necessary for next year's crop. Kakuo meticulously rubs the indigo dye into each and every strand of thread.

building and surrounding fields used by BUAISOU to grow their indigo are owned by a local dairy farmer who is happy to rent it to them because of their youth and determination to work in agriculture and with indigo. The local government has taken an active role in encouraging and supporting younger generations to move to rural areas like Tokushima and to revive traditional livelihoods. Places like Tokushima have an aging population, and the younger workforce tends to leave the area for bigger cities and more opportunity. The team at BUAISOU is a good example of the new generation using traditional techniques and applying them in new ways.

During the nineteenth century, Tokushima was the center of commercial indigo production in Japan, with thousands of people involved and about 1,800 farms. However, due to the labor-intensive process and the availability of more affordable alternatives, by 2019, the number had fallen to five farms. Blues made using natural indigo extract from India and synthetic indigo are cheaper, less intensive styles of dyeing. The lack of public knowledge and value for how the color blue is applied to cloth, in combination with the decreased demand for indigo-dyed goods using *Persicaria tinctoria* from Japan, has contributed to this decline. The high price of *sukumo* (composted *Persicaria tinctoria*) makes it difficult for successful overseas export, but as a national art, the style of indigo dyeing practiced by BUAISOU and others using *sukumo*, and the color blue created, is priceless.

BUAISOU was founded in 2015 by Kakuo Kaji, who studied textile design in Tokyo before moving to Tokushima in 2012, where he trained with indigo master Osamu Nii. In 2014, Kakuo dyed with the indigo he had processed from start to finish for the first time. Kakuo had a realization that the color blue he achieved was so much more than just a color; it represented time, labor, and care and was the embodiment of the long-standing history of cultivating indigo in the Tokushima region.

The week we were with BUAISOU, Nii-san received a Medal of Honor from the Japanese government for preserving the art of making *sukumo*. We were honored to visit him alongside BUAISOU. Nii-san's family has been working with indigo for six generations and is one of the remaining five families that still perform this kind of work.

The indigo growing season starts in December with plowing and fertilizing the fields to prepare the soil. In March, BUAISOU start their seeds in the greenhouse that sits across from the studio. Beginning in April, they transplant the seedlings using a small machine. From June through September, they harvest each plant twice by cutting very close to the ground four weeks apart. A day after the indigo is harvested, it is chopped and laid on the floor; large fans are used to separate the leaves from the stems—the leaves, being lighter, float through the air and are caught with a bag. The stems, too heavy to float, are swept up and discarded. The leaves are then brought to the greenhouse to dry. The dried leaves are collected into a bag and stored until it is time to begin making *sukumo*. To process the large amount of indigo they grow, they harvest a portion of their field every day, and repeat the above process of cutting, drying, and storing from June to September. After both harvests are completed, some plants are left in the field to flower and produce seed for next year's crop—which, accompanied by the studio dog Sakura, was the stage we saw.

The work to make *sukumo* is very laborious and takes 120 days of attention. The composting process is done onsite in a room adjacent to the dye studio called a *nedoko*, or bedroom, so called because the dried indigo leaves "are put to sleep." From this point on, the dried leaves are turned once a week. When we visited in early November, the 3,527 pound (1,600 kg) *sukumo* pile was at the point in the process where it needed to be turned.

Ken applies many layers of indigo to achieve the dark blue threads that will soon be woven into denim.

We watched as every pound of the hot compost pile was thoroughly rotated through raking. This process releases an incredible amount of steam, and the smell of ammonia permeates the air.

Throughout the composting process, water is added to the dry leaves to activate decomposition; however, too much water or poor air circulation can ruin the compost. It is important to rotate the pile regularly to make sure the compost remains moist throughout. The floor of the *nedoko* is made of unfired clay, which helps air circulation around the compost pile and avoids buildup of moisture along the bottom of the pile. While rotating the compost, the team inspects the floor to make sure it is in good condition and to scrape off any compost that may have adhered to the floor. Once done, the compost is shoveled back into place and tamped down to form the iconic rectangular shape with ever-so-slightly slanted sides. The sides are covered with straw mats and a decorative vase with a sakaki (*Cleyera japonica*) cutting placed on top. The turning of the compost is incredibly labor intensive but necessary to keep the bacteria healthy enough to fully break down the leaves. After 120 days, the *sukumo* will have millions of colonies of bacteria—a necessary component of the dyeing process.

Although growing and composting happen at specific times during the season, indigo dyeing is done year round. The indigo vats used by BUAISOU are completely organic with no synthetic elements. The only ingredients used to make the vat are *sukumo*, ash water, shell lime, and wheat bran. This vat creates what is commonly called "Japan blue," a special blue with red undertones specific to *Persicaria tinctoria* and this style of dye process.

At the end of the day, the vats are stirred with a long stick in order to keep the bacteria living in the vat healthy. The 238-gallon (900-L) vessels are set into the floor of the studio and covered with flat wooden lids.

During our visit, they were hard at work dyeing fine cotton thread intended to be woven into cloth at a nearby mill, which would be sewn into their first line of jeans. Part of BUAISOU's business model is creating their own line of goods, including the dyeing but also design, pattern drafting, and sewing. Education and connecting with people from around the world who want to learn more about this unique style of indigo are other important components. They offer workshops where you can dye with indigo and learn about *katazome*, the use of rice-paste resist to create patterns, and *shibori*, the style of resist-dyeing using pressure to create patterns.

After witnessing Kakuo's hard work, we asked him what keeps him motivated to continue working with indigo: "There are so many possibilities and decisions to be made when growing, composting, creating indigo fermentation vats, and dyeing with indigo, in order to create the optimal color. I am motivated by learning more about these possibilities through engaging in the process and how all of these steps relate to one another." Kakuo has often wondered how to best make things that embody or communicate everything that goes into making the indigo dye. How is it possible to truly capture the essence of the entire process through only the color blue?

When asked what his advice would be to new dyers or those interested in growing, composting, and fermenting indigo, Kakuo replied, "I think we have to consider not only the old-fashioned method but also how to innovate and create new styles of working with indigo." Leaving Tokushima, we took Kakuo's words to heart and began brainstorming new ways to innovate, such as how to work with this process on a smaller scale, making it more accessible for our own practice and for others.

BUAISOU
www.buaisou-i.com

Ken and Kakuo work hard to turn every pound of the composting *Persicaria tinctoria*. Yuya prepares to stir the indigo vat.

pathways: from gardens to textiles //
letters from kyoto

THE FIRST TIME WE VISITED KYOTO, WE were struck by the ways in which nature was honored throughout the city. As we wandered for hours, following the small, meandering streets from one textile gallery, studio, and shop to the next, tucked along the way were small, beautiful gardens. Even within this compact setting, space was made for nature, offering a moment to reflect and to gather oneself. One afternoon, taking a break from the bustle of city life, we spent some time in the grand gardens located in the northwestern corner of Kyoto, where the grounds were carefully cultivated to highlight the plants in season. It was early spring, and cherry blossom season was just about to start. The city was alive with anticipation: a small sprig appeared on the lid of a bowl of soup, preserved cherry blossoms adorned the top of a creamy spiral of soft serve ice cream—small touches alluded to the celebration of the cherry blossoms everywhere we went.

One afternoon, we made a stop at Gallery Kei. The founder, Kei Kawasaki, specializes in collecting exquisite textiles made from bast fibers like hemp, ramie, wisteria, linden, banana fiber, paper mulberry, nettle, and elm. These plants have been used in Japan for thousands of years to create textiles. The fibers from these plants are made from the inner bark, and they are known to be soft, flexible, and strong.

A panel of cloth made about 150 to 200 years ago, in the Edo period, held our attention. This piece is thought to be an example of *echigo jofu*, a fabric made of very fine, handspun, handwoven ramie from the area that is now known as Niigata Prefecture, an area northeast of Kyoto. This is the first type of Japanese fabric registered as Intangible Cultural Heritage by UNESCO. To make this fabric, the ramie plant was grown and laboriously processed into fiber, spun finely by hand, and finally hand woven on a back strap loom. The finished weaving was laid flat on the snow for multiple days, bleaching the fabric. It was typically sent to Kyoto or Tokyo to be dyed and embroidered. During the Edo period, pieces like these were made for summer kimonos to keep cool. The panel, dyed with indigo, features an illustration of a garden. Through the use of rice paste, the scene comes to life: A stream of water flows through the garden, past a gate and pine trees; flecks of fine iridescent silk embroidery highlight leaves and bark. Remarkably, the piece resembled a garden we had seen earlier in the day and brought us right back to the moment we were walking along the path through the trees.

Gallery Kei
gallerykei.jp

A portrait of a garden adorns a textile from Gallery Kei. Moments of nature seen around Kyoto.

an autumn journey to a persimmon dyer's private studio // letters from oharashorinincho village

ONE RAINY FALL AFTERNOON, OUR FRIEND Masaaki Aoki of Tezomeya natural dye studio in Kyoto took us to visit the studio of Kazue Yasui, an artist who has used fermented persimmon juice for more than thirty years to paint pictures upon long, narrow panels of ramie fabric. The drive from Kyoto to Oharashorinincho Village was particularly spectacular because we were visiting at the height of fall colors in Japan.

After an hour of driving, we got out of the car to find ourselves in a misty pine and maple forest village. The dark and stormy sky framed the showy maples' brilliant orange leaves in a dramatic display of natural beauty.

We were greeted by Kazue, and she welcomed us to her covered outdoor studio where she paints wall hangings and *noren*, a cloth door commonly used in Japan. The studio's clear corrugated roof let in lots of natural light while shielding us from the rain. Long, narrow pieces of fabric hung from one end of the studio to the other, all in different stages of completion.

Kazue first encountered persimmon dyeing, known as *kakishibu* in Japanese, as a young newlywed. Her husband's family were persimmon dyers. Intrigued, she began painting with persimmon dye. Her passion for the process guided her toward making many works of art throughout the years. She showed us a piece that she had painted freehand with a rice paste resist design, covered lightly with fine sawdust. She was preparing to begin dyeing it with persimmon juice. She then guided us to another work in progress: a stunning portrait of the trees found right outside her studio. Her brushwork was incredible. Nearby, on top of a small cart were vessels filled with persimmon dye in various strengths. She explained the process of painting on layers of the dye and waiting for each layer to dry before adding more. Because of the high tannin content of the dye, after many layers, the color deepens and will continue to deepen as it ages. In addition to being used to create images, this type of fermented persimmon juice has been used by craftspeople for hundreds of years to waterproof fabric and paper, as well as to stain wood.

After our tour, Kazue brought us inside the showroom, where her family was having tea. We enjoyed looking through the beautiful persimmon-dyed textiles as the rain softly tapped on the roof above, and at the *noren* and wall hangings displayed lovingly, all with images of nature or animals. We left that day with a glowing feeling—of witnessing something very special in the world, a close-knit family living and working together and making beauty to be shared. Sadly, we found out recently that Kazue passed away since we last saw her, making it all too clear that these crafts are hanging on generation by generation. Thankfully, her family continues the textile legacy and to breathe new life into old traditions, keeping them alive to be shared again and again.

In memory of Kazue Yasui.

Mitsuru Crafts
60 Oharakusao-cho, Sakyo-ku, Kyoto 601-1248
Telephone / WA: +81 75 744 2069
info@kakishibuzome.com

From her misty mountainside studio, Kazue shows us the sawdust she uses as part of her process. Nearby hangs her in-progress painting. Persimmons hang in a tree. A *noren*, painted with persimmon dye, mimics the shape of the roof of Kazue's studio and the surrounding mountains.

japan-inspired palette

The ingredients featured on these pages are those we saw used in Japan and are those used in this chapter. You will learn how to create many shades using just two dyes, *Persicaria tinctoria* and persimmons, through layering the dyes, pH shifts, and using iron, and how to create patterns by making paste with sweet rice paste. See the shade cards on the following pages to view the colors made from these dyes.

1 Fresh *Persicaria tinctoria*

2 Dry *Persicaria tinctoria*

3 Composted *Persicaria tinctoria*

4 Indigo seeds

5 Hardwood ash

6 Wheat bran

7 Limestone

8 Green persimmons

9 Iron

10 Sweet rice flour

11 Rice bran

12 Baking soda

our tiny indigo farm

IN TOKUSHIMA, BUAISOU GROWS INDIGO using one hectare of land, which is 107,639 square feet. Their compost pile on average is a whopping 3,527 pounds (1,600 kg) of dried *Persicaria tinctoria* leaves!

In our previous work with composting indigo, the average amount of the compost has been about 300 pounds, and the vats we made were approximately 50 gallons. This requires quite a bit of space and work; for example, you need about 2,000 pounds of fresh *Persicaria tinctoria* leaves.

We came home from Tokushima very inspired and curious as to whether we could re-create the process of composting and creating an indigo fermentation vat using *Persicaria tinctoria* on a smaller, home-garden-size scale.

In our front yard, we have a sunny hundred-square-foot plot, which at the time was home to a tomato plant, a scraggly aphid-ridden artichoke, and a gigantic jade plant. We decided to remove these plants and create a tiny indigo farm. The first challenge was to see how much *Persicaria tinctoria* we could grow within our plot, which would then dictate how many pounds of dry leaf we would have to experiment with in the composting process.

Luckily, *Persicaria tinctoria* grows well in clusters, so we were able to plant four seedlings in one hole. And each group of four seedlings needs only about a six-inch radius. This means we could grow four hundred plants in our small plot. We were off to a good start!

We harvested our first batch of *Persicaria tinctoria* once the plants reached 3 feet (1 m) high, with leaves measuring 6 inches (15 cm) in length. We allowed the plants to continue growing, and once again, when they reached 3 feet (1 m) tall, we made our second harvest. From these two harvests, our small indigo patch yielded 40 pounds (18 kg) of fresh leaves, which, when dried, weighed 20 pounds (9 kg). It was from this starting weight that we began to try composting. To make it easier to turn the compost, we used a compost tumbler.

We placed our tumbler in the sun to keep it warm. We took diligent notes on the temperature of the compost, when we added water, and when we rotated the leaves by turning the tumbler and recorded observations of mold growth and the smell: whether it was earthy or more like ammonia.

After the first week, the compost grew a soft, fuzzy white mold all over, a good sign that the decomposition of the leaves had begun. Because of the relatively small size of our compost pile, sometimes our compost was cooler than we liked. To maintain the necessary heat for successful decomposition, we kept the tumbler in the sun during the day and covered it with blankets at night. After ninety days, the compost shrunk from 20 pounds (9 kg) of crushed, dry leaves to 11 pounds (5 kg) of dark brown, rich, crumbly compost. We allowed the compost to dry for a month, and then set out to make an indigo vat with it.

We decided to create a 10-gallon (38-L) vat using 3.7 pounds (1.7 kg) of composted indigo; a size we feel is easier to maintain from a physical standpoint (stirring is labor-intensive), has a smaller footprint so easier to store, and makes it possible to create multiple vats from a single year's yield of indigo. We have kept this size vat in our kitchen and bathroom because of the easy access to water and electricity. Through trial and error, we developed a recipe for this size of vat that creates a wide range of blues. We love having a vat made of indigo grown right in our front yard and hope the instructions we have created guide you to creating your very own home-garden-sized fermented indigo vat.

Adrienne uses a scythe to harvest *Persicaria tinctoria*.

THE LIFE CYCLE OF GROWING
PERSICARIA TINCTORIA

Seedling

Plant growing

Flowering

Seeds

GROWING TIMELINE

ONE MONTH PRIOR TO PLANTING:
Start seeds indoors.

DATE OF LAST FROST IN YOUR AREA:
Transplant seedlings outside.

APPROX 2–2½ MONTHS LATER:
Harvest plants.

APPROX 1–2 MONTHS LATER:
Harvest plants.

APPROX 1–2 MONTHS LATER:
Before first frost, harvest seeds.

COMPOSTING TIMELINE

WEEK 1: Add 18 pounds (8 kg) crushed leaves and water to compost tumbler.

WEEK 2: Add 2 pounds (1 kg) crushed leaves and water to compost tumbler, start to emit ammonia smell, white mold starts to grow.

WEEKS 2–12: Keep moist, rotate every week, keep compost warm.

WEEK 13: Compost is done, take out to dry.

MAKING A FERMENTED INDIGO VAT FROM COMPOSTED *PERSICARIA TINCTORIA*

Dried indigo leaves

Compost

Surface of the vat

Dyed goods

MAKING A FERMENTED INDIGO VAT TIMELINE

Allow 1 to 2 weeks to gather the necessary materials and tools to make the ash water and vat. From starting the ash water to completing the vat, it will take at least nine days, and may take up to nineteen days.

Day 1: Make the first batch of ash water. Allow 3 to 4 hours to complete.

Day 2: Make the second batch of ash water and fine-tune it. Allow 5 to 6 hours.

Day 3: Begin to make the vat. This is marked as Day 1 in the vat's life. Allow 3 to 4 hours.

Day 4 and beyond: You will take the vat's vitals for the life of the vat. Allow a half hour each time you take the vat's vitals. When taking vitals, look to see if the swatch turns blue. This could happen on Day 4, but it could also take 4 to 5 more days. As soon as the swatch turns blue, allow an additional hour per day to complete making the vat. Based upon the pH, the bacteria in the compost, and your ambient temperature, this could take 5 to 15 days. Though this gives you a rough estimate of how many days it will take and how many hours per day to set aside to make a vat, you will learn more about the intricacies and nuances of this process on pages 122–231.

growing
persicaria tinctoria

TOOLS

Hand trowel

Tub/bucket for soil

Pencil and paper

Ruler

Hose and sprayer

MATERIALS

420 *Persicaria tinctoria* seeds

Soil (seed starter soil mix)

Water

One 128 cell plug flat

One standard 1020 greenhouse flat without drainage slots

Heated seed mat

ONE OF THE AMAZING THINGS about *Persicaria tinctoria* is that four plants can be grown in a single spot, which means you can really pack a lot into a small space. The leaves are harvested at most twice per season for the most reliable results. If you are following the instructions in this book to grow *Persicaria tinctoria* with the intention of composting (page 120) and creating fermentation vats from it (page 122), you will need 100 square feet (9 sq m) of growing space. The following instructions for growing indigo have been written for this amount of space and after two harvests will yield enough leaves, when composted, to create three fermented indigo vats. If you are growing *Persicaria tinctoria* to use the fresh leaves for dyeing (page 119) or to extract pigment (page 190), refer to each of these instructions to understand how much indigo you will need to grow.

INSTRUCTIONS

CHOOSE A LOCATION
Persicaria tinctoria loves full sun but tolerates part shade. Choose a level, sunny location with good drainage.

PREPARE THE SOIL
Nitrogen-rich soil is necessary for *Persicaria tinctoria* to grow indigo-rich leaves. Two weeks before transplanting the seedlings, prepare the soil: Combine nitrogen-rich fertilizer like cow, pig, or chicken manure with the soil in your planting area. If you would like to use a cover crop instead, see the Cover Crop Timeline.

PLANT SEEDS
We recommend starting your seeds indoors, which will give you a solid start and provide better insurance that you will be able to fit all three harvests (two for leaves, one for seeds) in a season.

1. Use a 128 cell plug flat. Fill all the cells in the tray to the top with well-draining seed-starting soil mix. Gently water the tray by softly spraying. Wait 5 minutes for the water to saturate the soil, and then water again and wait an additional 5 minutes. This will moisten the soil prior to adding the seeds and prevent them from floating away with the water.

2. Plant four seeds per plug by using a pencil tip to make a ⅛-inch (3-mm) deep hole and dropping the seeds in. Cover the hole with soil.

3. Keep the soil moist and warm at 60°F (16°C) or warmer (use a heated seed mat if necessary) until the seeds germinate. Add water to the tray below the cell plug flat to not wash away seeds, or spray with a very fine mist.

4. The seeds should germinate in 14 days. The seedlings have two small, oval leaves and a red stalk. Over the course of 4 weeks, the seedlings will grow an additional four leaves. Once this has happened and they are 3 inches (7.5 cm) tall, the seedlings are ready to plant.

MAP OUT YOUR PLOT

Measure your plot. Use paper and a pencil to map out where each spot will be located within your plot. Refer to your map when outside planting. To use every inch of the growing space, it is ok to plant seedlings within 6 inches of the edge of the plot. Allow 12 inches of space between plants. To grow the amount of indigo necessary to follow the composting instructions, you will need to plant 100 plugs of 4 seedlings.

COVER CROP TIMELINE

Green manure or cover crops, like fava beans, peas, and clover, can be used to add nitrogen to your soil in addition to manure and fertilizer, but they will need a longer prep time. If you would like to plant a cover crop, add this timeline onto the Indigo Growing Timeline (page 112). If you live in an area with a shorter growing season, and want to grow a cover crop, you can consider growing a larger plot of *Persicaria tinctoria* and completing one harvest for the plants, and one harvest for the seeds.

3 months before transplanting *Persicaria tinctoria* seedlings: Sow cover crop.

2 months later: Harvest cover crop and chop into 1-inch (2.5-cm) pieces. Turn the cover crop into the soil. Allow the soil to rest, giving the cover crop time to break down and combine with the soil, adding nutrients, specifically nitrogen, which *Persicaria tinctoria* thrives on.

4 weeks later: Plant *Persicaria tinctoria* seedlings.

TRANSPLANT

Ideally, because you have sown four seeds per cell, you will now have four seedlings per cell. However, it is possible that one of the seeds did not sprout. If this is the case, combine cells (you started 128 but you only have to plant 100) to create a total of four seedlings per cell. Transplant the seedlings according to the map you have created.

TEND THE PLANTS

The plants require moderate watering. Signs of stress include red leaves and sometimes puckering of the leaves. This may indicate they need more water more consistently or more nutrients. Using a drip irrigation system to maintain moisture levels is helpful. Fish fertilizer works gently without burning the plant.

HARVEST

The plants will be ready to harvest approximately 2 to 3 months after transplanting. They should be at least 30 inches (76 cm) tall with dark green leaves measuring up to 6 inches (15 cm) in length. You can test the indigo pigment in the leaf by putting one in the freezer for 10 minutes and then pressing it between your hands and letting it air dry. The leaf will dry a dark blue if the indigo is present. To harvest the indigo, cut the entire plant at the base 6 inches (15 cm) from the ground. This will allow the plant to grow again for a second harvest.

After harvesting, add fertilizer to the soil again with an organic nitrogen (blood meal, fish meal, or manure) and a well-balanced organic general-purpose fertilizer (5-5-5). Mix the fertilizer in the soil and water well. This will ensure your second growth will have a strong start.

Because the plant is well rooted, typically the second harvest will occur more quickly than the first. Harvest 1 to 2 months after the first harvest but prior to the plant flowering. In the two cycles of growing, in which you are focused on growing leaves, do not allow your plants to flower. If they begin to flower, pluck the buds off the plant.

DRY THE LEAVES FOR COMPOSTING

Remove the leaves from the stems and dry immediately after harvesting so they do not mold. (It's a good idea to harvest the plants over the course of a couple of days so you can keep up with the process of bundling and stripping the leaves.) You can strip the leaves from the stalk immediately after harvesting and lay the leaves to dry on a tarp or cloth in a protected, dry area. Or you can bundle the fresh plants and hang them to dry, removing the leaves later. Keep an eye on the leaves, making sure they have enough air flow and turning them as needed to dry thoroughly. Store the completely dry leaves in a small trash can with a lid. This way you can accumulate the indigo leaves from each harvest and store them until you reach the amount you need to compost. To compost the leaves, they must be ground finely; to save on space, it can be helpful to grind the leaves as you go. See the instructions regarding grinding leaves on page 120.

SAVE SEEDS AND WIND DOWN THE CROP FOR WINTER

The seeds are ready to be harvested when their outer covering is brown and dry. To test, pick a few seeds and rub off the dried brown covering—the seed is ripe when it is hard, dark brown, and plump, not green and soft. The seeds must be fully dried before storing. Air-dry the seeds in a warm location with good air circulation away from birds, insects, and rodents that may eat them. After they are dried completely, store the seeds in an airtight glass jar in a cool, dark, dry area. This will ensure bugs and pests will not eat them and they won't mold. Use your seeds within one year of harvesting, since germination rates fall rapidly after the first year. Make sure the seed storage container is labeled with the contents and date harvested. Note that ¼ teaspoon of *Persicaria tinctoria* seeds equals approximately 300 seeds.

When you are ready to plant, make sure your seeds are free from all dried flower debris and chaff. To clean the seeds, use a sieve or small screen, rubbing the seeds against it until all the seeds are free of their dried skins. This is a messy process and best done outside.

shade card: dyeing with fresh *persicaria tinctoria*

GOODS: Swatches of scoured white wool yarn, silk fabric, cotton fabric, and linen fabric

SCOUR: Applicable scouring recipes based upon fiber content (pages 217–219)

MORDANT: Not applicable

DYE: Swatches dyed with freshly harvested *Persicaria tinctoria* leaves, 3½ ounces (100 g) and 7 ounces (200 g), blended with ice. The range of colors was created by repeatedly dipping the swatches, as noted, into the indigo dyebath. See page 119 for full instructions.

	1 DIP	2 DIPS	3 DIPS	4 DIPS	5 DIPS	6 DIPS
100 G						
200 G						

dyeing with fresh *persicaria tinctoria* using a blender and ice

MATERIALS

2 cups (150 g) ice

3½ ounces (100 g) or
7 ounces (200 g) fresh
Persicaria tinctoria
leaves

2 cups (480 ml)
cold water

Silk or wool goods,
scoured (page 217)

TOOLS

Scale

Measuring cup

Blender (6-cup/
1.5-L capacity)

Fine-mesh strainer

Bowl

Rubber gloves
(optional)

Clothesline and
clothespins

THIS IS A VERY QUICK AND simple method of working with fresh *Persicaria tinctoria* leaves. It is possible to create a dyebath with the *Persicaria tinctoria* leaves as soon as they are harvested, but work fast, use ice, and begin dyeing immediately, as it is extremely perishable and can only reliably dye goods within one hour of harvest.

To use this recipe, you will need at least 3½ ounces of fresh, mature leaves, which is about 2 plants' worth of leaves. Harvest leaves by cutting the stalk of the plant 5 inches (12 cm) from the ground, then remove the leaves and compost the stalks. Refer to the shade card on page 117 to learn more about the colors that can be achieved.

INSTRUCTIONS

1. Soak the goods in warm water until fully saturated.

2. Fill the blender with the ice and all of the leaves.

3. Add the water to the blender.

4. Blend the ice, leaves, and water for approximately 2 minutes, until it is fully macerated and resembles the consistency of a smoothie.

5. Strain the mixture through the strainer into the bowl to catch the dye liquid. Discard the strained leaves.

6. Gently squeeze excess water from the wet goods. Submerge the goods into the dyebath. Massage the goods under the surface of the liquid for 5 minutes.

7. Remove the goods from the dyebath, squeezing excess dye liquid back into the bowl. Immediately rinse the goods in cool water. Hang the goods on a clothesline and allow to rest for 5 minutes before dipping again.

8. Repeat steps 6 and 7 until the desired color has been achieved.

9. Wash the goods (page 236).

composting
persicaria tinctoria

YIELD

Makes 13 pounds
(6 kg) composted
Persicaria tinctoria

MATERIALS

20 pounds (9 kg)
dry *Persicaria tinctoria*
leaves, crushed into
fine flakes and powder

2 gallons (11 L)
unchlorinated,
filtered water

TOOLS

Scale

Bucket

17-gallon (64-L)
tumbler composter
(recommended)

Leaf shredder/mulcher
(recommended)

Thermometer

32-ounce (1-L)
spray bottle

Hand trowel
(recommended)

Tarp

TO CREATE THE FERMENTATION vats on page 122, composted *Persicaria tinctoria* leaves are required. During the composting process the dry leaves reduce in mass and create a concentrated form of indigo. Bacteria is cultivated, which, during the dyeing process, aids in transforming the indigo from an insoluble to soluble state, allowing it to dye goods.

In this process, dried leaves are placed in a pile and sprayed with water. The leaves begin to decompose and generate heat. This is the beginning of the composting process. Over the next ninety days, the decomposing leaves, now referred to as compost, are kept damp, and bacteria forms, contributing to the decomposition and contributing to the heat. To keep the compost moving along so that the leaves are fully decomposed and to aid in the growth of bacteria, ideally, during this time, the compost temperature measures at least 100°F (37°C) and below 200°F (93°C)—the ideal temperature is between 150 and 185°F (65 and 85°C). With a compost pile this small, it is more difficult to control the temperature. When you are making your first few batches of compost, we suggest recording the high and low temperatures for your location as well as the temperature of your compost on a daily basis, so you can understand the relationship. If you are having trouble keeping the temperature above 100°F (37°C), wrap the tumbler with an insulated moving blanket, set it in a sunny spot, and consider composting during the warmer months of the year. If your compost is too hot, open the door of the tumbler, keep it in the shade, and consider composting during the colder months of the year.

A tumbler composter is highly recommended and is used in this recipe due to the ease of turning the compost and the ability to move the compost as needed to help control the temperature. However, feel free to experiment with other forms of composting.

To begin composting, the dried leaves must be crushed into fine flakes and powder. This is most easily done using a leaf shredder, a tool found at the hardware store, but it can also be done by stomping, cutting with scissors, crushing with your hands, or using a spice grinder.

INSTRUCTIONS

1. From the 20 pounds of crushed leaves, set aside 2 pounds (1 kg). These will be added to the compost in a week.

2. Working with the remaining 18 pounds, add a layer of crushed leaves to the compost tumbler. Spray with water until damp. The leaves should feel like a damp piece of fabric, but when squeezed, no water should drip from them. Add more layers of leaves, spraying as you go, until all 18 pounds (8 kg) of dry leaves have been added to the tumbler.

3. In one week, add the crushed leaves you set aside in step 1. Moisten the leaves the same as above. Using your hands or a hand trowel, rotate all the leaves, integrating the new leaves into the pile and breaking up any large clumps that may have formed. Doing this by hand ensures even decomposition and distribution of heat and water.

4. Check the compost every week for about 90 days. As long as leaf matter is present, turn the compost and keep it moist by spraying with water. Within the first two weeks of composting, ideally there will be white mold growing along the surface of the compost. You will notice the compost will smell quite strongly of ammonia throughout the composting process. This is normal. Monitor the temperature and keep the compost at least 100°F (37°C) and below 200°F (93°C)—the ideal temperature is between 150 and 185°F (65 and 85°C).

5. After about 90 days, the compost will be dark brown, resemble dirt, and have reduced in size. The leaf matter will no longer be present. The strong smell of ammonia will lessen and the compost will smell sweet and drop in temperature. These are all signs that the compost is done.

6. Dry the compost by laying it out on a tarp.

7. Use immediately or store for the future. It is important to keep the compost dry and to allow it to continue to release moisture. Store in a breathable container, such as a burlap bag, a pillowcase, or a 5-gallon plastic bucket with the lid set on top (do not tighten the lid).

creating a fermented indigo vat using composted *persicaria tinctoria*

Though this is the most labor-intensive vat we have ever encountered, taking about ten days to build and continuous daily upkeep throughout the life of the vat, it is also our absolute favorite. It produces an incredible array of shades of blue with red and purple undertones. The key to success with this vat is to create space in your schedule to really focus on the slight shifts and nuances arising due to time and use of the vat, taking the steps to maintain the vat morning and night, and taking consistent notes. Please read through the instructions before beginning, so you can understand an overview of the process and plan accordingly.

This vat is made with composted *Persicaria tinctoria* (also known as *sukumo*) either made by you (page 120) or purchased. At the time of writing this book, it is difficult to find composted *Persicaria tinctoria* for sale in the United States; however, perhaps now that these instructions exist, more people may create it to sell. To make this vat, you will first make high-pH water through combining hardwood ash with non-chlorinated water. Then you will begin to combine the compost with this ash water over the course of a few days. Starting on Day 2 of the vat's life, you will stir the vat twice a day, ideally once in the morning and once in the evening, take its vitals, and record them in your journal. Once the vat is completed, which takes anywhere from nine to nineteen days, you can begin dyeing in it.

In order to keep the bacteria healthy, which is crucial to keep this vat working, this type of vat has a limit on how much can be dyed in one day. For the size of the vat in this recipe, you can dye up to 100 g of goods a day. It is best suited to dyeing small pieces of fabric and yarn. If you are interested in dyeing large pieces of fabric or clothing, use this recipe as a basis to scale up and make a larger vat.

BEFORE YOU BEGIN

Creating the ash water for this recipe requires obtaining hardwood ash; either burn hardwood in your fireplace or grill and collect the ashes. If you do not have a fireplace or grill, ask a friend or neighbor with a fireplace or look to your local wood-fired pizza restaurant, which most likely uses hardwood. We find that the ash we get from our local restaurants is a combination of fine ash and charcoal. The ash used in this recipe needs to be fine and clear of any pieces of charcoal. We pass the ash through a sieve and discard all charcoal pieces. We ask for 1 to 2 pounds (0.5 to 1 kg) of extra ash to compensate for the loss in weight due to the removal of the charcoal. The ash water created in this recipe can be used as a substitute for limestone and water throughout the book. If substituting, take note of the required pH called for in the applicable recipe, and if different from your ash water's pH, dilute with fresh water, until you reach the correct pH.

You will need to heat a batch of water measuring 10 gallons (38 L) to 200°F (93°C). Ideally, this entire measurement of water would be heated at one time, though we recognize this is a lot of water and most people do not have pots big enough to do this. When we heat this much water, we use our kitchen stove and the largest pots we own. Because plain water is used, both kitchen pots and dyepots can be used. If you do not have the size of pots necessary to heat this much water at once, it is OK to heat multiple batches of water, but try to heat as much water as possible at one time.

Using an electronic pH meter is a surefire way to read the pH of your vat and is highly recommended, but the pH can be detected through sensing how slippery the dyebath is. Many dyers who use this type of vat do not wear rubber gloves, preferring to feel the liquid and stay in touch with the pH. Due to the viscosity of this type of vat, it is nearly impossible to read pH strips. Be attentive to the recommended temperatures when taking pH, as pH is affected by heat.

While we have given instructions to the best of our knowledge, your vat is going to be impacted by the temperature and bacteria in your environment, similar to the process of baking sourdough bread. So keeping a dye journal as you create, maintain, and dye with a fermented indigo vat is absolutely essential to understanding the health and life cycle of your vat. You will use this journal to compare the health of the vat from one day to the next. The same format can be applied any time you use an indigo vat to understand its behavior (for example, a vat made with fructose and limestone).

When we decide to make a fermentation vat, we start planning our projects to dip into the vat before we even begin to make the vat. This is because the vat makes the clearest, most colorfast blues as soon as it is created. So we want to be prepared to use the vat as soon as it is made. As the vat ferments, it is natural for the pH to drop, and when it does, limestone will need to be added to keep the pH up. This addition of limestone can affect the clarity of the blue. It is nice to have multiple vats, created at different times, to produce a wide array of blues.

WHERE TO MAKE AND KEEP YOUR VAT

When planning where to make and keep your vat, there are a few things to take into account.

To make the vat, you will need to heat 20 gallons of water, and the vat must stay around 82–95°F (28–35°C) for the first few days. Thereafter, for the life of the vat, which could be three months or longer, the vat must be kept at 75°F (24°C). In most circumstances, unless you live in an incredibly warm area, the vat will need to be heated to maintain this temperature. Therefore, being near a source for heating water and an electrical outlet is a must. It is also helpful to be near a source of water and a sink or tub to rinse indigo-dyed pieces. We have found our kitchen works well as a place to make and keep the vat.

When making and maintaining the vat, you will need enough space to accommodate the footprint of three 10-gallon (38-L) buckets, one for the vat and two for ash water. These are not easy to move, due to their size and weight. You will most likely have your vat for at least three months, so find a place where these items can stay put for this duration. Or place the buckets housing your vat and ash water on dollies, which will enable you to move them easily if need be. Because the vat is alive and needs to be taken care of like a pet, we recommend a spot where you can greet the vat each morning and wish it good night at the end of each day.

Though we have a particular fondness for the smell of this vat—we also like stinky cheese—some find the smell quite potent, especially when stirred. You may want to consider this when planning where to store your vat. If you are concerned about the smell, consider keeping your vat in a bathroom, laundry room, or other room that has a door that can be closed to help contain the smell.

22 gallons (83 L)
non-chlorinated water

5 pounds (2.3 kg) fine,
hardwood ash, such as
oak, cherry, or almond

7 ounces (198 g) lime-
stone (this is enough to
build the vat plus extra
for maintaining the pH)

3 pounds 7 ounces
(1.5 kg) composted *Per-
sicaria tinctoria* leaves

5 ounces (141 g) wheat
bran (this is enough to
build the vat plus extra
for maintaining the pH)

TOOLS

Sieve

Scale

Face mask (recom-
mended when making
ash water)

Three 10-gallon (38-L)
buckets with lids (two
for making ash water,
one for the vat)

Stainless steel pots to
warm water

Digital food
thermometer

Large stirring stick, 4
feet long × 1¼ inches
diameter (1.2 m × 3 cm)
(a large dowel from the
hardware store or a
broomstick works well)

MAKING ASH WATER

Two 10-gallon (38-L) batches of ash water are required to complete and care for the vat. The first is used to make the indigo vat. Once the vat is made, add any remaining ash water from the first batch to the second batch of ash water. This is used to prewet goods before dyeing them, to combine with the wheat bran to feed the vat, and to top off the vat as the water decreases from dyeing. The ash water can be stored indefinitely at room temperature. Making ash water will take at least two days to complete.

1. Heat 10 gallons (38 L) non-chlorinated water to 200°F (93°C).

2. Place the ash in one of the 10-gallon (38-L) buckets.

3. Pour the heated water into the container. Using the large stirring stick, stir vigorously for 5 minutes.

4. Cover and let rest for at least 24 hours.

5. When all of the ash is settled and the water is clear, transfer the water to an-other 10-gallon (38-L) bucket using the 5-gallon (19-L) bucket, carefully scoop-ing the clear water and being careful to avoid disturbing the ash. Check and record the pH, then cover with the lid. Label this Batch 1.

6. Repeat steps 1–4 with a second of the 10-gallon (38-L buckets). Cover with the lid. Label this Batch 2.

FINE-TUNING YOUR ASH WATER

To start making the vat, there are two strengths of ash water required, both of which are lower than the ash water you just made. You can use the trial-and-error method to combine the non-chlorinated water with the ash water until you get the correct pH. Though we have found it is helpful and more efficient to first calculate the ratio needed beforehand and then scale up the ratio to the amount of ash water needed to begin building the vats.

DETERMINE THE RATIO

The following process is going to determine the ratio of Batch 1 ash water to non-chlorinated water needed to create the required lower pH blends.

1. Add 1 cup (240 ml) of Batch 1 ash water to a 3- to 5- quart (2.8- to 4.7-L) stainless steel pot and heat to 113°F (45°C).

2. At the same time, heat 10 cups (2.3 L) non-chlorinated water to 113°F (45°C).

3. Test the pH of the heated ash water. The goal is to establish a pH of 11–11.5. Most likely your ash water will measure too high and will need to be diluted with the heat-

5-gallon (19-L) bucket

Electronic pH meter, pH buffer calibration solution, electrode storage solution

Masking tape and Sharpie

2-cup (480-ml) liquid measuring cup with a handle

Notebook and pencil for record-keeping

3- to 5-quart (2.8- to 4.7-L) stainless steel pot with lid to heat ash water and wheat bran

Wooden or stainless steel spoon

20 × 48-inch (50 × 122-cm) heated seed mat

Duct tape or bungee cord

72 × 54-inch (183 × 137-cm) moving blanket

Two A-clamps

Plenty of 2 × 4-inch (5 × 10-cm) swatches of linen fabric to test the health of the vat

Rubber gloves (optional)

ed non-chlorinated water. If this is the case, add the non-chlorinated water in ¼-cup (60-ml) increments. Note how much you add to establish a pH of 11–11.5 at 113°F (45°C). This ratio of ash water to non-chlorinated water is going to be the blend of water you will use in step 4 of Day 1, Making the Vat (page 126).

4. Further lower the pH to 10.5–11 by adding more heated non-chlorinated water in ¼ cup (60-ml) increments. Note how much you add to establish a pH of 10.5–11 at 113°F (45°C). This ratio of ash water to non-chlorinated water is going to be the blend of water you will use in step 6 of Day 1, Making the Vat (page 126).

NOTE: It is better to have the pH of your blend be a little high rather than low.

SCALING UP

Now that you understand the ratios of how much to dilute your ash water to obtain the appropriate pH to begin building the vat, the following equations will help you scale up the recipe so you will have enough of this water at the correct pH to make the vat.

1. Start with the numbers you have gathered in step 3 of Determine the Ratio and the final volume that you need in step 4 of Day 1, Making the Vat (page 126), which is 7½ cups (1.8 L):

A = amount of ash water needed to reach the desired pH

B = volume of non-chlorinated water needed to reach the desired pH

C = A + B

D = final volume needed

2. Next, fill in the values of the variables into the following equations to calculate the volume of ash water and non-chlorinated water needed to scale up your recipe:

Volume of ash water to scale up = D × (A / C) = E

Volume of non-chlorinated water to scale up = (B /A) × E = F

3. Mix E and F. Heat to 113°F (45°C) and test the pH. Repeat this process with the numbers you have gathered in step 4 of Determine the Ratio and the final volume needed in step 6 of Day 1, Making the Vat (page 126), which is 80 cups (19 L).

Here is an example of how this equation works:

Let's say you have established in step 4 of Determine the Ratio it takes 1 cup (240 ml) ash water (A) and 2 cups (480 ml) non-chlorinated water (B) to reach your desired pH. You have 3 cups (720 ml) of this blend of water (C). Step 6 of Day 1, Making the Vat requires 80 cups (19 L) of this blend (D).

Volume of ash water to scale up = 80 cups x (1 cup / 3 cups) = 26.7 cups (E)

Volume of non-chlorinated water to scale up = (2 cups / 1 cup) x 26.7 cups = 53.4 cups (F)

Mix 26.7 cups ash water with 53.4 cups non-chlorinated water. Heat to 113°F (45°C) and test the pH.

DAY 1, MAKING THE VAT

1. Create a paste using ¼ cup (60 ml) non-chlorinated water and approximately 1 ounce (28 g) limestone. Take the bucket intended for the indigo vat and spread the paste over the entire surface of the inside to sterilize. Do not rinse.

2. Pour the 3 pounds 7 ounces (1.5 kg) composted *Persicaria tinctoria* into the bucket.

3. Sprinkle 1.1 ounces (31.25 g) limestone over the compost.

4. Heat 7½ cups (1.8 L) of the blend of water as established in step 3 of Determine the Ratio to 113°F (45°C). Once the temperature is reached, test the pH. Make sure you are at a pH of 11–11.5. Add ash water or non-chlorinated water to adjust if needed.

5. Pour 7½ cups (1.8 L) of this blend of water into the bucket over the compost and limestone. Using your hands, mix well.

6. Heat 80 cups (19 L) of the blend of water as established in step 4 of Determine the Ratio to 113°F (45°C). Once the temperature is reached, test the pH. Make sure you are at a pH of 10.5–11. Add ash water or non-chlorinated water to adjust if needed. Add 80 cups (19 L) of this blend of water to the bucket. The bucket will only be half full; over the course of the next few days, you will add more ash water to bring the water level to the top of the bucket.

7. Using the large stirring stick, stir vigorously for 5 minutes.

8. Cook 2.2 ounces (62.5 g) wheat bran in a small stainless steel pot with 1⅓ cups (315 ml) ash water from Batch 1 over low heat for 5 minutes, or until the wheat bran turns golden brown and the mixture has gone from soupy to mushy. Add the wheat bran mixture by spoonfuls to the bucket. Do not stir. (**A**, opposite)

9. Wrap the container with a heated seed mat, and use either duct tape or a bungee cord to secure the seed mat to the outside of the vat. Then wrap the moving blanket around the seed mat and the vat, secure by clipping the blanket to the seed mat using the two A-clamps, and cover with the lid.

DAY 2 AND BEYOND

Starting on Day 2 of the vat's life, take the vat's vitals throughout the life of the vat two times a day, once in the morning and once in the evening—see Taking the Vat's Vitals and Stirring Instructions on page 128. As part of these instructions, you will begin to dip a swatch of fabric into the vat to check its health. You are now looking and waiting for the swatch of fabric to turn blue. This may happen on Day 2, but it could take 4 or 5 days. As soon as it turns blue, you can resume making and completing the vat. See Continue Making the Vat on page 130.

From Day 2 until the swatch turns blue, maintain the temperature at 86–95°F (30–35°C). Keep the seed mat turned on until you reach this temperature, then turn off the seed mat. Every 8 to 12 hours, check the temperature; turn the seed mat on and off as necessary. It helps to set a timer as a reminder.

TAKING THE VAT'S VITALS AND STIRRING INSTRUCTIONS

1. Record the date and time in your dye journal.

2. Take the vat's temperature. If the temperature is below the recommended temperature for that stage, heat it up by turning on the seed mat, covered with the lid. We found that our seed mats increase the vat temperature by 4–6°F (3–4°C) per hour.

- From Day 2 until the swatch turns blue: 86–95°F (30–35°C)
- Once the swatch turns blue until making the vat is complete: 82°F (28°C)
- Once making the vat is complete: 75°F (24°C)

3. Once the vat's temperature has reached the recommended temperature, take the vat's pH and record it in your journal.

4. Presoak one swatch of fabric in either batch of ash water. Dip it into the vat, rubbing it gently under the surface of the dyebath for 30 seconds. Remove and rinse in cool water. Allow to dry and place it in your journal. These swatches are an important indicator of the vat's health and will act as a guide for what to do to keep the vat healthy. (B, page 127)

5. Stir the vat thoroughly for 3 minutes, moving from the sides to the center. Create a strong swirling motion. It is very important to lift all of the sediment from the bottom of the vat and to mix it well. (C, page 127)

6. Repeat daily, making swatches each day.

FERMENTED INDIGO VAT DYE JOURNAL

These are the key pieces of information to record on a daily basis:

- Day in the life cycle of the vat (Day 1 is the day the vat is built)
- Date and time
- Temperature
- pH
- Swatch color
- Limestone: If limestone was added, how much
- Wheat bran: If wheat bran was added, how much
- Goods dyed: Description of goods dyed, weight of goods, length of time, and number of dips
- Additional notes and observations

Each pair of swatches represent one day in the life of the vat, starting with Making the Vat Day 1. The top swatch is from taking the vat's vitals in the morning, the bottom swatch is from taking the vat's vitals in the evening. By the evening of Day 2 of the vat's life, our swatch began to turn blue, so we proceeded to follow the instructions for continuing to make the vat. The blue swatches represent a healthy vat. On Day 12 of the vat's life, the swatches began to lighten, we stopped using the vat, and followed the instructions for maintaining the health of the vat. Our vat responded positively and our swatches turned brighter blue, and we resumed dyeing.

CONTINUE MAKING THE VAT

As soon as the swatch turns blue, begin the following process. Remember to stir your vat every morning and every night.

1. Add 0.7 ounce (19 grams) limestone and stir for 3 minutes.

2. Allow the vat's temperature to drop to 82°F (28°C) by heating it only as needed. Keep it at this temperature until you have completed building the vat.

3. 24 hours after adding the limestone, after checking the vat's vitals and dyeing the swatch, you will add more ash water to the vat: If your pH tested lower than 10.5, use whichever batch of ash water has the higher pH. If the pH was higher than 10.5, use whichever batch of ash water has the lower pH. Heat 12½ cups (3 L) ash water to 82°F (28°C), add it to the vat, and stir.

4. 24 hours after adding the ash water, heat 12½ cups (3 L) of ash water to 82°F (28°C), following the same guidelines as described in step 3. Repeat this 2 more times (adding a total of 49 cups [12 L] of ash water).

5. 24 hours after adding the last 12½ cups (3 L) of ash water, add 0.7 ounce (19 g) limestone and stir for 3 minutes.

6. Repeat step 5 until the pH of the vat has reached 10.2–10.3. This might take multiple days of adding limestone in this manner.

7. Once the vat has reached a pH of 10.2–10.3, repeat step 3. The vat is now full, done being built, and ready to dye. (D, page 127)

Now that the vat is complete, remember to take the vat's vitals and stir it every morning and night. Always make sure the vat is at 75°F (24°C) when measuring its pH and dyeing the swatch. The ideal pH is 10.2–10.5. When you are done taking its vitals and the vat is resting, it is OK for the vat's temperature to be around 72–75°F (22–24°C).

DYEING WITH A FERMENTED INDIGO VAT

To dye in a fermented indigo vat, follow the steps for Dyeing with Indigo (page 13), taking into account the following details:

• After taking the vat's vitals and stirring, wait for 1 hour before dyeing any goods.

• Use ash water for the pre-wetting alkaline bath. Fill a bucket with enough ash water to cover the goods.

• To protect the health of the bacteria in the vat, dye only 100 grams total a day in this vat. For example, if your piece weighs 50 grams, dip it only twice in one day. Allow your vat to rest until the next day. Place the piece you are in the middle of dyeing in cool non-chlorinated water overnight, until it is time to resume dyeing.

• For every 2 days of consecutive dyeing, allow the vat to rest for 1 day.

• When dyeing, keep the vat at 75°F (24°C).

• Keep the vat covered when not in use, to keep the vat warm and to protect the vat from things falling into it.

MAINTAINING THE HEALTH OF THE VAT

Dyeing with the vat and the passing of time will both impact the health of the vat. The pH of the vat will drop. This is unavoidable. And it is highly likely that the bacteria in your vat will tire and need to be fed. You will be able to read the health of your vat by referring to the swatches created while taking the vat's vitals. If your vat is 75°F (24°C), the pH is at least 10.2, and your daily swatch is similar to the blue you have been getting, then your vat is healthy and you can dye if you would like to. Through the use of your indigo vat, and the fact that you are taking out indigo as you dye, some lightening of the swatch is normal, but if you find that your swatch has lightened drastically, it is most likely due to one or more of the following conditions:

- The pH has fallen below 10.2.
- The bacteria is tired.

If the pH has fallen below 10.2, add limestone to raise the pH. Take care! Add only as much limestone as needed. Adding too much limestone too fast can harm the bacteria and dull the color. For this size vat, if the vat is at a pH of 10, and 4.5 g limestone is added, in 24 hours the vat's pH will increase from 10 to 10.1. Do not add more than 30 grams of limestone at one time. If you have to add more than this, space it out over the course of multiple days. After adding limestone, wait at least 12 hours before dyeing. After 12 hours, take the vat's vitals, making sure the vat is 75°F (24°C) with a pH of at least 10.2 before dyeing. If the vat is still not at 10.2, repeat the addition of limestone, wait another 12 hours, and once again take the vat's vitals.

If the vat is 75°F (24°C), you have added limestone and established a pH of at least 10.2, and the swatch is still lighter blue than what you previously recorded, it may be time to give the bacteria a boost by feeding it wheat bran. Cook 30 grams of wheat bran in a stainless steel pot with ⅔ cup (165 ml) ash water from either batch over low heat for 5 minutes, or until the wheat bran turns golden brown and the mixture has gone from soupy to mushy. Add the wheat bran mixture in spoonfuls to the bucket. Do not stir. Cover the vat and allow to rest for 12 hours. Take the vat's vitals: The swatch should be a darker blue. If not, allow the vat to rest for another 12 hours and test again. Proceed to dyeing once the swatch turns a deeper blue.

Waking Up the Vat

Once you have started a vat, it is best to use it frequently and consistently. That said, let's say you go out of town and leave the vat. We have occasionally allowed our vats to "go to sleep"—times when they are not stirred nor are the vitals taken. Once we return from our time away, we check its vitals and always find that the pH has fallen and the bacteria is very tired. If the vat's pH has fallen below a 9, while we do not recommend doing this often, it is possible to do a hard reboot on the vat. Start by taking the vat's vitals and heating the vat to 75°F (24°C). In the case when the pH is low and the bacteria is weak, there is a bit of a dance between raising the pH and strengthening the bacteria.

1. Add 30 grams limestone to the vat and stir vigorously for 3 minutes.

2. Cook 30 grams wheat bran in a small stainless steel pot with ⅔ cup (165 ml) ash water from Batch 1 over low heat for 5 minutes, or until the wheat bran turns golden brown and the mixture has gone from soupy to mushy. Add the wheat bran mixture in spoonfuls to the bucket. Do not stir.

3. Cover and let rest for 12 hours. You should notice a difference: The surface of the vat will develop copper spots. When you take its vitals, your color swatch will be a deeper blue.

DISPOSAL OF THE VAT

If the vat's vitals are healthy but the vat is no longer producing color, this is an indicator that you have used all of the indigo in your vat. At this time, follow the instructions on disposal of the vat on page 237.

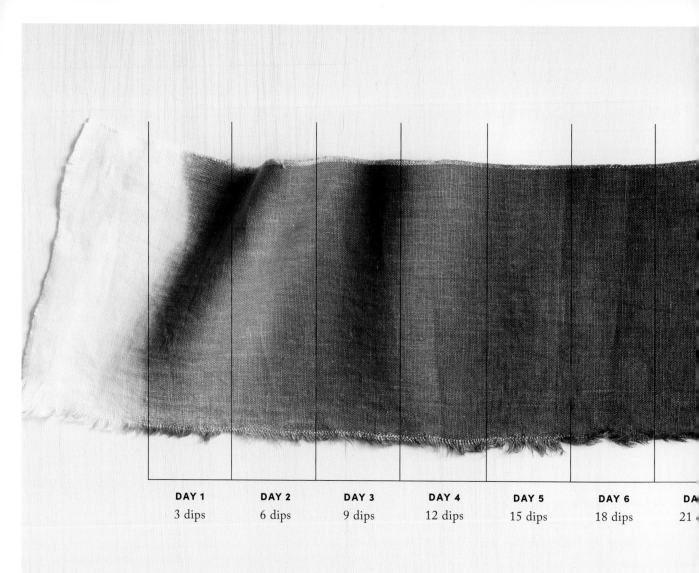

| DAY 1 | DAY 2 | DAY 3 | DAY 4 | DAY 5 | DAY 6 | DA |
| 3 dips | 6 dips | 9 dips | 12 dips | 15 dips | 18 dips | 21 |

shade card: blues made using a fermented indigo vat

GOODS: Merchant & Mills Laundered Linen (100% linen), milk

SCOUR: Scouring Cellulose-Based Goods (page 218)

MORDANT: Not applicable

DYE: Dyed with a fermented indigo vat using composted *Persicaria tinctoria* (page 122). This piece of fabric was dipped into the vat three times a day for fifteen days, successively moving down the cloth, to show the breadth of colors this kind of indigo vat can produce.

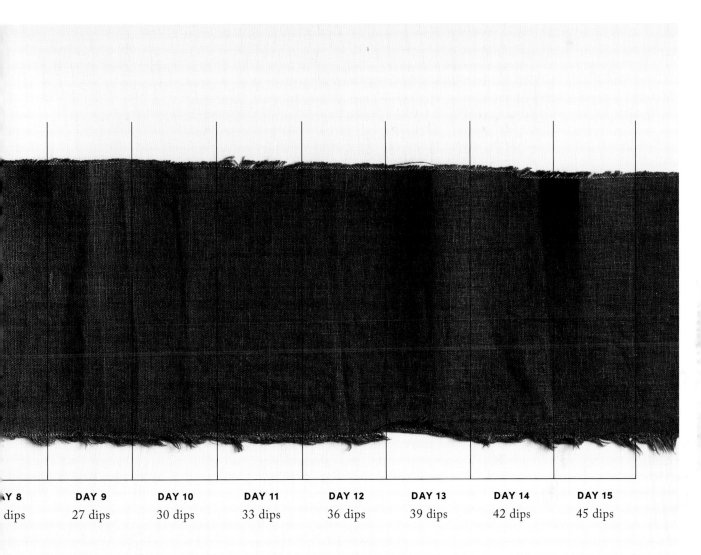

Y 8	DAY 9	DAY 10	DAY 11	DAY 12	DAY 13	DAY 14	DAY 15
dips	27 dips	30 dips	33 dips	36 dips	39 dips	42 dips	45 dips

skyline scarf

NATURE IS OUR FAVORITE place to find inspiration. Taking a moment out of our day to look at the sky, or an hour to take a walk in the park, provides us with a spaciousness to reflect on our connection to the earth and others. Inspired by this spaciousness and shared connection, we used the sky here in Oakland to inform the design on the Skyline Scarf using the *katazome* method of rice-paste resist.

To create this stencil, a photograph of our view was taken, printed out, and drawn onto tracing paper. Then it was set over a piece of persimmon-tanned paper. The clouds were cut out using an X-Acto knife and self-healing mat.

Scarves made by Fog Linen provide a wonderful canvas for trying katazome; they come in a wide range of weights. The one chosen for this piece has quite an open weave, which gives an airy effect to the clouds. The stencil was used twice. Both times the top of the stencil was aligned with the center fold of the scarf, right side up, creating a mirror reflection. In the second stenciling, the screen overlapped areas of the first print, which is OK because the finely ground rice bran sprinkled over the paste protects the paste from smudging. Once the reflection was completed, the scarf was hung on a drying rack for 24 hours to dry.

We used our fermented indigo vat to dye this piece. The vat's vitals were taken and the vat was stirred in the morning. Though the vat was heated to 75°F (24°C) to take the vitals, once the vitals had been taken, we stopped heating the vat and waited for a few hours, allowing the vat's temperature to drop to 73°F (23°C) to help preserve the connection between the rice paste and the scarf during the dyeing process. The more shades of indigo on a piece of cloth, adding depth and nuance, the more intriguing the piece is to the eye. So when dyeing this piece, we created an ombre that was very similar to the photo of the sky being used as inspiration. The scarf was folded in half. The fold and about 3 inches (7.5 cm) of the scarf were placed into the indigo vat and allowed to sit for 1 minute, and then removed from the vat for 1 minute. This was repeated two more times, each time placing more fabric on either side of the fold into the vat until the entire sky was covered with indigo. Immediately after the third and last dip, the scarf was placed into a bucket of cold water and gently massaged to remove the rice paste and rinse away excess indigo. The rinse water was changed frequently until the scarf stopped releasing indigo dye. The scarf sat in cold water overnight and was fully rinsed the next morning and dried. You will learn more about how to create your own katazome-treated pieces on the following pages.

katazome: using rice paste, stencils, and indigo to create patterns on cloth

IN JAPAN, THE PROCESS OF using a stencil and paste to create patterns on cloth is called *katazome*. In this section, you will learn how to carve stencils, make rice paste, and apply rice paste to cloth. In this case, the focus is on dyeing the fabric using indigo. If you study examples of katazome-treated fabrics, you can see an incredible array of colors and dyes used for this process. We recommend reading through the complete section to understand the entire process before beginning.

CARVING THE STENCIL

Stencils used for the katazome process in Japan are traditionally made from a special type of paper. Fine layers of paper are bonded together with persimmon juice, making the paper waterproof, and smoked. This paper can be hard to find and expensive due to the labor-intensive process of making it and the small number of people making it, but it is well worth the price. It is very enjoyable to work with this type of paper. When cutting the shapes easily fall away, the cut line is very crisp, the persimmon waterproofing treatment process makes the paper durable, and it is so nice to support artisans still making this type of paper and working with a product made from natural materials. To experiment with this process, card stock, Mylar, stencil paper, or the synthetic version of persimmon-dyed paper can be used. After a few uses, card stock will begin to come apart, so if you plan to spend a lot of time carving a stencil and would like to use it many times, it is best to use one of the other options listed.

MATERIALS

Persimmon-dyed paper, card stock, Mylar, or stencil paper

TOOLS

X-Acto knife and extra blades

Cutting mat

Pencil and eraser

Ruler

INSTRUCTIONS

1. Draw your design, including a 1-inch (2.5-cm) border.

2. Carve the design using an X-Acto knife. Remember all carved spaces will stay undyed. Keep your knife at a 90-degree angle while carving. By doing so, the top of the stencil will be the same as the bottom of the stencil. If the angle of your blade is not at a 90-degree angle, the bottom of your stencil will be smaller than the top of your stencil.

MATERIALS

⅓ cup (105 g) sweet
rice flour (known as
mochiko)

½ cup (60 g) finely
ground rice bran
(known as komon-nuka)

2 teaspoons (5 g)
limestone

2 teaspoons (5 g)
table salt

TOOLS

Flour sifter

Suribachi and accom-
panying wooden pestle
(recommended)
or mixing bowl and
wooden spoon

Measuring cups

Liquid measuring cup

Measuring spoons

Steamer

3-quart (2.8-L) stainless
steel pot with lid

2 small jars or bowls to
be used for the lime-
stone and salt solutions

Cotton towel

Tongs

MAKING RICE PASTE

Sweet rice flour and finely ground rice bran are combined into a dough, made into donuts, and steamed. Immediately after steaming, the donuts are mashed to create a paste. Using a *suribachi* set, a ceramic bowl with grooves along the inside of the bowl and accompanying wooden pestle, is very helpful during this process. The grooves in the bowl really help to pull the dough apart and make it into paste. However, a mixing bowl and wooden spoon can also be used. When the donut is first mashed, the dough is very elastic and resists being made into a paste. To pull the donut apart and mash it into paste, it can be helpful to have a friend hold the bowl. Allow two hours to make rice paste.

INSTRUCTIONS

1. Sift the sweet rice flour and rice bran into the suribachi or bowl 3 times.

2. Gradually add ¼ cup (60 ml) lukewarm water and mix thoroughly to form a dough. Knead until smooth and firm. The dough will resemble bread dough and will hold its shape. It should not stick to your hands. If the dough is not holding together, add a few more drops of water and continue to knead. If the dough is sticky, there is too much water: Add a bit more of each flour.

3. Form the dough into a ball. Press the ball between your hands to form a patty and lightly press your thumb through the center to make a 1-inch (2.5-cm) hole. The patty will be approximately ¾ inch (2 cm) thick and 3½ inches (9 cm) wide. (A, page 138)

4. Add 1 inch (2.5 cm) of water to the pot and place the steamer in the pot. Make sure the water does not touch the steamer—pour out some of the water if it does. Wet a kitchen towel or cloth, and line the steamer with it. Place the rice flour "donut" in the steamer and bring the towel ends up and over it. Cover the pot with its lid. The towel protects the donut from condensation while steaming.

5. Bring the water to a simmer. Steam the dough for 30 minutes. Check on the pot periodically to make sure there is still water in the pot. You may have to add more; if so, carefully pull the towel to the side, add water, taking care to not splash the donut or the towel, and resume cooking. Avoid getting the donut wet or exposing it to air. When the donut is done steaming it will be caramel in color and the dough will be elastic. You can test this by pinching a little piece of dough from the donut and pulling it apart. If the dough stretches, it is done.

6. While the donut is cooking, in a small jar, combine the limestone with ¾ cup (180 ml) hot water. Allow to rest. Any undissolved limestone will separate from the water and fall to the bottom of the glass. Set aside.

A

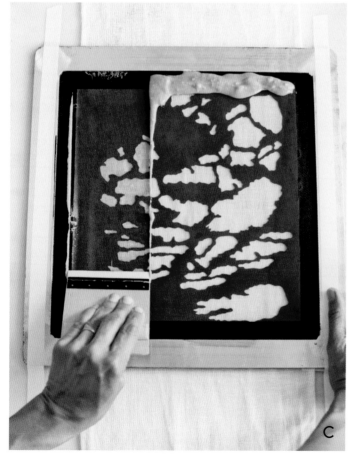

C

7. In a small jar, dissolve the table salt in ¾ cup (180 ml) hot water. Set aside.

8. As soon as the donut is done steaming, using tongs, carefully unwrap the cloth (taking care to not burn yourself) covering the donut and immediately place the donut in the suribachi or bowl. While the donut is still warm, mash it with the wooden pestle or wooden spoon. It is very important to do this quickly, or the dough will be lumpy and impede the printing process. As you mash, gradually add ¼ cup (60 ml) hot water from the pot you were just using to steam the donut, and keep mashing until smooth and glossy. This is when it can be helpful to have a friend hold the bowl as you mash to keep the bowl stable. (B, opposite)

9. Take a dab of the paste out of the bowl and set it aside to use as a comparative color sample. Gradually add 2 teaspoons of the limestone solution to the paste and combine using the pestle. The dough's color will change from brown caramel to straw yellow. If the paste is still not straw yellow, add another teaspoon of the limestone solution. As you are mashing, air bubbles will form in the paste. You will hear a popping sound as you mash the paste; this indicates you are on the right path.

10. Gradually add 2 teaspoons of the salt solution to the paste. Salt helps the paste retain moisture and helps keep the paste from cracking in the stenciling process. If you find your paste is cracking after applying it in the katazome process, add more of the salt solution. If you find that it is taking too long for the rice paste to dry, in the future add less salt solution. The way the paste responds in the stenciling process is related to the climate and weather. Experiment and find what the paste needs in your climate.

11. The paste is now complete. You can either use it now or you can place it in a glass container, cover it with ⅛ inch (3 mm) of water, cover the container with a lid, and store it in the refrigerator. Bring the paste to room temperature when you are ready to use it. If kept refrigerated, the paste can last 2 to 3 months.

Rice paste

Finely ground rice bran (komon-nuka or nuka) or fine sawdust

Cloth made of 100 percent natural fibers, scoured (page 217)

TOOLS

Screen-printing squeegee, tongue depressor, or spatula

Screen-printing screen (recommended if using a fine, detailed stencil)

Stencil

Painter's tape or masking tape

APPLYING THE RICE PASTE

The stencil is placed upon a piece of cloth. Rice paste is applied on top of the stencil and smoothed to cover the stencil. The stencil is removed and the rice paste is allowed to dry.

Just as a stencil can be as simple as a piece of card stock, the process of applying rice paste can be just as simple by using your finger, the edge of a credit card, or a folded piece of card stock. You don't even need a stencil: You can paint with the rice paste directly onto fabric. However, if you are using a finely cut stencil, one with thin lines or sharp angles that could get caught when spreading the rice paste across the stencil, using a screen-printing screen and squeegee is helpful in protecting the stencil and aids in applying an even, thin layer of rice paste.

INSTRUCTIONS

1. If using a stencil made from persimmon-tanned paper, soak it in water until saturated, approximately 20–30 minutes. Remove excess moisture by blotting with a cloth.

2. Tape the dry cloth to a smooth, flat work surface using painter's tape.

3. Tape the stencil to the cloth where desired. If using a stencil with fine lines, place a screen-printing screen over the top of the stencil.

4. Apply a line of paste along the top of the stencil (or screen).

5. Use a screen-printing squeegee or spatula to spread a thin, solid layer of rice paste over the stencil. Start at the top of the stencil, apply firm, consistent pressure, and pull the squeegee at a 45-degree angle toward yourself. Try to do this in one pass; this will help prevent the paste from spreading under the stencil. (C, page 138)

6. Make sure the layer of rice paste has covered the stencil completely.

7. After you have covered the entire stencil with rice paste, slowly lift the stencil (and screen) from the cloth.

8. Sprinkle nuka or fine sawdust across the surface of the cloth.

9. If you would like to add another repeat of your design, check the back of the stencil to make sure there isn't any rice paste attached to it, and remove it with a warm, wet cloth if so. Move the stencil into the position desired. Repeat steps 3–8. If the stencil is overlapping where you last applied rice paste, this is OK, as the sprinkling of nuka (or fine sawdust) will help sustain the pressure and prevent the rice paste from being smudged or removed. When placing the stencil onto the cloth, make sure to lower it directly down, and when lifting it off the cloth, make sure to lift it directly up to avoid smudging the previously applied paste.

10. Make sure to clean your stencil immediately, before the rice paste can harden, as it is difficult to remove once hardened and you risk weakening or, worse, tearing your stencil.

11. Allow the paste on the cloth to dry for at least 12 hours, preferably 24. Brush the cloth lightly to remove excess nuka or sawdust. The cloth is now ready for dyeing.

MATERIALS

Clothespins and clothesline

Thermometer

TOOLS

Indigo vat

Cloth treated with rice paste

INDIGO-DYEING FABRIC TREATED WITH RICE PASTE

When the dyeing is completed, the areas covered by rice paste will be white and all other areas will be blue. For the greatest contrast between the blue and white, and if you are using a fermented indigo vat, dye your katazome-treated cloth early in your indigo vat's life, when there is the greatest amount of indigo in your vat. If you are using an indigo-fructose-limestone vat, use the recipe for indigo vat #5 (page 195). This will give you the darkest shades of blue.

Rice paste is easily removed from the cloth with water, especially warm water, so it is important to work quickly and efficiently during the dyeing process and expose the rice paste to water only as much as needed during the dyeing process. Only dye in a vat of 75°F (24°C) or cooler. We have found that dipping the fabric into the indigo vat three to four times creates a rich color and preserves the rice paste's connection to the fabric; anything beyond this can cause the paste to loosen, allowing the dye to reach the areas once covered by paste.

INSTRUCTIONS

1. Place the stenciled cloth into the indigo vat and keep submerged for 1 minute. Remove the cloth from the vat and allow the cloth to oxidize for 1 minute. Do not wring the fabric; instead allow the fabric to drip into the vat. Repeat 2 more times. (D, page 138)

2. Rinse the fabric in cool water, removing excess indigo and rice paste.

3. Follow the finishing instructions on page 236.

persimmon-dyed
tote bag

JUICE SQUEEZED FROM GREEN persimmons makes an incredibly potent dye. The goods you plan to dye do not need to be mordanted, only scoured. This process does not require heat; the goods are submerged into a room-temperature bath of the juice (or can be painted with the juice) until saturated. Because the dye is set by UV, the goods are placed outdoors in the sun until dry. If a darker color is desired, additional layers of dye are added to the goods, through repeating the process of submerging the goods in the dye and setting it with UV. Over time, the persimmon juice will darken. The persimmon juice coats the goods and makes them stiff. The more layers applied, the stiffer the fabric. Over time, with use, the goods soften. The addition of persimmon juice to the goods makes them water-resistant.

Cocoknits Four Corner Bags, made of rustic undyed linen, were used in this project. They come in three sizes and have detachable leather handles, making them easy to dye. We have created the following examples to showcase the breadth of results that can be achieved layering persimmon dye with other dyes and modifiers. Continue experimenting to widen the palette. You will learn more about how to use persimmon juice to dye on the following pages.

SMALL DARK RED–BROWN BAG WITH BLUE HANDLES
We dipped this bag into the persimmon juice 9 times, resulting in a dark red–brown bag. We dipped the leather handles, leather washers, and cords in our fermented indigo vat to achieve a medium shade of blue.

MEDIUM DARK BLUE BAG WITH BLUE HANDLES
For the medium bag, we layered indigo and persimmon dye. First we dipped the bag into our fermented indigo vat one time, rinsed it, then dipped it into the persimmon juice 6 times. The bag is a deep, dark blue with a unique sheen and patina from the persimmon juice, and it has blue handles, also dyed in our fermented indigo vat.

LARGE BLACK BAG WITH TAN HANDLES
For the large bag, we wanted to show off the exciting ability for persimmon to shift to black using an iron bath. We dipped the bag into the persimmon juice 3 times. It was then dipped in a concentrated iron bath. Slowly the bag went from red-brown to a dark gray to the final black color. The black has a rich dark-chocolate undertone that gives it a distinct depth of color. We left the leather handles undyed to showcase the organic look and feel of the bag.

shade card: green persimmon dye

GOODS: Merchant & Mills Laundered Linen (100% linen), milk
SCOUR: Scouring Cellulose-Based Goods (page 218)
MORDANT: Not applicable
DYE: Swatches dyed using juice from green Hachiya persimmons. The dye was applied in layers ranging from one layer to nine. Between each layer of dye, the fabric swatch was exposed to sunlight, the UV setting the dye. The first row of swatches was created using green persimmon juice only.
NOTES: Dyed swatches were dipped into a concentrated iron water solution (page 234) as well as a baking soda solution (page 230) to widen the spectrum.

	LAYER 1	LAYER 2	LAYER 3	LAYER 4	LAYER 5	LAYER 6	LAYER 7	LAYER 8	LAYER 9
PERSIMMON ONLY									
WITH IRON									
WITH BAKING SODA									

dyeing with green persimmons

THERE ARE TWO TYPES of persimmons commonly found growing in California: Hachiya and Fuyu. Oval-shaped Hachiya, because of their high tannin content, must be fully ripened to eat; when ripe the flesh turns very soft and pulpy. They are often used in baking or dried. Fuyu are flatter than Hachiya and are commonly eaten fresh like an apple. While the underripe, green persimmons of both varieties can be used as dye, the Hachiya variety has the most tannin and will produce the most saturated color, most quickly. In California, we harvest green persimmons toward the end of August, before the nights get too cool, which causes the persimmons to ripen and turn orange.

In Japan, it is possible to purchase fermented persimmon juice to use as dye. We tried a number of experiments to ferment and preserve our persimmon juice but had varying results, so we find it easiest to work with fresh persimmon juice, which still yields incredibly saturated colors very similar to those created by fermented persimmon juice. Once the persimmon juice has been extracted from the fruit, it is best to use it that day, though it can be kept in the refrigerator in an airtight container for about a week. The more the juice is exposed to air, the more it begins to congeal and bind to itself. We found that freezing whole green persimmons to store them for future use is a way to make dye outside persimmon season. When you are ready to use them, take them out of the freezer, allow them to defrost, and once they are soft enough, immediately chop and use them as instructed below.

Because green persimmon dye is set through exposure to UV, choose a sunny day so the dye dries fast and has maximum exposure to UV. Persimmon juice is very potent. Take care to cover your counter with paper to protect it from staining. For easy cleaning, wash your tools soon after using them.

We tried applying fewer layers of dye but left the fabric out for multiple days in the sun. While the color did develop, the colors achieved were not as dark as with multiple layers of dye. When experimenting, we found using 100% juice, undiluted, and applied in multiple layers produced the darkest, most beautiful colors.

INSTRUCTIONS

1. Sew a 2-inch (5-cm) loop onto the goods with a needle and thread; when hanging the goods to dry, hang it from these loops, to avoid pressing the cloth with clothespins and leaving a mark.

5 to 7 persimmons
weigh about 1 pound
(.5 kg) and yield about
1 cup (240 ml) juice

MATERIALS

Green Hachiya
persimmons

Goods, scoured

TOOLS

Sewing needle

Thread

Bucket for pre-wetting

Knife

Cutting board

Food processor, juicer,
or cheese grater

Cheesecloth

Butcher tray (7½ × 11
inches/19 × 28 cm) or
stainless steel bowl

Flexible spatula
(recommended)

Pint mason jar with lid

Clothesline or drying
rack with clothespins

Rubber gloves

2. Wet the goods with tap water for 15 minutes to saturate, then squeeze excess water out before dyeing.

3. Wash the persimmons (A) and cut them into 1-inch (2.5-cm) pieces. Place the pieces in a food processor in batches and pulse to chop finely.

4. Lay the cheesecloth on your work surface, place the chopped persimmons in the center, and draw up the fabric to make a bundle. (B)

5. Squeeze the bundle as hard as you can over the butcher tray or bowl to catch all the juice. (C)

6. Dip the pre-wet goods into the juice in the butcher tray, using your hands (wear gloves to keep your hands from drying out) to gently rub the juice into the goods, ensuring the goods become fully saturated with juice. Lift the goods from the tray and, using your fingers, press excess juice back into the butcher's tray. (D)

7. Hang the goods on a clothesline in the sun. If you desire even color, review the goods for dry spots, where the juice was unable to penetrate thoroughly, and rub your fingers over this area, working to distribute the juice into the goods. This must be done at this step or else the dry spots will create permanent white splotches. Store the excess juice in a jar, covered with a lid, in the refrigerator while the goods dry. A flexible spatula is helpful to scrape excess dye out of the tray or bowl into the jar.

8. Once the dripping has stopped, rotate the goods to fully expose them to the sun to ensure even color. Allow the goods to dry fully before dipping again.

9. Repeat steps 6–8 to achieve a darker color (see shade card on page 148). Remember, the color will darken with continued UV exposure. On average, we find it is possible to complete 3 layers of dye per day.

10. When done dyeing for the day, place the leftover juice in a mason jar, seal with a lid, and keep it in the refrigerator.

WIDENING THE SPECTRUM

By raising the pH using baking soda, it is possible to shift the terra-cotta color to brown. By using iron water, it is possible to shift the terra-cotta color to gray and black. To do so, complete your final layer of dye and once the goods have dried, dip the goods using the baking soda solution and the room-temperature bath (page 233) or concentrated iron water solution (page 234).

A

B

C

D

CHAPTER FOUR

INDONESIA

batik dyeing with dalmini //
letters from kebon

FOR YEARS, WE HAVE BEEN CURIOUS ABOUT ways to apply natural dyes without heat. One prime example of textiles that may be dyed in such a way is naturally dyed batik, a process in which patterns are drawn onto cloth with wax, layers of dye are applied to the cloth, the wax is removed with hot water, and the patterns are revealed. This process requires room-temperature dyes, because using hot water in the dyeing process, as we would normally do, would remove the wax. We had been invited to Indonesia to share our natural dyeing work, and were hoping to meet with someone who creates naturally dyed batik fabric. After researching high and low, we were unable to locate anyone. Then, all of a sudden, we received an email newsletter from Daniel Gundlach, the founder of San Francisco–based company Language of Cloth. Daniel has traveled regularly to Indonesia to study batik and is an advocate for those in Indonesia who create textiles. In his email was an announcement that an acclaimed artist, named Dalmini, who uses natural dyes to create batik and is the cofounder of a cooperative named Batik Tulis Kebon Indah, would be visiting the Bay Area. Through Daniel, we were able to meet Dalmini, and she toured our studio. We expressed our desire to learn more about naturally dyed batik and asked her advice. She welcomed us to visit her and stay in her home to learn more about batik. We could not believe it—to be able to work and study with Dalmini was a dream come true.

Three weeks later, we landed in Yogyakarta, just five hundred miles south of the equator. As we walked down the stairs, off the plane, and onto the tarmac, the air was warm and thick with humidity, the heat rising off the blacktop. We collected our bags and exited the airport; people surrounded the exit, shouting the names of their loved ones. We scanned the crowd, looking for Dalmini, and there she stood with her family, waving. We hugged, laughed, and piled into their car. As we made the hour drive from the airport to Kebon, the village where Dalmini lives, the city lights dropped away and trees filled the horizon. Java's natural environment is tropical rain forest, and Dalmini's's bright lime-green home is cradled by tall teak trees and abundant flora. Upon entering her home, we were greeted by more family members and a spread of home-cooked food: salted goose eggs, crackers embedded with sardines, rice, tempeh, and fermented hot sauce. Tired from traveling and well-fed, we fell fast asleep.

The Batik Tulis Kebon Indah cooperative consists of 180 women creating naturally dyed batik fabrics. Dalmini tells us they named the cooperative because "Kebon is the name of our village, and indah means beautiful, so we named our collective Kebon Indah because we want our batik to be beautiful just like our village." Dalmini's role within the cooperative is to dye and promote their naturally dyed cloth. Two members of the cooperative create

---

Dalmini uses wood, bark, and dried fruit to create the colors found upon her batik fabric. Members of the Batik Tulis Kebon Indah cooperative use hot wax and a small tool called a canting to draw designs such as swirls, diamonds, flowers, and vines upon fabric.

the designs and draw them onto the fabric in pencil, and the rest of the members draw with wax onto the fabric.

In the early hours of the day, just as light was peeking through the window, we could hear one scooter after another pulling up outside the house—women, on their way to drop their children off at school, were stopping at Dalmini's to deliver stacks of fabric they had drawn on with wax so they could be dyed. As we walked through the house, what we thought was just a back door leading to a backyard revealed Dalmini's large, open-air dye studio. Dalmini was already hard at work. She had her dyepots going and was planning the dyeing to be completed that day. Her studio, integrated with the family's small farm, was alive with activity; chickens ran past, their chicks close behind, a rogue rooster every now and then coming through to bellow, a young goat in the corner eating hay, and a family of geese squawking should you get too close.

Dalmini immediately started teaching us how to create batik. The first step was to take a piece of scoured and mordanted, 100 percent cotton fabric measuring 36 inches (91 cm) long and 45 inches (114 cm) wide, and to choose a design created by her sister-in-law. Many of the designs depicted the local flora and fauna, including vines, flowers, birds, and butterflies, all of which can be seen in the village. We each transferred drawings to the fabric by using a glass table, natural light, and a pencil.

A tiled veranda wrapped around the side and front of Dalmini's home. A formal sitting area was to the right of the front door, where a table with tea was available all day long to guests. The rest of the veranda was open, where various gatherings would occur, and where we spent a lot of time learning how to draw using a canting. We watched those around us easily dip the copper bowl of their canting tool into the hot wax, bring the spout of the canting tool toward their mouth, blow into the spout to clear the passage, and then bring the tool down to the fabric and begin to draw, smoothly and beautifully. Once they had used all of the wax in their bowl, they returned the canting to the dish of hot

wax and repeated the process. We felt confident in our approach—*OK, just get the hot wax in the bowl, now blow in the spout . . . uh, where is the spout? Finally, get the canting tool to the fabric—oh no, now that's just a blob of wax.* Luckily, everyone around us was really encouraging, and as we kept trying, we did get better.

Later in the morning, a group of schoolgirls arrived on motorbikes, wearing the classic uniform commonly seen in that area—a light blue shirt tucked into a navy blue skirt. Each girl went to the dye studio, found her piece of fabric, and joined us on the veranda to draw with wax. Learning batik is part of their education. Along each girl's sleeve there were patches showing what she was learning in school, including one featuring a canting.

A few hours went by; we diligently tried to cover all the pencil-drawn lines on our fabric with wax. As lunchtime approached, a group of women riding motorbikes arrived. About thirty women, all members of the co-op, were meeting to have lunch and to look at photos. It was an exciting time—Dalmini's oldest daughter had recently gotten married and she had just received the photos back from the ceremony. The group passed along the photos oooing and ahhing. Though we were newcomers, we were welcomed into the group. Each woman greeted us by shaking our hand, pulling us into a hug, and kissing each cheek. We ate together, and once we finished, the women took off on their scooters to continue their day; we returned to canting, and Dalmini returned to dyeing.

The historical use of resist dyeing with wax is an ancient art form more than two thousand years old. Batik in Java was first recorded in the twelfth century, though many believe it was used earlier. In Java, batik was used primarily for ceremonial clothing. Due to the labor-intensive process of creating intricate designs by hand, coupled with the rich colors made by applying multiple layers of dye to the cloth, batik was expensive, a status symbol worn mainly by those in the royal court. When asked which batik fabrics today have cultural significance, Dalmini responded, "Batik with the motifs named *klasih wahyu temurun* and *sido mukti* are worn during the wedding ceremony, and the motif named *trutum* is worn by the bride and groom's parents. The color is up to the one who wears it." Javanese batik is typically made using a 2½-yard (2.25-meter) length of cloth worn as a sarong around the hips or made into a hat. In 2009, UNESCO added Indonesian batik to the list of the Intangible Cultural Heritage of Humanity, making batik a vital part of Indonesia's history and culture.

In 2006, a major earthquake hit Java, and the region where Dalmini lives was in great distress. Prior to the earthquake, Dalmini and the women who are now in the collective participated in only one part of the process: drawing with wax. There were men who came to the region who would give them fabric with designs drawn onto it in pencil. The women would draw with wax, and then they would give the fabric back to the men, who would then take the fabric to be dyed and sold. Dalmini never knew where the fabric went, what it looked like dyed, or where it was sold. After the earthquake, the men stopped coming. This left Dalmini and the other women without an income stream. As often happens, when a natural disaster strikes an area, relief organizations and nonprofits are drawn there to help stabilize and support the region. One of these organizations located in Yogyakarta came to speak to the women about starting their own collective to design, dye, and sell their own batik fabrics, and they did just that. Dalmini said, "Kebon Indah Cooperative is made for the empowerment of women who live in the village, so the economy of the village will improve, as will the welfare of the members and their families."

Dalmini was drawn to using natural dyes because it is environmentally friendly and the dyes can be sourced in and around their village. Dyes the collective uses most often include indigo, *soga tinggi* bark (mangrove, *Ceriops tagal*), *tegeran* wood, (cockspurn thorn, *Maclura cochinchinensis*), *soga jambal* bark (*Peltophorum ptero-carpum*), *jalawe* (myrobalan, *Terminalia chebula*) fruit, *mahoni* (mahogany, *Toona sureni*) wood, *jati* (teak, *Tectona grandis*) leaves, mango tree leaves, mangosteen peels, and rambutan peels. Using natural dyes also preserves the traditional color palette of Javanese batiks. Once the dye has been extracted from the plants, the remains are then turned into compost or used as firewood.

When the light got too low to continue working, we walked around the village with Dalmini, visiting the homes of her friends and collaborators, where we were invited to sit on their verandas and drink tea. When they saw us, we were greeted with open arms, and Dalmini would tell them what we did that day. We would sit quietly, smiling, enjoying everyone's company, casually relaxed and relishing the night air.

One night while walking home on the dirt road through the neighborhood, a member of the cooperative came up to us with a stack of fabric she had drawn on with wax for Dalmini to review. Dalmini looked the fabric over closely under the tiny streetlight and gave a few words of feedback and direction, the woman nodded, and we continued on our way. It felt like the entire village was a studio working toward the common goal of uplifting one another. With the moon high in the night sky and the chirps of the geckos growing to a full chorus, we rested while eagerly awaiting the next day's lessons.

Once we had traced all of the pencil lines with wax, we went back to the dye studio to join Dalmini. She was in the process of creating batches of dye concentrates—she added whole plants and bark to a pot of water, then slowly over the course of the day, she heated the dyebath and added more water until the dyebath formed a viscous concentrate. Once complete, Dalmini strained the concentrate and allowed it to cool to be used the next day for dyeing. While the dye concentrate simmered, Dalmini dyed the cloth one piece at a time. In a wooden basin, she poured the cool dye concentrate and added the length of fabric. Using her hands, she massaged the dye into the surface of the fabric until the entire piece was thoroughly coated with dye. She then hung each piece of fabric; the ambient heat caused the fabric to dry fairly quickly, at which point Dalmini returned the fabric to the dyebath and repeated the dyeing process.

Once we had completed covering the outline in pencil with wax, we dipped our cloths into indigo three times. Then we added more wax to the areas of the cloth that we wanted to stay blue. Next, we applied three layers of *jalawe* (a yellow dye)—combined with the indigo, this created green. We set the *jalawe* with a bath of aluminum–potassium sulfate mordant and added more wax to all the areas of the cloth we wanted to stay green. For the last stage of dyeing, we submerged the cloth in a bath of iron, turning all areas not covered with wax black. Finally, to complete the process, we dropped our fabric into a cauldron of boiling-hot water and quickly, using a long stick, pulled it out again, up and down; we continued until all the wax was removed.

The entire process of creating our batik fabric spanned the course of four days, working all day into the final minutes of sunlight. The process of canting can be quite addictive, and at times Dalmini had to force us to stop and rest. That being said, it was certainly a window into the incredibly labor- and time-intensive practice of batik, and it gave us greater insight into the value of these incredible textiles.

While we worked on our fabrics, Dalmini continued to accept fabrics with wax drawn on them from women in the collective, and she began the process of dyeing them. Walking through the dye studio during that week, we saw endless variations of designs and color combinations. It was absolutely awe-inspiring. There were times when indigo-dyed cloth filled the space, and other times the palette shifted to deep terra-cotta, and then there was the magic of seeing the cloth with the wax removed. It was hard to decide which was more beautiful—the fabric hanging mid-process, heavy with multiple layers of dye and wax, exuded a sculptural quality, but also deeply impressive was the supple, soft completed cloth, all the layers of wax removed, revealing the intricate lines and myriad colors.

Toward the end of our time with Dalmini, we visited the Batik Tulis Kebon Indah co-op headquarters. The space includes a shop where their batik is displayed, a community center for the women to gather, and a batik dye studio where members of the co-op can demonstrate the process to visitors. Much of our week was spent with the fabrics in mid-process, so it was really incredible to see the stacks of completed fabrics and to recognize the vast array of finished designs and color combinations on display.

It was hard to leave Dalmini and the family she has created through the co-op. Though we do not speak each other's language, through gestures, smiling, our shared love of textiles, and a little help from Google Translate, we were able to create a friendship.

We are so grateful to Dalmini and the members of Batik Tulis Kebon Indah for allowing us to spend time with them and to learn from them. Batik Tulis Kebon Indah accepts students who would like to learn the process, and they enjoy traveling within Indonesia and abroad to teach others. Dalmini said, "I love talking about batik to other people." And we are incredibly thankful she does.

Dalmini c/o
Batik Tulis Kebon Indah
Kebon, Java
Telephone / WA: +62 857 2569 1539

Language of Cloth
www.languageofcloth.com

Fabric mid-process covered in multiple layers of dye and wax hangs in Dalmini's outdoor studio. Dalmini rubs the thick dye concentrates into the surface of the cloth. The wax is removed from the cloth by boiling water and vigorous up-and-down movements. Dalmini (far left) meets with members of the Batik Tulis Kebon Indah cooperative for lunch.

one farmer's journey to preserve indigo // letters from ambarawa village

IN OUR DYE STUDIO, WE HAVE MAINLY relied on indigo that has been grown and processed in India and imported into the United States. Desiring to grow and process our own indigo, so we can cut down on our carbon footprint and be more self-reliant, we have been studying various methods for a few years and are always excited to meet others who have this same interest. So when we learned of Saiful Nurudin and his farm, Tinctori, which specializes in growing and extracting indigo, and learned we could visit, we jumped at the chance to meet him and hear more about his work.

To get to Saiful's farm, located about an hour and a half north of Yogyakarta, we hired Faisal and Ahmad, two college students studying English to help as translators. They were excited for the road trip and the chance to work on their English, and we were excited to see more of Java. We had verbal directions to the farm, and the four of us attempted to decipher them; after a few wrong turns and phone calls, we finally made it. It was a fun drive, full of chatting as we went along, sharing what we saw and watching the landscape shift and change.

As we pulled up to the house, Saiful greeted us and introduced us to the property, which was an indigo paradise. Surrounded by lush bright-green rice fields, there were bushes of *Indigofera tinctoria* growing, a greenhouse filled with young *Persicaria tinctoria*, an impressively sized compost pile composed of spent indigo stalks and leaves, and large cement basins used to extract the indigo. Saiful began the tour by teaching us about the types of plants they grow that contain indigotin: *Indigofera tinctoria*, *Persicaria tinctoria*, *Strobilanthes cusia*, and *Isatis tinctoria*. Though *Indigofera tinctoria* is what has grown in the area historically, Saiful and his father are interested in these other varieties that have the potential to grow equally as well or better.

Saiful's father began growing indigo in 2008 with support and training from the government. In 2010, Saiful also became interested in growing and processing indigo and joined his father's efforts. Currently, Saiful and his father work with twelve partner farms to grow indigo, and more are interested in joining. Saiful and his father give seed to the farmers, and once the indigo is harvested, they buy the indigo from the farmer. Saiful and his father also rent land to grow indigo.

Saifu stands with his *Indigofera tinctoria* plants. A basin full of indigo pigment Saiful has extracted from his plants is then used to dye cloth. *Persicaria tinctoria* blooms nearby.

To create indigo dye, Saiful starts growing in November, during the rainy season. The first harvest takes place in February, followed by three more harvests to complete the cycle. Once the plants are harvested, they are submerged in water inside a large tub (depending on the ambient temperature, this may take place for a few hours to a couple of days), the plant is removed (and added to his compost pile), the pH of the water is increased by adding limestone, and the water is aerated. This causes the indigo dye to separate from the water (if you look closely, you can see little bits of indigo particles floating in the water). The indigo dye will then settle along the bottom of the tub. Saiful next drains the water from the tub, being careful to not disturb the indigo pigment, and there, finally, once all the water has been siphoned off, is the concentrated indigo pigment. This indigo, in the form of paste, is packaged and sold to local dyers. In Indonesia, this is known as *pasta*. It is similar to the indigo pigment we use in our studio imported from India, though the pigment we use has been dried and ground. Once the dyer receives the indigo, they create an indigo vat; a variety of methods can be used, such as combining the indigo with fructose and limestone (as is instructed in this book on page 196), to dye a gorgeous array of blues that we all know and love—resembling everything from the palest of skies to the deep, dark ocean.

In addition to selling his indigo paste to local dyers, he also uses it in his indigo and batik studio. Saiful has his own line of indigo-dyed goods, featuring patterns created with wax and *shibori*-style resist dyeing. Tinctori also accepts outside dye commissions. They indigo dye cloth, wood, and leather. Standing in awe of all the things Saiful and his family are accomplishing, we asked Saiful what advice he would give to others who would like to start an indigo farm or natural dyeing practice. He replied, "Keep trying, and don't give up." And that is exactly what Saiful is doing as he preserves the tradition of growing and processing indigo in Indonesia.

Tinctori
Saiful Nurudin
Dusun Jlamprang Wetan rt03/06, Gemawang, Jambu,
Kan Semarang, Central Java 50663
Telephone / WA: +081 32 713 8835
Ifulbatik@gmail.com

mordanting with plants, dyeing with roots, and weaving ikat // letters from ubud and tenganan

YEARS AGO, WHILE VISITING THE RENOWNED natural dyeing center Maiwa in Vancouver, British Columbia, we happened across a container with *Symplocos* written across it. Curious, we read further and learned that *Symplocos* is the genus of a tree whose leaves can be used in place of metallic salts, such as aluminum potassium sulfate, in the mordanting process. Through reading about *Symplocos*, we learned about the Bebali Foundation's Plant Mordant Project, led by I Made Maduarta, who goes by Pung. The Bebali Foundation strives to preserve the use of *Symplocos* as a traditional plant mordant used by weavers in Indonesia. Pung is also the cofounder of Threads of Life, a for-profit social enterprise located in Bali consisting of a gallery and shop located in Ubud and a dye studio, located just north of Ubud, featuring the Bebali Foundation natural dye garden. Both organizations aim to provide education about the textiles of Indonesia, to support those creating traditional textiles with natural dyes, and to encourage environmental stewardship within the natural dyeing practice.

Inspired and intrigued, we picked up a container of *Symplocos*, hoping to experiment and learn more about the process. Threads of Life and the Bebali Foundation

went on our list of places we hoped to visit one day. So years later, when we received the opportunity to travel to Indonesia, visiting Threads of Life, understanding more about the Bebali Foundation, and learning about *Symplocos* were at the top of our list.

In addition to *Symplocos*, for years we had been studying Indonesian ikat textiles and were captivated by the warm, rusty reds. From reading about these textiles in books and seeing them in museums, we learned about the many dye traditions of working with cotton yarn and *Morinda*, a tree that grows in the tropics, whose root produces a red dye similar to madder. The traditional practices of working with cotton and *Morinda* are elaborate, involving vegetable oil, tannin, *Symplocos*, limestone, and *Morinda* root, in a series of applications that are repeated for days, weeks, months, and even years. This dyeing process does not require heat.

Early one morning, we traveled to the Threads of Life dye studio and met with William Ingram, another cofounder of Threads of Life. The team at Threads of Life have been working for many years on studying the tradition of mordanting with plants. Knowing we were interested in the process of mordanting with with

Curcuma domestika

Datura fastuosa

Calotropis gigantea

Carica papaya

Eryth

Gossypium hirsutum

Aleurites moluccana

Symplocos and dyeing with *Morinda* root, William showed us a three-ring binder filled with red swatches, where they have meticulously recorded their experiments. Their dedication, diligence, and commitment to understanding the relationship between *Symplocos* and *Morinda* were incredibly inspiring.

To mordant cotton with *Symplocos* and dye with *Morinda*, the first step is to apply a saponified oil and tannin to the cotton threads. Under instructions from Pung, a series of leaves and roots are gathered from the lush Bebali dye garden located right next to the studio. The leaves and roots are chopped and combined with candlenut, which has a high oil content, in a mortar and pestle. A bit of water is added to create a bath, and then the cotton yarn is submerged. Once the oiling process is complete, the yarn is hung to dry for one to two months, so the oils can saponify and oxidize. Then a dyebath is created containing *Symplocos* and *Morinda* root.

William explains that the leaves of the *Symplocos* tree, found on the island of Flores, turn bright yellow at the end of the season and fall to the ground. The leaves must be gathered at that time, before they are rained upon. If rained upon, the aluminum in the leaves is washed away, and the leaves cannot be used as a mordant. Threads of Life and the Bebali Foundation find it important to support the conservation of these trees, so that the traditional textiles made by the local communities, which play an important role in their culture and heritage, can continue to be made.

It was clear from this demonstration that a deep knowledge of plants, in combination with time, is necessary to fully understand the process. Though this was a peek into the process, it would take many more years of study for us to understand it in full. We were in awe of Pung's breadth of knowledge and reminded of the vast styles of natural dyeing practiced around the world,

the importance of studying one's local plants, and the acknowledgment that no matter how much we want to learn about natural dyeing, some things may take a lifetime to understand or perhaps may never be fully understood, but instead can be honored.

One day, we went with William to meet Wayan Mudana, the owner of Morinda Art, located in the village of Tenganan, one of the last places on Bali where naturally dyed textiles are still being made and one of the only places in the world where double-ikat cloth is woven. Called *geringsing*, these cloths—yellow, red, and black in color—are woven in various rectangular shapes and are worn by women and men for ceremonial purposes. They feature geometric patterns, stylized floral motifs, and remarkable imagery of human figures. When asked what the motifs found in the textiles represent, Wayan replied, "There are twenty-four designs we have inherited from our ancestors. All of those designs have their own meaning and magical aspects."

Ikat, meaning "to bunch" or "to bind" in Indonesian, is a type of resist-dyeing. Resist-dyeing is a form of surface design in which pressure is applied to yarn or fabric before being dyed. During the dyeing process, the dye cannot seep into the areas of yarn or fabric under pressure. Once the dyeing is complete, the materials applying pressure are removed and a pattern emerges.

Typically, resist-dyeing is done to cloth that has already been woven. However, to make the cloth at Morinda Art, and to create the complex designs found upon the *geringsing*, the thread that makes up the cloth is resist-dyed *before* it is woven. When weaving any cloth, there are threads tied vertically under tension, called the "warp." The weaver passes a thread, called the "weft," at a 90-degree angle, through the warp, to create the cloth. At Morinda Art, before they become cloth, both the warp and the weft threads are gathered in clusters, according

The lush Bebali Dye Garden—from which a selection of tannin-rich roots and leaves have been gathered to mordant and dye the red cotton yarn shown.

to a predetermined pattern, and wrapped with fine pieces of thread and plastic, which resist the dye. Double-ikat refers to the fact that both the warp and weft ikat threads are wrapped.

To create *geringsing*, first, the warp and the weft are kneaded in a mixture of candlenut oil and a wood ash lye solution and soaked for more than a month. Then the warp and weft are removed from the oil and lye solution and hung to dry. They are now a soft yellow color due to the oil. The warp and weft are both carefully measured, and small bundles of threads are gathered and tied with thin pieces of plastic. The areas that have been tied are protected from the dye and will stay yellow. The warp and weft are sent to a neighboring village and are dyed with indigo, and then returned to Tenganan. A portion of the ikat bindings are removed, and then the warp and weft are dyed again, this time with the bark of the *Morinda* root. Wayan said, "The last color, *mengkudu* (*Morinda*) red, is dyed repeatedly for three months until we get the desired color." The areas that had been tied during the indigo dyeing were soft yellow going into the *Morinda* dyebath, and emerged a red. The areas that are blue from the indigo dyeing emerge from the *Morinda* dyebath nearly black. Wayan and his wife work on design and apply the yellow and red dyes. Women in the village add the resist ties and do the weaving. There are some pieces that can take ten years to complete.

Once the dyeing is finished, the ties are removed from the warp and the weft. The warp is added to the loom, and the weaving process begins. Ni Wayan Juniani, one of the weavers in the village, will spend at least two months weaving this particular piece. The weaving is plain weave, and though it is relatively simple in the lexicon of weaving patterns, she carefully lines up each warp thread and weft thread, one by one, using a small pick, to bring to life the human forms depicted in the cloth. Her attention to detail and patience are truly awe-inspiring.

Leaving Bali, taking our lessons learned from Threads of Life, the Bebali Foundation, and Morinda Art, we reflected on just how much our perspective on plants had widened. We looked forward to studying how we could re-create similar effects to those we saw, using plant mordants and dyes from our local area. And we were determined to understand ikat further, even if that meant creating a very small, much simpler sample, such as the Zigzag Ikat Woven Bracelet on page 204.

In memory of Ni Wayan Juniani.

Threads of Life
Gallery Location: Jalan Kajeng 24, Ubud, Bali 80571, Indonesia
info@threadsoflife.com
www.threadsoflife.com

Morinda Art
I Wayan Mudana
Desa Tenganan Pegringsingan, Bali, Indonesia
Telephone / WA: +082 23 779 6311
morindaart@yahoo.co.id

Clockwise from bottom left: The warp thread oiled using candlenut, before being dyed, sits next to a full warp that has been dyed with *Morinda* root and indigo, right before being placed upon the loom to be woven. Ni Wayan Juniani carefully places each and every thread in just the right place, making the imagery come to life. Examples of double ikat woven fabric, woven and dyed at Morinda Art. Even the architecture of the homes of Tenganan displays layers of handmade nuances, like the bricks in the wall, molded by hand.

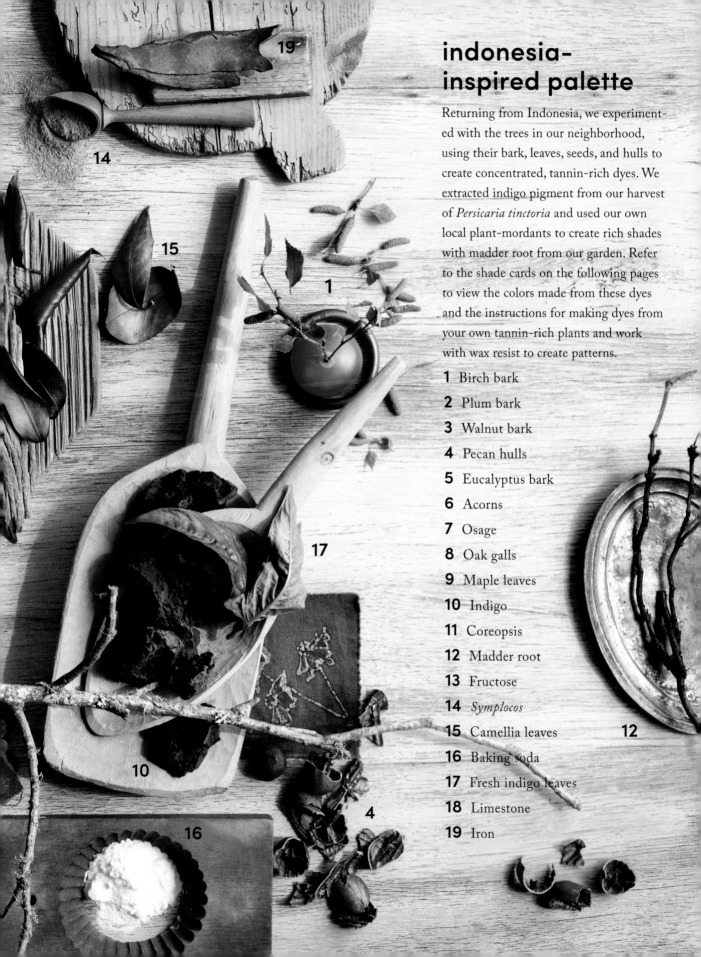

indonesia-inspired palette

Returning from Indonesia, we experimented with the trees in our neighborhood, using their bark, leaves, seeds, and hulls to create concentrated, tannin-rich dyes. We extracted indigo pigment from our harvest of *Persicaria tinctoria* and used our own local plant-mordants to create rich shades with madder root from our garden. Refer to the shade cards on the following pages to view the colors made from these dyes and the instructions for making dyes from your own tannin-rich plants and work with wax resist to create patterns.

1 Birch bark
2 Plum bark
3 Walnut bark
4 Pecan hulls
5 Eucalyptus bark
6 Acorns
7 Osage
8 Oak galls
9 Maple leaves
10 Indigo
11 Coreopsis
12 Madder root
13 Fructose
14 *Symplocos*
15 Camellia leaves
16 Baking soda
17 Fresh indigo leaves
18 Limestone
19 Iron

batik: layering wax and dye concentrates to create patterns

Batik is the process of taking wax, applying it to fabric, dyeing the fabric using room temperature concentrates, and removing the wax. With batik it is possible to create thousands of patterns and color combinations. In this section, you will learn how to create naturally dyed batik fabrics using combinations of locally sourced barks, leaves, and indigo. We suggest that you read through all the steps to understand the whole process before beginning, as it is time intensive.

SELECTION AND PREPARATION OF FABRIC

Dalmini uses a very specific fabric: 100 percent cotton, tightly woven, and lightweight. Due to the construction, this fabric is very smooth and makes an ideal canvas for the time-intensive wax drawings her cooperative creates. A similar fabric easily found in the United States is Robert Kaufman Kona (100 percent cotton). For fun, we experimented with an array of cotton and linen fabrics ranging in thickness and in tightness of weave. The wax easily penetrated the surface of the lighter-weight fabrics and those with a looser weave, making it easy to create fabrics that were nearly reversible when complete. Also, it was easier to remove the wax from these fabrics, which is always a plus. When using thicker fabrics, such as Robert Kaufman Waterford Linen, the wax tended to sit on the surface rather than penetrate the fabric. Once the wax was removed, some of the dye reached under the wax, resulting in uneven lines and giving the design a rustic look. Though the results are quite different from the sharp lines created by Dalmini and her collective, the uneven faded lines provided another beautiful effect. One more thing to note: The wax was a bit harder to remove from the thicker fabrics, because that which did make it through the surface was more heavily embedded within the thicker threads.

Size of Fabric

To begin studying this technique, our recommendation is to start small. Butcher trays, size 7½ × 11 inches (19 × 28 cm), are inexpensive, widely available at local art supply stores, and ideal for the dyeing process. Fabric cut to 9 × 6 inches (13 × 15 cm) works nicely with these trays and is easy to handle while learning how to cant, dye, and remove wax. The Cleo Tool Roll on page 187 calls for this size of fabric and is a great project to showcase your dyeing experiments. Once you have tried the process from start to finish, then plan a bigger piece or continue experimenting and creating pieces the same or of similar size to learn about the vast array of possibilities.

Pre-Mordanting

When experimenting with room temperature dye concentrates, we tried a number of mordanting possibilities and analyzed the depth of color upon completion of dyeing as well as colorfastness, and we found that mordanting with aluminum acetate and chalk (page 221) provided the best lightfastness and colorfastness.

DESIGN: CREATING YOUR OWN NATURE-BASED VISUAL LANGUAGE

Depending on your skill set, you may be extremely excited to draw your own design or a bit overwhelmed when facing a blank canvas. Nature provides endless possibilities for inspiration. Take a walk around your yard and see which plants catch your eye. Either sit in your garden (if you don't have a garden, the community garden or public park works well, too) with paper and pencil and sketch, or choose a plant and gather four or five examples to bring inside, so you can look at it from different angles to really capture the essence of the plant. If you can, take a photo of the plant to understand the overall pattern of growth, which can be incorporated into your design. Through these simple steps, you can create your own visual language, which can be brought to life through the practice of batik.

Coreopsis growing in our dye garden provided the inspiration for the fabric used in the Cleo Tool Roll (page 187). By gathering a few flowers and studying the ways the petals lie, a pattern that is multidirectional emerged. Make sure when designing to think about whether you would like your design to be directional, and sewn as such, or multidirectional so it can be used in any orientation when sewing. Though the coreopsis are almost all nearly the same size, as on the plant, you can play with proportions to give a greater depth to the design. You can add leaves or small buds about to become flowers. Dalmini frequently uses decorative dashes, dots, and swirls to break up large swaths of space and to add intricate detail. These moments guide the eye through the design and are fun to draw with wax.

Transfer a Design to Fabric

Place your design on a window or lightboard, place your scoured and mordanted fabric over the design, and, using a pencil, lightly draw the design onto the fabric.

DESIGN TIPS

Three additional aspects to consider when creating a design:

- Think about how many colors you plan to use. If you are planning to dye with more than one color, make sure to read Creating Multiple-Color Designs on page 176.

- Drawing with wax using a canting can be challenging at first, but with practice it becomes easier. When first starting out, a simpler design may be easier to execute.

- The removal of wax can be tricky, so remember that the more lines you draw, the more wax you will apply, and the more wax you have to remove.

USING WAX TO CREATE PATTERNS

Dalmini and the members of the cooperative practice *batik tulis*, a style of batik using a special pen-like tool called a canting, to hand-draw designs. This process is mesmerizing to watch and to practice. It is the style of batik used to create the batik fabric featured in the Cleo Tool Roll (page 187). When using the canting tool to draw with wax, Dalmini taught us to watch for the wax to penetrate through both sides of the fabric. When looking at the back side of the fabric, the wax line should be nearly as strong as on the front side. This way, the wax will fully resist any dye, creating a clear line, and ensure the wax will not be accidentally removed during the multistage dyeing process. This is a little tricky at first, and will most likely take some time to perfect as you learn the balance between having the wax hot enough and being able to control drawing with the canting tool. An intermediary step in this process is to use a different applicator for the wax, for example a paintbrush, which you have most likely used before and are more familiar with than the canting tool, to understand the relationship between the temperature of the wax and making sure the wax penetrates the fabric thoroughly. But we think having skips and starts in the wax line due to the wax not penetrating thoroughly adds texture and nuance to the fabric, and this can be nice, too.

Preparing Your Workspace

Protect the surface of your work space from wax drips and dye splatter by covering it with layers of newspaper, butcher paper, or tightly woven cotton canvas. Place a drop cloth on the floor to catch any drips.

Choosing Wax

In Java, there are a number of waxes to choose from made from combinations of beeswax, paraffin, animal or plant waxes, and *gondorukem*—resin obtained from the milky white sap of *Pinus merkusii juhn*, a species of pine tree. An artist chooses wax based on what type of batik they are creating, what tools they are using, and their own personal preference after years of practice. Here are some options for waxes to use in your batik-making practice:

WAX FROM JAVA

Before leaving Java, we purchased wax to bring home with us. This wax has a very distinct smell, which we are quite fond of because it reminds us of being with Dalmini, but nevertheless it is best to use this wax with good ventilation—near an open window. This wax flows smoothly from the canting tool, and with practice, it is possible to get a thin line (thinner than the other waxes listed below). The wax heats evenly without smoking, and when heated and used in the canting tool, it stays warm, so the tool doesn't need to be refilled too often.

BEESWAX

This is a great choice of wax because it can be sourced locally and melts easily. Beeswax melts at a lower temperature than the wax from Indonesia, but at the temperature that allows it to write well with the canting tool and to penetrate the fabric, the wax creates a wider line. The wax cools faster, so the bowl of the canting tool has to be refilled more frequently.

SOY WAX

This wax has the least amount of smell, melts at the lowest temperature, and can easily be removed with hot tap water. It is also the hardest to control. This wax tends to spread when applied, so it is hard to get a crisp line. Because it can be used at a low temperature and can easily be removed, we recommend using it when working with children.

Coreopsis flowers provided inspiration for the design used in the Cleo Tool Roll.

Tools Used to Apply Wax

A canting is made of a small copper pot with a spout attached to a wooden or bamboo handle. The spouts range in size from fine, to draw a thin line, to wide, in order to fill larger areas with wax. Cap (pronounced *chop*), an ornate stamp made of copper, is another tool used in Java to apply wax. In addition to using a canting tool or cap, you can use any implement that can withstand heat to apply wax, such as kitchen utensils like a fork or spoon, or objects made of wood like a toothpick, tongue depressor, or wooden spoon—even a rock or leaf can be used.

Drawing with Wax

To successfully draw with wax, pay close attention to the fine balance between heat, wax, the canting tool, and the fabric you have chosen to work with. Have a piece of scrap fabric on hand to do a few warm-ups before approaching the main piece. Using the canting tool and hot wax, draw dots, lines, curves, and circles to practice. When drawing, it is helpful to tuck your arms close to your body or to rest them on the table for support and stability. Ideally, to achieve the crispest line on the finished fabric, the wax will glide out of the canting's copper spout and penetrate the fabric so that both sides of the fabric look nearly the same. Once you have drawn a few lines and tried this technique, make sure to read Tips (page 171) to develop a more thorough understanding of the practice.

MATERIALS

Scoured (page 217), mordanted (page 219) fabric made of cotton or linen

Wax (page 168)

TOOLS

Canting tool or heat-resistant tool of your choice

Pot to heat wax— there are special batik heaters designed for this process (recommended). Any heating device with a turn-dial heating source is a good option because even, constant heat and the ability to raise and lower the temperature easily is ideal. You can also use a hot plate with a saucepan.

Embroidery hoop (optional)

INSTRUCTIONS

1. Heat the wax until it is completely melted. Warning: The wax will be very hot, and you can burn yourself if it drips on your skin. Work over a table, so if the wax drips, it drips onto the tabletop rather than your lap.

2. Place the canting into the wax for at least 1 to 2 minutes before beginning to draw to warm the small copper bowl and spout.

3. Lay the fabric along the palm of your nondominant hand so it is tilted slightly, at about a 45-degree angle. If you find it difficult to hold the fabric this way, you can place the fabric within an embroidery hoop and hold the side of the hoop at a 45-degree angle.

4. Hold the end of the canting's handle. Dip the canting into the wax, filling the bowl with wax. Quickly take the tool down to your fabric and draw a wax line, following your transferred design.

5. After about 30 seconds to 1 minute of drawing, dip the tool back into the wax, refill the bowl, and continue drawing. Repeat until the entire design has been drawn with wax. Only apply wax to one side of the fabric.

Tips

If the wax does not penetrate the surface of the fabric, dye may seep under the wax, or wax may chip and dislodge entirely during the dyeing process, blurring the line and affecting the design. If you find that the wax is no longer penetrating the fabric and is instead sitting closer to the surface of the fabric, this means the small copper bowl and spout on the canting tool is not hot enough and/or the wax has cooled. Return the canting tool and the wax to the heater and allow it to warm for 30–60 seconds, then try drawing again.

If you find that the wax is coming out of the canting too fast, you may be pointing the canting at too steep of an angle. Adjust the tilt of your hand slightly, relaxing the angle. If you adjust the angle of your hand and you find this is continuing to happen, your wax may be too hot. Pause for a moment from drawing, hold the canting in your hand, allowing the wax to cool, and try drawing again. Turn the heat down a touch.

When you're first learning to draw with wax, it is easy to drip or create unintended blobs of wax on your fabric—sometimes this happens because you are moving your hand too slowly, you stop in the middle of drawing, or a drip of wax comes from the canting tool. Remember to keep moving once you start—don't stop mid-process. If you do need to pause while canting, angle the canting tool upward slightly to stop wax from flowing out of the spout. Move your canting away from the fabric, holding it over the tabletop, so if a drip happens, it hits the work surface instead of the fabric.

Sometimes, no matter what you try, wax will not come out of the spout of the canting. The tip of the tool may be clogged. Take a piece of straw from a broom or a pin and poke it into the tip of the tool to clear it. If the tool gets clogged repeatedly, this may mean that you are allowing the wax to get too cool in the bowl of the tool. Refill the tool more often and make sure your wax is hot.

When Dalmini and the others in the collective take the canting tool from the heated vessel and fill it with hot wax, they bring the tip of the canting close to their lips (not touching) and blow through the spout, creating a slight whistle and bubbling sound. This indicates the spout is clear and ready to draw. This technique also helps keep wax blobs from developing. If you would like to try this, we recommend you do so when you feel confident with the practice, because you can burn your lips if you come too close to the spout, and wax that sits alongside where the copper pot connects to the wooden handle of the canting can drip, potentially hitting your hand.

Over time, with practice, you will learn the balance between drawing fast enough to avoid a blob within your work and an erratic line caused by wax that has cooled. In the meantime, your fabric will still be beautiful, and it will tell the story that you are brave enough to try a new process.

Cleaning Up

When you are done for the day, take your canting out of the wax and turn off the heat. Do not worry about making sure your canting is clean, as when you heat up the wax and your canting tool the next time you make batik, any wax left on it will melt. If you are using the same heating element and wax for future sessions of batik, simply turn off the heat and allow it to cool. Next time you are ready to create batik, turn the heat on and start drawing.

If you need to transfer the wax out of the heating element and you would like to save it for future use, scoop the wax into either a clean empty can or a wax paper–lined egg carton and allow to cool. When you want to use it again, place the can in a pot of hot water to melt, then carefully pour the hot wax into the vessel you will use during the canting process. If you used the egg carton method, peel the paper off the wax, add it to your vessel, and reheat.

MAKING DYE CONCENTRATES

Heat cannot be used in the batik-making process, as it will melt the wax. Instead, highly concentrated dyes are created and applied in layers to the fabric without heat.

About Tannin-Rich Dyes

Inspired by Dalmini's use of tannin-rich dyes, and knowing that tannins and cellulose-based fibers, like cotton, work well together, we set out to learn more about to learn more about the widely available trees in our area and created the tannin-rich dyes featured on the shade cards on pages 180–185. Tannins and cellulose-based fibers have a natural affinity for one another, and by adding an aluminum-based mordant, it is possible to achieve longer-lasting naturally dyed color. We asked our friend, ethnobotanist and natural dyer Deepa Natarajan, to expound on the relationship between tannins and plants: "All plants have the potential to make tannins, which serve as a defense against disease. The presence of tannins can change with seasonality; for example, unripe fruits may have higher quantities of tannins to deter premature consumption, and, as they ripen [and sugar content increases] tannins decrease, and they become desirable for animals who eat and disperse their seeds. Tannins are also produced in response to injury, which is why oak galls contain high quantities of tannins—a response to gall wasps infecting the trees. Tannins can be produced in all parts of the plant but tend to be concentrated in those that require defenses and protections, such as fruits, leaves, or barks."

We began to experiment with the trees in our yard and on our block, focusing on their bark, leaves, seeds (such as acorns), and hulls to see what colors we could achieve. The colors ranged from tan to light gray mostly. So we began to shift the pH to see what would happen, and there was a wonderful surprise. By adding baking soda while extracting the color, the colors became more saturated, and in some cases undertones of pinks and purples began to emerge.

As you can see from the shade cards on pages 180–185, some plants, such as pecan hulls, oak acorns, oak galls, and eucalyptus bark, produce very similar colors and could be used interchangeably for a very similar effect. Use whichever one is easiest for you to obtain. This journey brought a whole new life and understanding of the trees found in our neighborhood. We hope these examples inspire you to look more closely at the trees in your own neighborhood and to create your own dye. And don't forget to check out your local grocery store for tannin-rich dyes like pecan hulls, walnut hulls, and black tea. Stay curious and create dyes using the methods described in this section to widen your palette.

Preparing Tannin-Rich Dyes

When using the bark of the tree for dyeing, focus on the inner bark, where the dye is located, which is the softer, spongier bit in between the outer bark and the wood. Avoid taking bark from the tree trunk, as it can permanently damage the tree. Using twigs is the easiest option, as they are easy to cut from the tree. Making friends with a local tree pruner is a great way to source twigs, leaves, and hulls for making dye.

Chop the twigs as finely as possible with a pair of garden shears or clippers to get the most dye. If dyeing with leaves, use a pair of scissors or a knife to cut them finely. When using seeds, hulls, or galls, a mortar and pestle will help you make a mash.

Extracting Dye to Create Concentrates

To create saturated colors like those featured on the shade cards (pages 180–185), we added baking soda to the extraction process. We believe the addition of baking soda is most effective with dyestuffs where tannins are present and when the plant material is thick or dense. If working with flowers, they may or may not respond to the addition of baking soda. Experiment both ways to learn more.

In addition to using these concentrates for batik, they can be used to paint on fabric or can be diluted with water and used as washes (page 183). Use an airtight container, like a mason jar, to store your dye. Add a drop of clove oil to prevent mold growth and to extend the shelf life of the dye.

YIELD

Makes 1½ cups (320 ml) dye

MATERIALS

100 g dye material

Baking soda

TOOLS

Garden clippers or shears

3-quart (2.8-L) stainless steel pot

Sieve

Quart-size (liter-size) mason jar with lid

INSTRUCTIONS

1. Rinse the dye material to remove any dirt or debris, then chop finely.

2. Add the dye material to the pot, then pour 5 cups (1.2 L) water into the pot.

3. Add ⅛ teaspoon baking soda for each 1 cup (240 ml) water to the pot and stir.

4. Over medium-high heat, bring the water to a simmer. If the dyebath begins to boil, reduce the heat. The goal is to slowly heat the plant material, so it softens and releases as much dye as possible, while also evaporating the water.

5. Let simmer for 60 minutes. At the end of this time, the liquid should measure somewhere between ½ cup (120 ml) and 1 cup (240 ml). If your liquid measures less, the heat was too high. For the next round, lower the heat. If the liquid measures more than this, place the liquid back into the dyepot, turn up the heat, and allow the water to simmer until you have 1 cup (240 ml) or less.

6. Strain the dye water into a jar, keeping the dye material aside.

7. Repeat steps 2–6 two more times, returning the dye material to the empty pot, with the following changes: For the second extraction, add 4 cups (960 ml) water, and for the third extraction, add 3 cups (720 ml) water. Each time, add ⅛ teaspoon baking soda for each 1 cup (240 ml) water.

8. Combine the 3 extractions. If the combined extractions measures more than 1½ cups (360 ml), pour all of the dye back into the pot and simmer until the dye reduces to 1½ cups (360 ml). See page 174 for instructions on dyeing with concentrates.

Dyeing with Concentrates/ Setting Dyes with Mordants

When creating batik-dyed fabrics, always scour and mordant your fabric before canting and dyeing to encourage long-lasting colors. Though the cloth has been pre-mordanted, because the dyes have been applied without heat, they must be set with either a solution of aluminum potassium sulfate or a concentrated iron water solution. An aluminum potassium sulfate solution will set the color and not change it (top swatch in right-hand photo), while a concentrated iron water solution will turn the color dark brown, gray, or black (bottom swatch in right-hand photo). See the shade cards on pages 180–185 to see the differences in these two treatments.

Indigo is the one exception: If you are dyeing your fabric with indigo, and you plan to use only indigo and not apply any other dyes, the fabric does not have to be pre-mordanted. The indigo dye is set during the dyeing process; do not set it with either of the post-mordant solutions. Refer to the instructions on page 13 to learn more about dyeing with indigo.

We recommend starting with one dye to understand the process and then proceeding to create designs with two or more dyes. If you are interested in creating designs with two or more dyes, read the section Creating Multiple-Color Designs (page 176) to develop a fuller understanding of the process.

APPLY DYE

1. Pour ½ cup (120 ml) dye concentrate into the butcher tray.

2. Place the dry fabric in the dye. Gently massage the dye into the fabric for 5 minutes, making sure the fabric is thoroughly saturated. If you have applied wax to your fabric, be careful to not remove, nick, or loosen the wax when massaging the dye into the fabric.

3. Remove the fabric and allow as much dye as possible to drip back into the dish. If you have applied wax to your fabric, do not wring the fabric. Instead, use your fingers to smooth the fabric, forcing the excess dye to drip back into the dish.

4. Hang the dyed fabric to drip-dry. Allow the fabric to dry completely.

5. Once the fabric has dried, dip the fabric another 2 times, repeating steps 2–4. Once the third layer of dye has been applied and the fabric is dry, set the dye.

SET THE DYE

To set the dye applied above, the fabric must be dipped into a post-mordant solution of aluminum potassium sulfate (page 221) or a concentrated iron water solution (page 234) before washing or applying additional layers of wax or dye. An aluminum

MATERIALS

Scoured (page 217) and mordanted (page 219) cotton or linen fabric

Dye concentrates (page 172)

Concentrated Iron Water Solution Using Ferrous Sulfate (page 235) or Post-Mordant Solution of Aluminum Potassium Sulfate (page 221)

TOOLS

Shallow dish such as a butcher tray, 7½ × 11 inches (19 × 28 cm); for larger pieces a rimmed baking sheet works well

Rubber gloves (recommended)

Clothesline and clothespins

potassium sulfate solution will set the color as seen on the swatch, while a concentrated iron water solution will turn the color dark brown, gray, or black. If you are planning on creating a design with two or more colors, use only a solution of aluminum potassium sulfate. See the shade cards on pages 180–185 to determine your desired outcome and which path to take.

1. Pour ½ cup (120 ml) of the solution into the butcher tray.

2. Place the dry fabric into the bath and leave for 5 minutes, making sure it is fully saturated.

3. Remove the fabric from the bath, rinse with cool water, and hang the goods to drip-dry over a drop cloth. Allow the fabric to dry completely.

4. Remove the wax.

Creating Multiple-Color Designs

Here are two examples of how you can create three-color designs.

USING ONE DYE AND TWO POST-MORDANT SOLUTIONS

1. Draw the design in wax.

2. Color A: Apply 3 layers of the first color. Set with aluminum potassium solution.

3. Apply wax over the areas in which you want to preserve Color A.

4. Dip the fabric into a concentrated iron solution. Allow the fabric to dry completely.

5. Remove the wax (page 177).

USING TWO DYES AND ONE OR TWO POST-MORDANT SOLUTIONS

Apply colors from lightest to darkest. Referring to the shade cards on pages 180–185, you can see the dye extracted from birch bark, walnut bark, and black tea are lighter than the other dyes and make ideal candidates to use as the first color applied in a multiple-color design. If using indigo in your design, apply the indigo first, to create the most light- and color-fast results, and then add other dyes that provide darker colors. Refer to the swatches on page 184 to see examples of designs made using multiple dyes and post-mordant solutions.

1. Draw the design in wax.

2. Color A: Apply 3 layers of the first color. Set with aluminum potassium solution.

3. Apply wax over the areas in which you want to preserve Color A.

4. Color B: Apply 3 layers of the second color. Set with either aluminum potassium sulfate or concentrated iron solution. Allow the fabric to dry completely.

5. Remove the wax (page 177).

FINISHING BATIK FABRICS

Removing Wax from the Fabric

For soy wax, simply hold the fabric under hot running tap water. Rub the wax until it is removed.

For beeswax and paraffin-based waxes, like those used in Indonesia, the way we have found most effective, as described below, is to use hot water with a bit of soda ash. While this removes the wax from the fabric, it is a harsh environment for the dye, so the key is to submerge the fabric in boiling water only as long as needed to melt and remove the wax. Finish by pressing with an iron as described in step 10.

MATERIALS
Baking soda

TOOLS
3- to 5-quart
(2.8- to 4.7-L) pot

Bowl

Tongs

Spoon

Clothesline and
clothespins

Iron and ironing board
(optional)

Newspaper or butcher
paper (optional)

INSTRUCTIONS

1. Fill the pot with water. Note how much water you added.

2. Add ⅛ teaspoon baking soda for every 4 cups (960 ml) water used and stir until dissolved completely.

3. Bring the water to a boil.

4. Meanwhile, fill a bowl with cool water and set it near the pot.

5. Submerge the fabric in the boiling water. Using a pair of tongs, move the fabric up and down in the pot to fully saturate. As the wax melts from the fabric, it will float to the top of the water. Use a spoon to scoop wax off the surface and discard. Continue moving the fabric up and down in the water until all the wax is removed; this takes about 5 minutes.

6. Place the fabric in the bowl of cool water to test if the wax is fully removed. The cool water makes it possible to touch the fabric and it solidifies any remaining wax. Touch the fabric and feel the surface—if you can feel wax, return the fabric to the boiling water, following the same motions as described in step 5, though for only 30 seconds.

7. Continue repeating step 6 until you can no longer feel wax on the surface of the fabric.

8. As you are removing the wax, especially if you are working on a larger piece or removing wax from multiple pieces, you may notice some of the dye coming off in the water, changing the water's color, and though you are removing wax from the surface of the water, as you work, at some point the water may become saturated with wax. If this becomes the case, make a second pot of boiling water and continue following step 6 to complete the process of removing the wax.

9. Once the wax has been removed from the fabric, rinse the fabric with clean cool water and hang to dry.

10. Once dry, if you feel any wax still on the fabric, use an iron and a piece of tissue paper or butcher paper to remove the remaining wax. Turn your iron to the cotton (hottest) setting. Sandwich your fabric between two pieces of paper. Press in 15-second intervals, checking the fabric often. Stop pressing when the wax has been removed.

Cleaning Up

Do not dump the wax and water down your drain or you can ruin your plumbing. Instead, use these precautions to remove as much wax as possible from the water. Once you have removed the fabric from the hot water, allow the water to cool. A layer of wax will form on the surface of the water. Using a spoon, skim the surface to remove the wax. Then pour the water through a fine-mesh sieve to collect any remaining wax and dispose of the water down the drain.

If a layer of wax remains at the level of the waterline in the pot, heat the empty pot to melt the wax and use a paper towel to remove the wax fully. Be careful to not burn yourself. If you are having trouble removing the layer of wax, add a dab of oil to your paper towel. It is important to clean your pot thoroughly so future projects stay wax-free.

Caring For Batik-Dyed Fabrics

Wash on the gentle cycle with like colors using cold water and gentle detergent. Air dry.

AN OVERVIEW OF CREATING A TWO-COLOR FABRIC

Here are the steps used to make a two-color batik-dyed fabric featured in the Cleo Tool Roll (page 187):

1. Scour (page 217) and mordant (page 219) the fabric. (A)

2. Draw a design and transfer it (page 167) onto the fabric. (B)

3. Trace over the design with wax (page 168). (C)

4. Make two dyes: one from birch bark and one from plum bark (page 172). (D)

5. Apply 3 layers of birch dye. Dry fully between each layer of dye (page 174). (E)

6. Set the dye with aluminum potassium sulfate solution and dry (page 174). (F)

7. Apply more wax, covering the flower motif. (G)

8. Apply 3 layers of plum bark dye. Dry fully between each layer. (E)

9. Dip the fabric into concentrated iron water solution and rinse well. (H)

10. Remove the wax (page 177). (I)

shade card: cold bath dyeing with concentrates set with aluminum potassium sulfate and iron

GOODS: Robert Kaufman Kona (100% cotton) fabric, white

SCOUR: Scouring Cellulose-Based Goods (page 218)

MORDANT: Mordanting Cellulose-Based Goods with Aluminum Acetate and Chalk (page 221)

DYE: Swatches dyed with concentrates made using the method described in Making Dye Concentrates (page 172) and using the technique of Dyeing with Concentrates (page 174). The dye has been applied three times, which is the recommended amount of applications to create batik fabrics. The dye is then set with either a bath of aluminum potassium sulfate or iron. All colors have been created by raising the pH in the extraction process (page 232).

	SET WITH ALUMINUM POTASSIUM SULFATE	SET WITH IRON		SET WITH ALUMINUM POTASSIUM SULFATE	SET WITH IRON
BIRCH BARK, FRESH			OSAGE SAWDUST, DRIED		
PLUM BARK, FRESH			MAPLE LEAVES, DRIED		
WALNUT BARK, FRESH			BLACK TEA, DRIED		
PECAN HULLS, DRIED			OAK GALLS, DRIED		
EUCALYPTUS BARK, FRESH			ACORNS, DRIED		

shade card: cold bath dyeing with washes set with aluminum potassium sulfate and iron

GOODS: Robert Kaufman Kona (100% cotton) fabric, white

SCOUR: Scouring Cellulose-Based Goods (page 218)

MORDANT: Mordanting Cellulose-Based Goods with Aluminum Acetate and Chalk (page 221)

DYE: Swatches were created by following the instructions in Making Dye Concentrates (page 172) and then diluting the concentrates as follows: 1 tablespoon dye concentrate to 2 tablespoons water. The swatches were dipped one time into this solution. The dyes were then set with either aluminum potassium sulfate solution (see page 221) or concentrated iron solution (page 234), as listed. All colors were created by raising the pH in the extraction process (page 232).

	SET WITH ALUMINUM POTASSIUM SULFATE	SET WITH IRON		SET WITH ALUMINUM POTASSIUM SULFATE	SET WITH IRON
BIRCH BARK, FRESH			OSAGE SAWDUST, DRIED		
PLUM BARK, FRESH			MAPLE LEAVES, DRIED		
WALNUT BARK, FRESH			BLACK TEA, DRIED		
PECAN HULLS, DRIED			OAK GALLS, DRIED		
EUCALYPTUS BARK, FRESH			ACORNS, DRIED		

shade card:
examples of two-color designs

GOODS: Robert Kaufman, Kona (100% cotton) fabric, white

SCOUR: Scouring Cellulose-Based Goods (page 218)

MORDANT: Mordanting Cellulose-Based Goods with Aluminum Acetate and Chalk (page 221)

DYE: The flower design was drawn with wax. The first dye listed was applied in three layers and set with a post-mordant solution of aluminum potassium sulfate (except for indigo, which does not need to be set). Then the flower motif was covered with wax. The dye listed second was applied in three layers. The mordant, listed last, was applied as the final layer to set the dye.

	COLUMN 1	COLUMN 2
FIRST DYE	Birch	Plum
MORDANT	Aluminum potassium sulfate	Aluminum potassium sulfate
SECOND DYE	Tea	Maple
MORDANT	Concentrated iron	Concentrated iron
FIRST DYE	Plum	Birch
MORDANT	Aluminum potassium sulfate	Aluminum potassium sulfate
SECOND DYE	Maple	Maple
MORDANT	Aluminum potassium sulfate	Aluminum potassium sulfate
FIRST DYE	Birch	Indigo
MORDANT	Aluminum potassium sulfate	n/a
SECOND DYE	Osage	Plum
MORDANT	Concentrated Iron	Aluminum potassium sulfate
FIRST DYE	Indigo	Walnut
MORDANT	n/a	Aluminum potassium sulfate
SECOND DYE	Osage	Plum
MORDANT	Aluminum potassium sulfate	Concentrated iron

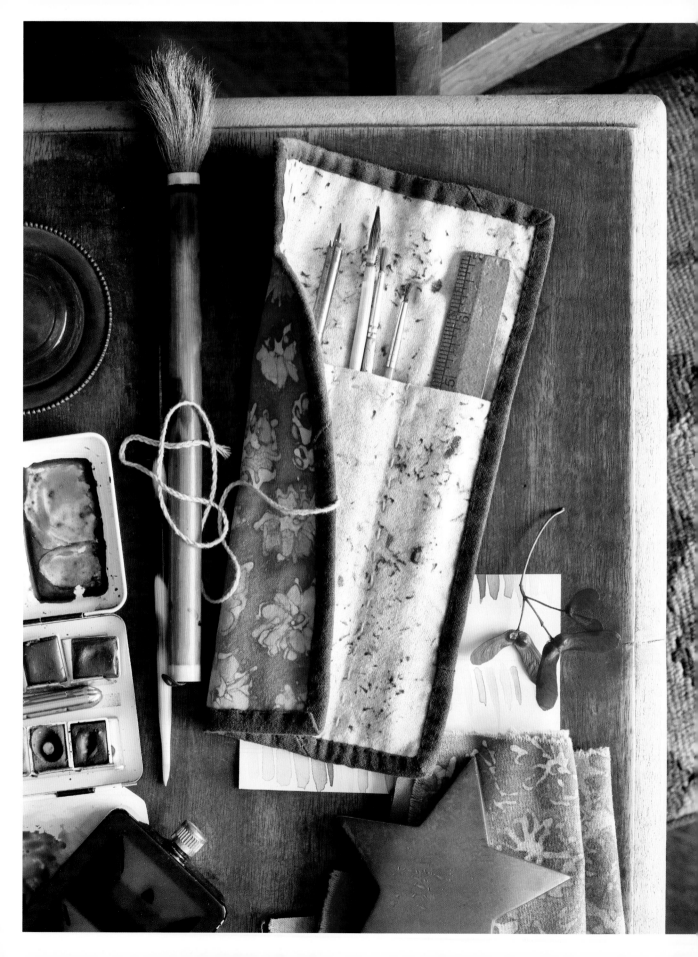

cleo tool roll

FINISHED MEASUREMENTS

9 × 6 inches (23 × 15 cm)

MATERIALS

Robert Kaufman Kona (100% cotton), white
two 9 × 6 inches (23 × 15 cm)

Robert Kaufman Essex (50% cotton, 50% linen), natural
one 9 × 6 inches (23 × 15 cm) for the interior
one 6½ × 6 inches (16.5 × 15 cm) for the pocket

1 hank of sashiko thread, white

Sewing thread, brown, or color to match project

TOOLS

Iron and ironing board

Sashiko needle

Sewing needle

Scissors

Ruler

Pins

THIS QUICK PROJECT IS A GREAT way to use small pieces of fabric that you are creating by trying out the batik process. Named after our cylinder-shaped dog, Cleo, this tool roll features four pockets and is the perfect carrying case for your favorite paintbrushes, pencils, and knitting needles. All the fabric was cut to size before dyeing. The floral batik fabric featured on the exterior of the roll was created by following the steps on page 179. The interior fabric was created by eco-printing with coreopsis seeds following the steps on page 179. The binding tape framing the tool roll was dyed with plum bark and set with iron water (page 234). The sashiko thread was scoured (page 217) and dyed using the One-Pot Dyeing method (page 227) with black tea.

SEW

1. Enclose the raw edge along the top of the pocket: Take the piece cut for the pocket, along one 6-inch (15-cm) edge, fold ¼ inch (6 mm) toward the wrong side, and press, repeat, enclosing the raw edge. Taking the sashiko thread and needle and using a running stitch, sew down the folded edge ¼ inch (6 mm) from the top of the pocket piece.

2. Fold the pocket piece in half lengthwise and press a line down the center.

3. Lay the interior piece right side up on your work surface. Lay the pocket, right side up, atop the interior piece with the bottom edges aligned. Using the fold line on the pocket piece as a guide, with the sashiko thread and needle, starting at the top of the pocket, use a running stitch to sew a line to the bottom of the fabric. Measure 1¼ inches (3 cm) to the left of this line and sew a line. Measure 1¼ inches (3 cm) to the right of the center line and sew a line.

4. Lay the interior fabric on the exterior fabric, wrong sides facing.

5. Make binding to finish the edges using the narrow strips. Sew them together, right side facing, to make one strip 33 inches (84 cm) long. With wrong side up, fold the long edges in ¼ inch (6 mm) and press. Fold the strip in half lengthwise and press.

6. Starting near the midpoint of the pocket on the left side, sandwich the binding around the raw edges of the tool roll, pinning if necessary, and stitch the binding down. When you reach a corner, fold the binding into a miter and continue stitching. When you reach the starting point of the binding, overlap by ½ inch (12 mm), trim the tape if needed, fold under the raw end, and stitch it down.

7. Cut three lengths of sashiko thread, each 17 inches (43 cm) long, and braid to make a cord. Stitch the cord to one side of the tool roll 4 inches (10 cm) from the bottom.

aerial view
throw pillows

FINISHED MEASUREMENTS

22 × 22 inches
(56 × 56 cm)

MATERIALS

Hemp or linen
grain sacks

Dye concentrates

Aluminum potassium
sulfate post-mordant
solution (page 221)

Concentrated iron water
solution (page 235)

Pillow form (1–2 inches/
2.5–5 cm larger than the
finished measurements
of the pillowcase)

Sewing thread, white

TOOLS

Paintbrushes

Small jars (for diluting
concentrates)

Hand sewing needle

Scissors

Ruler

Pins

ON THE FIRST SUNDAY of the month, near our house, there is a bustling flea market where we collect vintage handspun and handwoven hemp and linen grain sacks. Their long, narrow shape makes them perfect as covers for throw pillows. If you are unable to find vintage grain sacks, use any fabric made of natural materials to create these pillows. The Aerial View Throw Pillows are a simple, fast project that does not require pre-mordanting or heat to set the dye. We figure if the color fades over time, it is easy to apply more layers of dye and set them again. The beautiful watercolor-esque lines are created simply by diluting dye concentrates with water and painting them onto the fabric using a paintbrush. On the pillow pictured, the rust color was made from walnut bark and set with aluminum potassium sulfate water, and the charcoal color was made from eucalyptus bark set with iron water. Refer to the shade card on pages 180–181 for additional color options.

INSTRUCTIONS

1. Wash and dry the linen sacks on the hottest setting.

2. Measure the width of the sack along the bottom edge. Measure that same length along the side, add ½ inch (12 mm) for the seam allowance, and cut across the sack. This will give you a square-shaped sack, already sewn on three sides.

3. Dilute each dye concentrate in its own jar by combining 1 tablespoon dye concentrate with 2 tablespoons water.

4. Twist only the front of the pillowcase's fabric, careful to not catch the fabric on the back of the pillowcase, unless you want dye on both sides of the pillowcase.

5. Using a paintbrush, apply the diluted dye to the folds made by the twist. The sculptural line created by the twist provides an organic shape that is easy to follow.

6. Set the dye by painting a solution of either aluminum potassium sulfate (page 221) or iron (page 235) over the painted line. Allow the painted line to dry.

7. Repeat steps 4–6 with new twists and different dyes.

8. Place the pillow form inside the pillowcase. Fold the raw edges in ½ inch (12 mm). Using needle and thread, whip stitch the pillow closed.

extracting indigo pigment from fresh *persicaria tinctoria* to dry or dye

MATERIALS

35 ounces (1,000 g) mature, freshly harvested *Persicaria tinctoria* indigo leaves

10½ quarts (10 L) non-chlorinated water

1–2 tablespoons (7.5–15 g) limestone

TOOLS

Garden shears for cutting indigo

Two 5-gallon (19-L) buckets

Kitchen scale

12-quart (11.4-L) stainless steel pot and lid

Thermometer

Liquid measuring cup

Measuring spoons

Timer

pH strips

Fine mesh strainer

Silk habotai fabric, 16 × 16 inches (40.5 × 40.5 cm)

Clothespins to hold filter in place (recommended)

Butcher tray or baking sheet

TO EXTRACT INDIGO pigment from fresh *Persicaria tinctoria* leaves, it must go through the following process: The fresh leaves are soaked in water and removed from the water, the water is aerated, the pH of the water is raised, the indigo pigment separates from the water and settles along the bottom of the bucket. Once the indigo pigment is in this state, you have two choices: proceed to strain the pigment from the water and then dry the pigment and store to use at a later date (page 192); or make an indigo dyebath directly after aeration (page 192), in which case, please read through the entirety of the instructions before beginning.

A single mature *Persicaria tinctoria* leaf weighs about 1 to 1.5 grams, so you will need about 1,000 leaves to complete this recipe. This will require 5 to 6 spots worth of 3-foot (1-m) tall plants—in other words, 20 to 24 plants. To learn more about growing your own indigo, see pages 114–116.

INSTRUCTIONS

1. Heat 10½ quarts (10 L) of water to 120°F (49°C) in the pot.

2. Place the indigo leaves in one of the buckets.

3. Pour the hot water into the bucket to cover the leaves.

4. Allow the leaves to soak for 3 hours, covered. After 1 hour, stir. At the end of 3 hours, the liquid will be red-brown and the leaves will be wilted. (**A**)

5. Using your hands or a strainer, remove the leaves from the water. Pour the liquid from one bucket to another through a fine-mesh strainer to remove all dirt and small particles of leaves.

6. Aerate the liquid by pouring it from bucket to bucket for 10 minutes, or until you have poured it back and forth 50 times. (**B**)

7. Add enough limestone to reach a pH of 10. This amount will vary depending on the pH of your water; we recommend starting with 2 teaspoons of limestone. Remove 1 cup (240 ml) liquid from the bucket. Add 2 teaspoons limestone to the cup of liquid and mix well. Pour the liquid back into the bucket and mix well. Record the amount of limestone added.

A

B

est the pH, and if it is still below 10, repeat step 7, add-
more limestone ¼ teaspoon at a time until the pH is 10.
ord the amount of limestone added.

erate the liquid again by pouring from bucket to bucket
2 minutes. The liquid's color will shift to dark blue.

Decide whether you would like to dry the pigment you
extracted or create an indigo vat. See the following
s for applicable instructions.

C

TO DRY

1. Cover the bucket and let rest for 24 hours to allow the pigment to settle.

2. After 24 hours, the water will be red-brown, resembling iced tea. If the water does not look like this, test the pH. If it is below 10, repeat step 7 on page 190. If it is at 10 or above, aerate for 10 more minutes, or until you have poured the liquid from one bucket to the next 50 times. Cover the bucket and let rest for 24 hours.

3. Line the fine-mesh strainer with the silk fabric and pour the liquid and pigment through the strainer. Straining the pigment is a slow process—it can take 4 to 6 hours for all of the water to strain through the silk.

4. Once all the water has drained, keeping the silk and pigment in the strainer, transfer it to a butcher tray. Keeping the silk in the strainer helps with air circulation. Allow to dry fully. (**C**, page 191) Dispose of the liquid.

5. Once dry, scrape the pigment off the silk fabric, grind it into a powder in a mortar and pestle, and weigh it to understand the relationship between your indigo plants and how much indigo pigment they produce. Store in an airtight container.

MATERIALS

Limestone

Fructose or iron

TOOLS

15-inch (38-cm) spoon or dowel for stirring

White spoon

TO MAKE A VAT

When making a vat from your aerated solution, instead of straining and drying the pigment, you will add limestone and either fructose or ferrous sulfate (also known as iron) to raise the pH and to shift the indigo into a soluble state, making it possible to use as a dye. The amount you add of each of these things is based upon the amount of indigo in your aerated solution. Ideally, for the best results, you would follow the drying steps in the previous section to understand how many grams of indigo you have extracted. If you would like to skip the drying step, you can use our numbers and hope that you have extracted a similar amount of indigo.

Based on the weight of indigo extracted from 1,000 g of fresh leaves, calculate the amount of limestone and reducing agent to add to your vat. Follow one of these recipes:

FRUCTOSE / LIMESTONE

• Add two times as much limestone*

• Add three times as much fructose

FERROUS SULFATE / LIMESTONE

• Add two times as much ferrous sulfate

• Add three times as much limestone*

*NOTE: Because you added limestone in order to extract the indigo, your water is already at a high pH. Therefore, you may not need to add more limestone.

FRUCTOSE VS. FERROUS SULFATE?

When we first set out to create this recipe, we used the instructions for Making an Indigo-Fructose-Limestone Vat (page 196), and our results yielded a very light blue color due to the low amount of indigo compared with the amount of water. After all that hard work of extracting the indigo, we wanted to make the most of our extracted indigo and create a darker shade of blue. So we made a second vat using ferrous sulfate. The benefits of using ferrous sulfate are that it provides deeper shades of blue and does not require heat to dye. However, take care when dyeing protein fibers in the vat made with ferrous sulfate, as the iron content can make the fibers brittle. The vat made using fructose and limestone is gentler on protein-based fibers. Choose the recipe that is best for your situation.

OUR NUMBERS

From 35 ounces (1,000 g) of leaves, we have extracted an average of 6 grams of indigo pigment.

To create a vat using fructose/limestone, 12 g of limestone and 18 g of fructose are required. However, because 7 g limestone was added during the extraction process, only 5 g of limestone is necessary to complete the vat, along with the 18 g fructose.

To create a ferrous sulfate/limestone vat, 18 g limestone and 12 g ferrous sulfate are required. Again, as in the previous example, because 7 g limestone are added during the extraction process, only 11 g of limestone are necessary to complete the vat, along with the 12 g ferrous sulfate.

Once you have decided whether to use fructose/limestone or ferrous sulfate/limestone, and have calculated the amounts needed, follow the instructions below to make your vat.

INSTRUCTIONS

1. Pour the aerated indigo liquid into the stainless steel pot, cover, and heat to 120°F (49°C).

2. Remove 1 cup (240 ml) liquid from the pot. Add fructose (to achieve a lighter blue) or iron (to achieve a darker blue) to the cup of liquid and stir to dissolve. Pour the solution back into the pot and stir gently to combine.

3. If by your calculations you need to add more limestone to your vat, remove 1 cup (240 ml) liquid from the pot. Add limestone to the cup of liquid and stir to dissolve. Pour the solution back into the pot and stir gently to combine.

4. Allow the vat to rest for 1 hour. Hold the white spoon just under the surface of the vat: The liquid should have shifted from opaque blue-green to yellow-green, yellow, amber, or dark yellow–red, and the liquid should have very few dark particles floating in it, indicating that the sediment of indigo pigment and limestone has settled at the bottom. If so, it is ready to dye, but we have found waiting a total of 24 hours yields the most saturated, long-lasting color. Proceed to pages 198–200 to learn how to dye in this kind of vat. The fructose/limestone vat and the ferrous sulfate/limestone vat are incredibly similar to each other, and the instructions on the listed pages are applicable to both, with one main difference: the ferrous sulfate/limestone vat does not need to be heated or recalibrated.

shade card: indigo-fructose-limestone vat on cotton and linen

GOODS: Robert Kaufman Kona (100% cotton), white, and Antwerp (100% linen), white

SCOUR: Scouring Cellulose-Based Goods (page 217)

MORDANT: Not applicable

DYE: Swatches dyed in an indigo-fructose-limestone vat in five different strengths of vat. The range of colors was created by altering how many grams of indigo were added to the vat and by the number of times the sample was dipped into the vat. See page 198 for full instructions.

NOTE: To see examples of wool and silk dyed in an indigo-fructose-limestone vat, see pages 78 and 86, respectively.

	COTTON FABRIC				
INDIGO 3 DIPS	#1	#2	#3	#4	#5
INDIGO 6 DIPS	#1	#2	#3	#4	#5
INDIGO 9 DIPS	#1	#2	#3	#4	#5
INDIGO 12 DIPS	#1	#2	#3	#4	#5
	LINEN FABRIC				
INDIGO 3 DIPS	#1	#2	#3	#4	#5
INDIGO 6 DIPS	#1	#2	#3	#4	#5
INDIGO 9 DIPS	#1	#2	#3	#4	#5
INDIGO 12 DIPS	#1	#2	#3	#4	#5

	#1	#2	#3	#4	#5
INDIGO	6.5 g	13 g	39 g	78 g	117 g
LIMESTONE	13 g	26 g	78 g	156 g	234 g
FRUCTOSE	19.5 g	39 g	117 g	234 g	351 g

making an indigo-fructose-limestone vat

MATERIALS

Natural indigo powder*

Fructose*

Limestone*

*Refer to the shade card on page 195 for amounts of indigo, fructose, and limestone.

TOOLS

1 (2) ½-gallon (500-ml) mason jar(s) to create vats #1–4 (to create vat #5)

Liquid measuring cup

Whisk

Small white spoon

16-quart (15-L) stainless steel pot

15-inch (13-cm) spoon or dowel for stirring

Bucket (large enough to hold your goods, for pre-wetting)

YOU CAN USE THIS RECIPE with indigo you have extracted from your home-grown *Persicaria tinctoria* or with purchased natural indigo extract. We recommend reading through all of the instructions before beginning, so you have a sense of the entire process.

When dyeing with indigo, Dalmini uses a combination of indigo, palm sugar, and limestone. Her indigo is processed with limestone into a paste, called *pasta*. She combines this paste with palm sugar and waits 24 hours before using her indigo vat. Our variation of this kind of vat uses natural indigo powder, fructose crystals, and limestone powder. If you wish, in place of fructose crystals, you can experiment with palm sugar, dates, ripe pears, banana peels, and other, similar materials. The ratio is 1 part natural indigo powder, 2 parts limestone, and 3 parts fructose crystals. We were first introduced to this ratio by natural dyer Michel Garcia.

VAT SIZE

This recipe is for a 14-quart (13-L) vat, which is best for full-size skeins of yarn (up to 200 grams at a time) and pieces of fabric (approximately 12" × 9" [30 × 23 cm]). We focused on this size of vat because we believe it to be a good fit for the home dyer, but if you plan to do a lot of indigo dyeing or want to dye garments, a bigger vat is recommended, to avoid touching the bottom of the vat and disturbing the sediment. Simply decide what size vat you are making; adapt the amount of indigo, limestone, fructose, and water according to the recipes listed; and follow the instructions below using your new measurements.

CHOICE OF VESSEL: BUCKET OR POT

This style of vat works best heated. If you are using a bucket, gently heat it by wrapping it in a seed mat or attach an immersion heater. But we prefer to use a pot and warm the vat on the stove because it is quicker, so we have written the instructions below to be used with a pot.

CHOOSE YOUR FAVORITE SHADE OF BLUE

See the shade card (pages 194-195) to learn how the amount of indigo in the vat along with the number of dips impacts the color. There are five vats to choose from. Decide which color you like best, refer to the ingredients necessary to create the vat, and follow the instructions below to make the vat and to dye.

INSTRUCTIONS

MAKE THE INDIGO CONCENTRATE (SOMETIMES REFERRED TO AS THE MOTHER)

NOTE: When making the #5 vat, you will need two ½-gallon (500-ml) ball jars in order to ensure there is enough water to mix and dissolve the dry ingredients. In that case, use the water amounts listed below for each ball jar, and split your dry ingredients evenly between the two jars.

1. Heat 8 cups (2 L) water to 120°F (49°C). Pour 5 cups (1.2 L) of this water into the jar and ¼ cup (60 ml) into the measuring cup. Keep the remaining water hot.

2. Add the powdered indigo to the measuring cup. Use a pestle (preferred) or small whisk to thoroughly mix the indigo. (If the indigo is clumping, add more water from your pot.)

3. Pour the indigo mixture into the jar.

4. Rinse the measuring cup with about ¼ cup (60 ml) hot water to remove any indigo left in the measuring cup and pour it into the jar. Stir.

5. Add the fructose to the jar and stir.

6. Gradually add the limestone to the jar, stirring as you add it to avoid clumps. Stir thoroughly until all the powders are combined.

7. Add the remaining hot water to the jar to bring the volume up to 8 cups (2 L).

8. Allow the jar to sit for 24 hours, stirring once or twice during this time.

MAKE THE VAT

NOTE: When you see amounts given in brackets below, these refer to the indigo concentrate being in 1 ball jar [2 ball jars].

1. Add 11 L [9 L] water to the stainless steel pot and heat to 120°F (49°C). Turn off the heat.

2. Reserve 1 L of this water to rinse your jar out.

3. Gently pour your indigo mother into the pot.

4. Rinse your jar(s) with the reserved hot water and pour into the pot. If you find clumps at the bottom or stuck to the sides, use a spoon to gently dislodge them and pour them into the pot.

5. Stir the indigo vat in a circular motion gently for 20–30 seconds.

6. Allow the vat to rest for at least 1 hour. Take the white spoon and hold it just under the surface of the vat: the liquid will have shifted from opaque blue-green to yellow-green, yellow, amber, or dark yellow-red, and the liquid will have very few dark particles floating in it, indicating that the sediment of indigo pigment and limestone has settled to the bottom of the vat.

DYEING IN THE INDIGO VAT

Follow the steps for Dyeing with Indigo (page 13), taking into account the following details:

• Use a soda ash bath for the pre-wetting alkaline bath. Take a bucket and create a bath using warm water (110°F/43°C) and soda ash (⅛ teaspoon/0.6 g) per 1 gallon (4 L) water.

• Make sure the vat stays at 95–100°F (35–38°C) for wool and 75°F (24°C) for silk and cellulose-based fibers. If the temperature drops while dyeing, and you notice the goods are not picking up the color, stop dyeing and warm the vat.

• When you start your dyeing session, the vat is in its prime state. Upon dipping the goods into the vat, and pulling them from the vat, the goods will be yellow-green. This is a good sign. As you continue dyeing, if you notice that the goods upon exiting the vat are blue, this means the sediment at the bottom of the vat may have be disturbed. When this happens, stop dyeing, and read the section below.

CARING FOR YOUR VAT

DURING DYEING

If the liquid in the vat turns blue and/or the goods exiting the vat are blue: Stop dyeing and let the vat sit for 30 minutes, allowing the sediment to settle. Once 30 minutes have passed, dip the white spoon just under the surface of the vat: The liquid will be translucent and yellow or yellow-red; it is now OK to continue dyeing. Sometimes this may take up to 1 hour.

AFTER DYEING

When you have completed your dye session, add approximately one tenth the amount of fructose you started with, stir well, and cover with a lid. Adding fructose will keep your vat working well longer and reduce the need for a more intense recalibration.

FOR YOUR NEXT DYE SESSION

1. Before dyeing, bring the temperature of your vat back to the temperature as recommended above.

2. If your vat has not been stirred in the last 12 hours, stir well, mixing the sediment resting along the bottom of the vat with the water. Allow to settle for at least 1 hour before dyeing.

White spoon showing a fructose vat ready for dyeing

RECALIBRATING

Over time, the conditions needed to dye properly shift. If you have if you have followed the steps listed in For Your Next Dye Session (page 198), and you still find the following things occurring, you may need to recalibrate:

• No color attaches to your goods when you dip them in the vat.

• When you dip the white spoon under the surface of the vat, the color of the liquid is no longer amber or yellow—it may appear as a dull dusty green or blue-green.

• Your yarn appears to be dyed, but more dye than usual comes off during washing.

TO RECALIBRATE THE VAT

1. Make sure the vat is at 95–100°F (35–38°C). Turn off the heat.

2. Add one-third of the original amount of fructose and stir.

3. Slowly add half of the original amount of limestone, stirring as you add it to avoid clumps.

4. Allow to settle and reduce for 24 hours.

5. Take the white spoon and hold it just under the surface of the vat: The liquid should have shifted from opaque blue-green to yellow-green, yellow, amber, or dark yellow–red, and the liquid should have very few dark particles floating in it, indicating that the sediment of indigo pigment and limestone has settled to the bottom of the vat. If your liquid is this color, heat the vat to the temperature recommended for the type of fiber you are dyeing (page 198), and proceed to Dyeing in the Indigo Vat (page 198) above and dip your goods. If when dipping your goods they are coming out white or very light blue, stop dyeing, and repeat steps 1–5.

layering mordant and madder to create darker shades

The root of the Madder (*Rubia tinctorum*) produces a red dye, and is the version we grow of Indonesia's dye plant *Morinda citrifolia*. They are in the same family, *Rubiaceae*, and the main dye molecules in both plants (moridone in morinda and alizarin in madder) are anthraquinones that are closely related.

Madder is easy to grow in well-draining soil and full sun, and is considered drought tolerant. As a perennial it will grow year after year and goes dormant in the winter, bouncing back with fresh green leaves in the spring. Madder is a sprawling, prickly, weedy plant, so we suggest giving it a raised bed of its own. It can be grown by seed, sowing either directly outside or starting indoors, to transplant later. Younger roots produce a soft pink. To achieve the richest reds, harvest the roots when they reach the thickness of a pencil, when the plant is approximately two years old. When the plant is mature it can easily be divided to propagate and grow new plants, a great gift for your friends who also dye with plants.

When dyeing cotton fiber with our mature madder root, we had difficulty getting a strong, repeatable red shade when applying only one layer of mordant and one layer of madder. We tried increasing the percentage of dye in the dyebath. We also tried mordanting once and adding the yarn to multiple dyebaths—similar to how we applied layers of dye in the Mexico chapter (page 52). But still, the color did not darken.

Thinking about the way mordant and *Morinda* root are applied in Indonesia, and the theme in our research of applying dye in layers, we wondered if applying multiple layers of mordant and dye would produce darker shades. Through our experiments, we confirmed indeed it does.

In addition to applying multiple layers of mordant and dye, we took things a step further and experimented with using only local plants as our mordant. We learned that plants such as camellia and hydrangea leaves have the ability to accumulate aluminum similarly to *Symplocos*—as long as the soil they grow in is acidic. So we began to experiment with leaves from our neighborhood to create the samples shown on the following shade card.

To mordant cellulose-based goods with *Symplocos* or another bioaccumulator of aluminum and dye it with fresh madder root, follow these steps:

1. Scour (page 217) your goods.

2. Mordant your goods using tannin and *Symplocos* according to the instructions on page 224.

3. Create a dyebath using fresh madder root, following the directions for whichever of the Two Basic Methods of Dyeing (page 227) suits the size of project you are completing. Make sure your dyebath remains at 180°F (82°C).

4. If, after applying one layer of mordant and madder, you would like a darker shade, give your goods a quick rinse with water and repeat steps 2 and 3 to apply a second mordant layer and a second madder layer.

5. Repeat step 4 again as desired. To create the madder shade card on pages 202–203, we repeated steps 2–5 up to three times total.

shade card: madder + plant mordants

GOODS: Blue Sky Fibers, Organic Cotton Skinny (100% organic cotton) yarn, birch (white)

SCOUR: Scouring Cellulose-Based Goods (page 218)

MORDANT: Listed in the first, left column

DYE: Swatches dyed using 100% freshly harvested madder root (the equivalent amount of madder extract to achieve these shades is 6%) using 100 g of goods and 8–9 cups (1.9–2 L) water in a 3-quart (2.8-L) pot.

NOTES: "1 layer" indicates the goods were mordanted, dyed, and rinsed. "2 layers" means the goods were mordanted, dyed, rinsed, and then mordanted and dyed again using fresh mordant and dye (see page 201 to learn more about layering with madder), and so forth.

	1 LAYER	2 LAYERS	3 LAYERS
6% ALUMINUM ACETATE AND CHALK			
15% OAK GALLS AND 14% ALUMINUM POTASSIUM SULFATE			
15% OAK GALLS AND 50% SYMPLOCOS			
15% OAK GALLS AND 50% CAMELLIA LEAVES			
15% OAK GALLS AND 50% HYDRANGEA LEAVES			

TIPS FOR WORKING WITH MADDER ROOT

Tips for working with madder root:

• Only harvest the amount you need to dye to keep the plant healthy.

• To achieve red, harvest roots that are at least ¼ inch (6 mm) thick because they are older and have more dye in them.

• Keep your dyepot at 180°F (82°C); if hotter, other components can be extracted from the madder roots, adding a brown hue to your goods.

• Madder is easily impacted by raising and lowering pH. Follow the methods used on page 230 to experiment and discover new shades of oranges, reds, and pinks.

zigzag ikat woven bracelet

SIZE
One size fits most

FINISHED MEASUREMENTS
⅓ inch (8 mm) wide × 13¼ inches (33.5 cm) long

MATERIALS
Blue Sky Fibers Organic Cotton Skinny (100% organic cotton; 150 yards [137 m/65 g]): 1 skein birch

WE WERE INSPIRED BY THE incredible weavings of Tenganan when we designed this much simpler warp-faced ikat bracelet. Though we chose to dye our bracelet with madder, you can dye yours any color you wish. Indigo blue would look incredible!

To create this bracelet, you will warp the loom with undyed yarn, group warp threads and wrap them tightly with yarn in a zigzag pattern, remove the warp from the loom, dye the warp and the weft, remove the yarn used to create the zigzag pattern, re-warp the loom, and weave the bracelet. The bracelet is completed with a clever loop and tie closure made from the ends of the weaving, requiring no additional findings.

These directions make a bracelet that is 13¼ inches (33.5 cm) long. To lengthen or shorten, increase or decrease the loom length and weaving length by your desired amount. You will be working with a cardboard loom, which is easy to make but also bendable. We will give tips and tricks for working with this material.

With all weaving, there's a fine balance with tension. In this project, you will warp your loom twice: first in order to tie the resist yarn on before dyeing, and second after dyeing, in preparation to weave. In order for your resist pattern to line up properly when you are ready to weave, you will need to warp with a similar tension both times. This tension should be taut, but not as tight as possible, otherwise it will be difficult to weave.

The color of the bracelets were made by:
Darker bracelet: 3 layers of mordant (oak galls and Symplocos) and dye (madder)
Lighter bracelet: 3 layers of mordant (oak galls and camellia leaves) and dye (madder)

TOOLS

Sturdy cardboard cut to 8 × 1½ inches (20 × 4 cm) (corrugated cardboard, with corrugated lines running along the longer length is recommended)

Scissors or X-Acto knife and cutting mat

Tapestry needle

Tape

Ruler or measuring tape

Black pen (pencil may transfer to weaving)

Small scissors with pointed tips

TIP

• If your unprocessed yarn is losing its twist, add twist back in to make the yarn firm and increase its ability to resist.

• Keeping your loom flat on the table will allow you to hold the wraps securely with one hand while wrapping with the other. This will help keep the resist as tight as possible.

INSTRUCTIONS

PREPARE THE YARN

Wind off 2 yards (2 m) and set aside; do not scour or mordant this length. Scour (page 217) the remainder of the skein.

MAKE THE LOOM AND WARP

1. The cardboard piece will be your loom. With the ruler and pen, draw a line ¼ inch (6 mm) from the bottom of one short end. This marks the beginning of your weaving. Draw another line 5¼ inches (13 cm) from the bottom of the loom. This marks the end of your weaving. This is the front of your loom.

2. Take the scoured yarn and tie a knot at one end. This marks the beginning of your warp. On the back of your loom, in the middle along the right edge, mark an X. Tape the end of the yarn so the knot is on the X. In the middle along the left edge, mark an O. This is where you will tape the end of your yarn after warping.

3. Turn your loom with the front facing you. Starting at the left edge, wrap the yarn around the bottom of the loom and up over the top. Continue wrapping the yarn around the loom until you have 16 vertical warp yarns on the front of the loom. Keep your tension even; do not pull the yarn too tightly, but be careful that it is not loose either. Leave approximately ¹⁄₁₆ inch (2 mm) between each warp yarn, making sure they all fit on the loom.

4. Turn your loom so the back is facing you. Wrap the yarn around to the back of your loom to the O, and cut the yarn 1 inch (2.5 cm) past the O. Tie two knots at the end of the yarn to mark the end of your warp. Tape the yarn so the end is on the O.

CREATE ZIGZAG: TIE RESIST BY WRAPPING WARP YARNS IN PATTERN TIGHTLY

Warp yarns are numbered 1–16, starting with 1 on the left

1. Cut approximately 1 yard (1 m) of the unprocessed yarn and thread it onto your tapestry needle.

2. Starting at the beginning weaving line marked on your loom, begin to group and wrap the warp threads tightly by passing your tapestry needle underneath warp yarns 3–5. Pull yarn through, leaving a 2-inch (5-cm) tail. Wrap the yarn around the same yarns in the same direction again, and pull the yarn through snugly. Repeat until you have 5 wraps around the warp yarns, pulling tight after each wrap. Tie a square knot with the 2-inch (5-cm) tail.

3. Pass the tapestry needle underneath warp yarns 6–8, and pull the yarn through. Position the first wrap in the middle of the resist section you made on warp yarns 3–5, and pull it tight. Loop around the same yarns again until you have 5 wraps around the warp yarns, pulling tight after each wrap. Pass the yarn under the warp threads again, and before you pull the loop tight, pass the needle through the loop, creating a knot. Tighten the knot over the 5 wraps to hold them securely. (A)

4. Repeat this for warp yarns 9–11, then 12–14. You have created the first leg of the zigzag; now you will continue in the same manner, working back to the left side of the weaving as follows: Wrap around warp yarns 9–11, again overlapping the resist section with the one you just completed, then 6–8, and so on to the beginning. Make sure there is a gap of warp yarn visible between the two resist sections on yarns 9–11 so that when the yarn is dyed the zigzag pattern will be distinct.

5. Continue wrapping the resist yarn on the warp in this manner until you are ½–1 inch (12 mm–2.5 cm) past the end weaving line. Attach another length of unprocessed yarn when you need it.

6. To keep the yarn from tangling during dyeing, tie two loose figure-8 loops around all the warp yarns on the front of the loom, one at the beginning weaving line and one after the last resist. On the back of the loom, add one tight single loop securing the beginning and end of your warp and all the warp yarns in between.

7. Un-tape the ends and carefully slide the warp off of your loom.

MORDANT AND DYE

1. Cut 1½ yards (1.3 m) of the scoured yarn to use as the weft yarn.

2. Mordant and dye your warp and weft yarn using the instructions on page 201 (see the shade card on pages 202–203 to decide what color you would like and which method to use).

3. Rinse the yarn and hang to dry.

REMOVE RESIST TIES

1. Pull the knot away from the first resist you tied, and carefully cut it off using small scissors with pointed tips.

2. Unravel the resist ties, cutting knots as needed, and remove the resist ties.

As you weave, because
you are creating a
warp-faced fabric,
the warp begins to
shorten and narrow,
causing the cardboard
loom to bend slightly.
Keeping the loom flat
on the table as you
weave will help keep
the loom flat with
only a small bend. If
you are weaving and
you are finding your
loom to have bent to
the point where there
is a crease, or where it
has become impossi-
ble to weave, do not
lose hope! You can
insert a short card-
board strip (the same
width as the loom)
behind the warp on
the back of the loom,
making the loom once
again flat, so you can
keep weaving.

WEAVE

1. Locate the knot marking the beginning of your warp and tape it onto the X on the back of your loom. Repeat the warping process, making sure the resisted (undyed) areas line up in the same place as when you tied them while keeping the tension as even as possible. The first resist area should start at the beginning weaving line.

2. Tape the end of your weaving onto the O marked on the back of your loom.

3. (First Row) Thread the weft yarn onto a tapestry needle. Starting at the right side of your warp, begin weaving plain weave by passing the tapestry needle under the first warp yarn, over the second, under the third, etc., until you reach the end. The pathway of the needle and weft yarn through the warp yarns is called a shed. Pull the yarn through, leaving an 11-inch (28-cm) tail. If needed, push your weft down with your needle until it is at the beginning weaving line.

4. (Second Row) From the left side of your warp, pass your tapestry needle under the first warp yarn, over the second, under the third, etc. Note: You are creating a tightly woven fabric that will require the weft yarns to be packed tightly. To do so, beat each weft yarn two times so it will fit snugly within the weaving. Place the loom flat on the table, and carefully pull the weft through halfway so you can reinsert the needle into the shed you have created. With one hand, hold the loom flat; with the other hand, pull the tapestry needle down to beat (push) the weft yarn snugly into place. Remove the needle from the shed. Place your hand flat on your weaving where your weft yarn is and carefully pull the weft yarn through from left to right. Continue pulling the weft yarn until you can no longer see the weft yarns between the warp yarns. The goal is to use the weft yarn to pull the warp yarns together to form the warp-faced fabric. Insert the tapestry needle back into the same shed and beat again, while pushing the tapestry needle down toward the weaving; pull the weft thread tightly to create a snug fabric. (Beating twice, while pulling on the weft yarn, produc-es the most even and firm fabric.) **(B)**

5. Continue weaving in this manner until you reach the line marking the end of your weaving.

FINISH

1. Remove the weaving from the loom: With the back of the loom facing you, 3¾ inches (10 cm) from the bottom of your loom, cut through the warp yarns. The tails at the beginning of your weaving are 4 inches (10 cm) long and the tails at the end of your weaving are 6½ inches (16.5 cm) long.

2. Finish the beginning of your weaving by making two braids: Take the 17 strands (16 warp yarns and 1 weft end) at the beginning of the weaving and divide them into

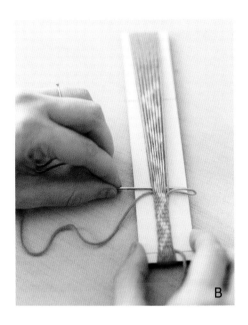

two groups, one with 8 strands and one with 9. Divide the group of 8 strands into three groups (3, 2, and 3 strands) and braid those groups for 1½ inches (4 cm). Choose your longest strand and wrap it once around the end of the braid, then thread that strand into a tapestry needle and pass the end through the wrap you created two times and pull tight to secure. Repeat for the group of 9. Trim these tassels to 1¾ inches (4.5 cm) or desired length.

3. Finish the end of your weaving by making one braid with a buttonhole at the end: Take the 17 strands (16 warp yarns and 1 weft end) at the end of the weaving and divide them into three groups (6, 5, and 6 strands) and braid those groups for 2½ inches (6 cm). Choose your longest strand and wrap it four times around the end of the braid, then thread that strand into a tapestry needle and pass the end through the four wraps you created, then through the last wrap once more and pull tight to secure.

4. Take the remaining length and divide the 17 strands in half into two groups. Twist each group in opposite directions from one another for ¾ inch (2 cm), then repeat four wraps using the longest strand as in step 3, creating a ⅝-inch (15-mm) buttonhole. After securing, trim tassels to 2 inches (5 cm) or desired length. (C)

WEAR

1. Thread the end with two braids through the buttonhole and pull the bracelet all the way through the buttonhole until the braid forms a ¾-inch (2-cm) loop.

2. Thread the end of the bracelet with two braids through this new loop (do not pull the bracelet all the way through this time).

3. Slide the bracelet onto your wrist and pull the two braids through the loop until it is the desired size. Tighten by pulling the new loop closed.

CHAPTER FIVE

FOUNDATIONS OF
NATURAL DYEING

The recipes and directions in the book are dependent upon the fiber type. To achieve the most long-lasting colors, predictable results, and saturated colors, and for a successful dyeing experience, it is important to pre-wash (scour) the materials and mordant (apply the binder, which is what the color attaches to) the undyed materials. In this chapter, you will find instructions on setting up your work space, recommended tools used widely throughout the book, instructions on preparing your fibers for the dyepot, recipes on how to scour and mordant your goods, and, finally, how to wash your dyed goods and properly dispose of used dyebaths.

setting up your work space

Before we get into the nitty-gritty of dyeing, let's examine the possibilities for creating a comfortable work space. All you need are a few important features, whether you work inside or outside.

INDOOR OPTIONS

Nearly everything dyed for this book was done so in our kitchen. We used our stovetop to scour, mordant, and dye and our kitchen sink to wash goods. We placed a drying rack over a drop cloth to hang goods to dry.

The key elements of a functional dyeing work space can be found in most kitchens:

• A counter for weighing, recording, and dyeing

• Easy access to water for creating dyebaths and pre-wetting/washing fibers

• A source for heating water to create dyebaths

• Good ventilation

• Surfaces that are easy to clean or protect

Other areas in the house with similar attributes might be a garage, a laundry room, a bathroom, or a basement.

OUTDOOR OPTIONS

Dyeing outdoors is always a great option. There's something wonderful about spending the day in the fresh air dyeing, enjoying the sunshine, and creating colors from nature.

To set up an outdoor work space:

• Use a folding table as a counter for weighing, recording, and dyeing

• Carry water from indoors or bring a garden hose to your work area

• Use a hot plate if you have access to electricity; if you don't, use a butane stove

tools

The tools listed here are only those that are used widely across most techniques discussed in this book. Allow the techniques you decide to try, and the tools listed, to inform which tools to acquire first. All the tools can be purchased at your local hardware or kitchen store or collected inexpensively at a garage sale or thrift store.

An important note: Natural dyes are sensitive to metal, and this can affect the color. To obtain colors similar to what is shown in this book, it's important to use tools made of nonreactive materials, such as stainless steel, glass, or plastic.

Never use a tool for cooking if it has been used for dyeing. Always keep the tools you use for dyeing separate from those that you use to cook—store them separately and mark them clearly.

Kitchen Scale You must weigh your goods to identify how much scour, mordant, and dye to use. Acquire a digital scale that measures in grams and can weigh up to 5 pounds (2.3 kg). A scale that measures to a tenth of a gram is highly recommended for the most reliable results.

Dye Journal This useful tool helps plan projects and re-create results. See page 215 for detailed information on organizing your journal.

Buckets Plastic buckets from the hardware store are useful for carrying water, holding wet goods, and washing them out after dyeing. An 11-quart (10-L) bucket is helpful to pre-wet and wash small- to medium-sized projects. Five-gallon (19-L) buckets are good for larger projects.

Stainless Steel Pots with Lids To create the best lightfastness and provide the most even application of dye, choose a dyepot big enough to allow water and dye to move freely and easily around the fiber.

It's nice to have three pots: one for scouring and mordanting, at least one for dyeing, and, if practicing the fructose-based indigo vat (page 192), one for indigo dyeing. However, you can use only one pot and wash it well between uses. Here are some suggested sizes:
- 3 quart (2.8 L)—for small projects and samples
- 5 quart (4.7 L)—for small to medium projects
- 12 quart (11.3 L)—for medium projects
- 16 quart (15.1 L)—for indigo dyeing or if working with 1-yard (90-cm) lengths of fabric
- 20 quart (18.9 L)—for working with 2- to 3-yard (1.8- to 2.8-m) lengths of fabric

Butcher Trays (7½ × 11 inches/19 × 28 cm) A shallow rimmed tray good for applying room temperature dye. These are inexpensive and can be found at your local art store.

Kettle A kettle, while not necessary, is helpful to warm water on your stovetop when dissolving agents such as those used in scouring and mordanting.

Canning Jars with Lids A variety of canning jars (including 1-quart [1-L] jars with lids and half-gallon [2-L] jars) is helpful for dying and storing dyes.

Liquid Measuring Cup A clear, glass liquid measuring cup comes in handy for measuring water and as a vessel for dissolving agents such as those used in scouring and mordanting.

Measuring Spoons You will need a set of measuring spoons to measure agents such as those used in scouring and mordanting, ranging from ⅛ teaspoon to 1 tablespoon.

Stirring Spoons or Small Stainless Steel Whisks
Use these tools to dissolve agents such as those used in scouring and mordanting.

Tongs To turn goods while dyeing, use a pair of nonreactive tongs.

Cooking Thermometer Water must reach the correct temperature to ensure colorfastness (the desired temperature will be provided in the project recipes). Use an all-purpose cooking thermometer to take the temperature of the water while scouring, mordanting, and dyeing.

Timer Once the designated temperature is reached, it is important to maintain that temperature for the correct amount of time to ensure lightfastness.

pH Strips pH strips measure the acidity or alkalinity of a water-based solution. To learn about how to use pH strips, see page 230.

pH Meter and Recalibration Solutions Like pH strips, a pH meter measures the acidity or alkalinity of water-based solutions. When properly calibrated, they are more accurate, precise, and objective than pH strips. We use an Oakton EcoTestr pH 2+ Pocket pH Meter. Don't forget to purchase recalibration and storage solutions. To learn about how to use pH meters, see page 230.

Clothesline, Drying Rack, or Shower Caddy and Clothespins Used in multiple dyeing processes and to dry goods. Use whichever of these makes most sense in your space.

Rubber Gloves Our favorite gloves are Casabella WaterBlock Premium. They have a rim that helps keep the water from dripping down your arm, and they fit nicely. Gloves help protect your hands from heat and keeps them soft.

Mask Wear a disposable N95 mask when weighing aluminum acetate (a mordant) and when weighing out ash to create ash water (page 122) to avoid breathing in fine particles.

Mortar and Pestle Helpful for grinding whole dyestuffs, such as cochineal, pine cones, acorns, and more.

Wooden Dowels A variety of unfinished wooden dowels are useful when stirring, eco-printing, and ombré-dyeing yarn.

Sieves, Colanders, and Cheesecloth It is helpful to have a variety of sieves with different sizes of mesh and colanders. Cheesecloth can also be used as a strainer, though we typically only use it to make persimmon dye.

Masking or Painter's Tape and Permanent Marker If you have multiple projects going at once, it's helpful to label pots and buckets with their contents.

Tyvek Sometimes we fill a scour, mordant, or dyebath with different types of yarn and fabric. When working with a variety of fabric and yarn in the same vessel, label the goods with Tyvek, a waterproof and heatproof material easily upcycled from United States Postal Service mailers. See the sidebar on page 216 to learn how to make and use the labels.

Calculator To calculate percentages.

Drop Cloth or Butcher Paper If using your kitchen table as a work space, cover it with newspaper or butcher paper to protect it from occasional spills. Place a drop cloth on the floor to catch extra drips of dye.

fiber characteristics

HOW FIBERS DIFFER

There are two types of natural fibers: protein-based fibers from animals or insects and cellulose-based fibers from plants. In order to create predictable, lightfast color, it is important to know the content of the yarn or fabric—the goods—you plan to dye. The differences between the two types of fiber affect the dyeing process and the colors you can achieve with natural dyes.

Protein-Based Fibers

Protein-based fibers come from the fur or hair of animals (such as sheep, alpaca, camel, angora rabbits, and goats) and the filament spun by one very special insect, the silkworm. These fibers are made mainly of protein, thus the name. In this book, we use wool yarn and silk yarn in the shade cards and projects.

Due to the chemical composition of animal-based fibers, there are many points at which mordant and dye can attach to the fiber, so very little dye is needed to create saturated, vibrant color in a wide variety of shades and hues.

Wool is often recommended to beginning dyers because it is easier to achieve a wide array of colors with than with silk or cellulose-based fibers. Special care should be taken to avoid felting, which is when the tiny scales that make up wool fiber attach and lock together. You can avoid felting by never allowing your woolen fiber to boil and never shocking it with temperature extremes.

Silk sits in a unique position in the fiber world as it is made by an insect, the silkworm. Though it is produced by an insect and considered a protein-based fiber, it shares more characteristics with cellulose-based fibers than all other protein-based fibers. Like cellulose-based fibers, silk cannot felt, can be affected negatively by acids used to lower the pH, and tends to take naturally dyed color in softer hues (so use more mordant and dye than

you would with animal-based fibers). However, unlike cellulose-based fibers, silk can be damaged by heat. Keep the temperature around 160°F (71°C) during the scouring, mordanting, and dyeing processes to ensure your silk goods stay strong and lustrous.

Silk fibers are composed of two proteins: fibroin and sericin. Fibroin is the structural part of the silk fiber, and sericin is a sticky coating that allows the fibers to stick together. Silk fiber that has had the sericin removed, such as chiffon or habotai, will dye a lighter shade than silk fiber that retains its sericin, such as organza. Refer to the shade card on pages 86–87 to learn more about dyeing silk.

Cellulose-Based Fibers

Fibers made from plants are composed mainly of cellulose, and are thus referred to as cellulose-based fibers. In this book, we use cotton yarn and fabric made from cotton, linen, or a blend of both.

On a microscopic level, cellulose-based fibers are very smooth and quite different from protein-based fibers. They require more dye and a different mordanting process than protein-based goods because of their difference in composition. Even with a greater amount of dye, colors tend to be more muted on plant-based fibers. Just as with protein fibers, each type of cellulose fiber will take dye differently. For example, bast fibers such as linen are porous and are the most responsive to natural dyes. They exhibit a wider range of shades than cotton.

Cellulose goods can endure boiling water without harm, and they won't felt. So you don't have to be as careful about shifts in water temperature as you do with protein-based goods, and you can jump from one step to the next faster without fear. Cellulose fibers can endure dyebaths with high alkalinity, unlike protein-based fibers, although acidic dyebaths weaken them. Use with caution. Cellulose-based fibers mildew quickly, so don't keep them in water for more than forty-eight hours.

keep good notes

We have found that documenting our dyeing process gives us a deep understanding of how dyes work with a wide variety of fibers. By recording in a journal, we are better able to understand our results and predict the outcome of colors. This is especially important when tackling complex dyeing projects such as multiple-color batik designs.

Documenting our dyeing process in a dye journal gives us a deep understanding of how dyes work with a wide variety of fibers, and enables us to better understand our results. Additional observations such as smells, textures, and a visual description of the dyebath will help you hone your skill as a dyer.

When working on more complex processes, such as extracting indigo pigment (page 190) or composting indigo (page 120), the same principles apply: The more information you record, the more guidance you will have when trying to understand or repeat your processes in the future.

INFORMATION TO RECORD

Here are a few key pieces of information you should record in your journal. Recording the date gives a frame of reference for your progress. The date indicates the season when the dyeing was done, which can be meaningful if you harvested the dyes, because the amount of pigment in the plant can fluctuate seasonally. Recording the date of when you complete each stage of the process can help you understand how long a process took from start to finish.

Content of goods The fiber content has a tremendous effect on the outcome of the color and also dictates the amount of dye needed.

Tools used Make a list of tools used—and take note of tools you wish you had!

Weight of goods Record the weight of dry fiber, yarn, or fabric.

Scour material and amount used/date Record the type and amount of soap and water used.

Mordant material and amount used/date Record the type and amount of mordant and water used.

Dye material/type and amount used/date Record what form your dye is in (leaves, flowers, seeds, stems, bark, roots, peel, wood chips, sawdust), whether your plant material is fresh or dried, and when and where it was gathered or grown.

Modifiers used/date Record any dyebath or post-dye modifiers, such as iron or baking soda solutions.

pH When shifting the pH of your dyebath, or dipping dyed goods in a bath to modify the color, or during any indigo process, record the pH to help you understand your results. Also record the temperature, as pH depends on temperature. Read more about pH on page 230.

Wash material and amount used/date Record the type and amount of soap or detergent and water used.

Sample Once your dyed goods are dry, take a little snip and attach it to your journal entry to record your results.

weighing and preparing your goods for dyeing

WEIGH THE GOODS

Weigh the goods you plan to dye before you get started. The amount of scour (page 217), mordant (page 219), and dye you will use is based on the weight of goods (WOG). Record this measurement.

PREPARE THE GOODS

Take the following precautions to make the goods easier to handle while dyeing.

Unspun Fiber

Unspun fiber is a particularly sensitive form, as it can easily tangle or come apart. It is best to separate it into 1- or 2-ounce (28- to 56-g) increments for ease of handling.

Yarn

Yarn can be found in two forms, a ball and a skein, but it should always be dyed in the skein form. To prepare the skein, lay it flat on a table and open it into a large loop. Take a piece of scrap yarn and thread it through the skein in the shape of a figure 8. In this manner, tie the skein snugly in four places that are spaced equally apart. Do not tie too tightly, the dye won't reach the yarn under the tie. Make sure the knots are secure so the ties do not fall off in the dyeing process. Preparing the yarn in this way keeps it from becoming tangled.

Fabric

Once fabric absorbs water, it can become quite heavy and unwieldy. Cutting a piece of fabric into sections before dyeing it makes the process more manageable. Be especially careful when dyeing knit fabric, as it can stretch out

BATCH SCOURING AND MORDANTING

It can be convenient to scour and mordant the materials for multiple projects simultaneously— it is OK to dry the goods and store them until you're ready to dye them. It's a good idea to mark them so you can identify them and to remember which stage the goods have gone through. This is especially important when mordanting protein-based fibers, because if they go through the mordanting step twice, the fiber will be permanently sticky. The solution is marking. Cut a strip of Tyvek recycled from a mailer and loosely tie it to the fiber or yarn. If working with fabric, make a small snip in the corner of the material, thread the strip through, and knot it. Use a permanent marker to record the fiber content and the weight of the item, and as you work through the process, continue to add information to the tape—an "S" for scour and an "M" for mordant is our system. Make a circle around the letter once the process is complete. If you have dried out any of the materials after scouring or mordanting, re-wet them and jump right into the next step of the process.

of shape. Make sure to always hold it with both hands when transferring it from one pot to the next, and try not to wring it or stretch it. Due to its construction, knit fabric takes dye more readily than woven fabric.

PRE-WET THE GOODS

It is necessary to thoroughly pre-wet all goods before starting scouring, mordanting, or dyeing.

To judge when the goods are thoroughly pre-wet, notice when they sink on their own accord. Once they sink, they are ready to scour, mordant, or dye.

recipes for scouring

SCOURING WOOL

MATERIALS

pH-neutral soap, or a gentle, biodegradable dishwashing detergent like Ecover

TOOLS

3-quart (2.8-L) or larger stainless steel pot with lid (size dependent on the amount of goods)

Measuring spoons

Thermometer

Tongs

Rubber gloves

Laundry detergents and soap are usually alkaline and can damage protein-based fibers. Use only mild dishwashing detergent with a neutral pH level.

INSTRUCTIONS

1. Fill the pot with enough water so the goods are covered and can move freely once added to the pot.

2. For every 500 g of dry goods, add ½ teaspoon (2.5 ml) dishwashing liquid to the pot of water and use your tongs to stir to combine.

3. Add the wet goods to the pot and cover. Slowly, over 30 minutes, bring the water in the pot to 180°F (82°C), keeping the water just under a simmer. Hold at this temperature for an additional 30 minutes, rotating the goods gently from the top to the bottom of the pot every 10 minutes. Make sure the goods remain submerged when rotating.

4. Turn off the heat. Allow the goods to cool in the water.

5. Squeeze excess scouring water from the goods and rinse with cool water to remove excess detergent. If the water in the pot is dark yellow or brown after scouring, repeat the process until the water is clear.

6. You can either proceed to mordanting the goods or store them wet in a plastic bag or bucket; if left in a cool, dark place, they will be fine for 2 to 3 days. If you need to wait longer than this, allow the goods to dry and store them until you are ready to mordant.

SCOURING SILK

MATERIALS

pH-neutral soap, or a gentle, biodegradable dishwashing detergent like Ecover

TOOLS

Bucket

Measuring spoons

Thermometer

Tongs

Rubber gloves

Silk fibers do not need as aggressive scouring as wool fibers, as they do not contain lanolin or accumulate debris the way wool fibers do. Because silk is more receptive to heat, lower temperatures are used to avoid damaging the fiber.

INSTRUCTIONS

1. Fill the bucket with enough 140°F (60°C) water so the goods are covered and can move freely once added to the bucket.

2. For every 500 g of dry goods, add ½ teaspoon (2.5 ml) dishwashing liquid to the pot of water and use your tongs to stir to combine.

3. Add the wet goods to the bucket. Gently agitate with your hands for about 5 minutes to make sure the silk is fully wet.

4. Squeeze excess scouring water from the goods and rinse with cool water to remove excess detergent. If the water in the pot is dark yellow or brown after scouring, repeat the process until the water is clear.

5. You can either proceed to mordanting the goods or store them wet in a plastic bag or bucket; if left in a cool, dark place, they will be fine for 2 to 3 days. If you need to wait longer than this, allow the goods to dry and store them until you are ready to mordant.

MATERIALS

Soda ash (also known as washing soda or sodium carbonate)

TOOLS

3-quart (2.8-L) or large stainless steel pot with lid (size dependent on the amount of goods)

Measuring spoons

Measuring cup

Stirrer, such as a whisk or spoon

Thermometer

Tongs

Rubber gloves

SCOURING CELLULOSE-BASED GOODS

Cellulose-based goods can endure, and in fact benefit from being washed in an alkaline environment. The stovetop method suggested is the best way to thoroughly scour. That said, it may be more convenient to use your washing machine to scour cellulose-based goods. Use the hot water/long cycle setting.

INSTRUCTIONS

1. Fill the pot with enough water so the goods are covered and can move freely when they are added to the pot.

2. For every 100 g of dry goods, combine ¼ cup (60 ml) hot water and 1¼ teaspoons (3 g) soda ash in a measuring cup. Stir with a small whisk or spoon until dissolved.

3. Add the dissolved soda ash mixture to the pot of water and stir.

4. Add the wet goods to the pot and cover. Slowly, over 30 minutes, bring the water in the pot to 180°F (82°C), keeping the water just under a simmer. Hold at this temperature for an additional 30 minutes, rotating the goods gently from the top to the bottom of the pot every 10 minutes. Make sure the goods remain submerged when rotating.

5. Turn off the heat. Allow the goods to cool in the water.

6. Squeeze excess mordant water from the goods and rinse with cool water to remove excess soda ash. If the water in the pot is dark yellow or brown after scouring, repeat the process until the water is clear.

7. You can either proceed to mordanting the goods or store them wet in a plastic bag or bucket; if left in a cool, dark place, they will be fine for 2 to 3 days. If you need to wait longer than this, allow the goods to dry and store them until you are ready to mordant.

recipes for mordanting

Aluminum potassium sulfate (14% WOG for wool, 20% for silk)

TOOLS

3-quart (2.8-L) or larger stainless steel pot with lid (size dependent on the amount of goods)

Measuring spoons or kitchen scale

Liquid measuring cup

Stirrer, such as a whisk or spoon

Thermometer

Tongs

Rubber gloves

PROTEIN-BASED WITH ALUMINUM POTASSIUM SULFATE

Use food-grade aluminum potassium sulfate for this step, because it is free of iron and other impurities. Because silk is more receptive to heat, lower temperatures are used to avoid damaging the fiber.

INSTRUCTIONS

1. Fill the pot with enough water so the goods are covered and can move freely once added to the pot.

2. Add ¼ cup (60 ml) 90°F (32°C) water to a measuring cup (or amount needed to dissolve the mordant). Determine the amount of aluminum potassium sulfate to use: measure out an amount that is 14% of the weight of the goods if using wool, and 20% of the weight of goods if using silk, and add to the measuring cup. Stir with a small whisk or spoon until dissolved.

3. Add the dissolved aluminum potassium sulfate to the pot of water and use your tongs to stir to combine.

4. Add the scoured, wet goods to the pot and cover. Slowly, over 30 minutes, bring the water in the pot to 160°F (71°C) for silk and 190°F (88°C) for wool, keeping the water just under a simmer. Hold at this temperature for an additional 60 minutes, rotating the goods gently from the top to the bottom of the pot every 10 minutes. Make sure the goods remain submerged when rotating and during the mordanting process.

5. Turn off the heat. Allow the goods to cool in the water.

6. Squeeze excess mordant water from the goods and rinse with cool water. You can either proceed to dyeing the goods or store them wet in a plastic bag or bucket; if left in a cool, dark place, they will be fine up to 3 days. If you need to wait longer than 3 days, allow the goods to dry and store them until you are ready to dye.

MATERIALS

Aluminum potassium
sulfate (14% WOG)

Cream of tartar
(10% WOG)

TOOLS

3-quart (2.8-L) or
larger stainless steel
pot with lid (size
dependent on the
amount of goods)

Measuring spoons
or kitchen scale

Liquid measuring cup

Stirrer, such as a
whisk or spoon

Thermometer

Tongs

Rubber gloves

MORDANTING WOOL WITH ALUMINUM POTASSIUM SULFATE AND CREAM OF TARTAR

This mordanting recipe is more acidic than the others. If you are using dyes that are sensitive to shifts in pH, this recipe will alter the outcome of the dyed colors. For example, when you use this recipe, goods dyed with cochineal will turn pink, and those dyed with madder will turn orange. Due to the high acidity of this mordant bath, we do not recommend using it with silk or cellulose-based fibers.

INSTRUCTIONS

1. Fill the pot with enough water so the goods are covered and can move freely once added to the pot.

2. Add ¼ cup (60 ml) hot water to a measuring cup (or amount needed to dissolve the mordant). Determine the amount of aluminum potassium sulfate to use: Measure out an amount that is 14% of the weight of the goods and add to the measuring cup. Stir with a small whisk or spoon until dissolved. Repeat for cream of tartar, but this time, measure an amount 10% of the weight of goods.

3. Add the dissolved aluminum potassium sulfate and cream of tartar mixture to the pot of water and use the tongs to stir to combine.

4. Add the scoured, wet goods to the pot and cover. Slowly, over 30 minutes, bring the water in the pot to 190°F (88°C), keeping the water just under a simmer. Hold at this temperature for an additional 60 minutes, rotating the goods gently from the top to the bottom of the pot every 15 minutes. Make sure the goods remain submerged when rotating and during the mordanting process.

5. Turn off the heat. Allow the goods to cool in the water.

6. Squeeze excess mordant water from the goods and rinse with cool water. You can either proceed to dyeing the goods or store them wet in a plastic bag or bucket; if left in a cool, dark place, they will be fine up to 3 days. If you need to wait longer than 3 days, allow the goods to dry and store them until you are ready to dye.

1-quart (1-L) mason jar

Kitchen scale

Liquid measuring cup

Stirrer, such as a whisk
or spoon

Thermometer

Butcher tray, 7½ × 11
inches (19 × 28 cm); for
larger pieces a rimmed
baking sheet works well

Rubber gloves

Clothesline and
clothespins

Drop cloth if dyeing
indoors

POST-MORDANT SOLUTION OF
ALUMINUM POTASSIUM SULFATE

When applying dye without heat, as done in the batik process (page 174), and when creating the Aerial View Throw Pillows (page 188), even if you have pre-mordanted the fabric, it is necessary to set the dye using either a solution of aluminum potassium sulfate or concentrated iron water (page 234). This solution can keep indefinitely if stored in an airtight container at room temperature.

INSTRUCTIONS

1. Fill the jar with 4 cups (960 ml) of 90°F (32°C) water, and then add 70 g aluminum potassium sulfate; stir with a small whisk or spoon until dissolved.

2. To use, pour the alum solution into the butcher tray. Soak the dry goods in the solution for 5 minutes, making sure they are fully submerged and saturated by the solution.

3. Remove the goods from the solution, rinse immediately with cool water, and hang the goods to drip-dry over a drop cloth.

CELLULOSE-BASED GOODS WITH
ALUMINUM ACETATE AND CHALK

After a series of tests, we have found that aluminum acetate, followed by a chalk bath, creates the brightest colors and the best colorfastness on plant-based fibers. The chalk bath can be used for up to 500 g of goods. Discard any remaining chalk bath after 1 week.

INSTRUCTIONS

1. You need only 90°F (32°C) hot tap water for this recipe, so you can use either a pot or a bucket. Fill the vessel with enough hot water so the goods are covered and can move freely once added to the pot.

2. Be sure to wear a mask when weighing and dissolving the aluminum acetate. Add ¼ cup (60 ml) hot water to a measuring cup (or amount needed to dissolve mordant). Determine the amount of aluminum acetate to use: Measure out an amount that is 6% of the weight of the goods and add to the measuring cup. Stir with a small whisk or spoon until dissolved.

3. Add the dissolved aluminum acetate mixture to the pot of water and use tongs to stir to combine.

3-quart (2.8-L) or
larger stainless steel
pot or bucket with lid
(size dependent on
the amount of goods)

11-quart (10.4-L)
bucket

Measuring spoons

Measuring cup

Stirrer, such as a
whisk or spoon

Thermometer

Tongs

Rubber gloves

Mask

4. Add the scoured, wet goods. Cover the pot to help retain the heat.

5. Stir the goods, rotating every 10 minutes. Make sure the goods remain submerged.

6. Let the goods sit for 2 to 24 hours in the mordant bath. The longer you allow the goods to sit, the better lightfastness you will achieve.

7. Squeeze excess mordant water from the goods and rinse with cold water. You can either proceed to applying the chalk bath and to dyeing, or you can store the goods wet in a plastic bag or bucket in a cool, dark place for up to 3 days. If you need more than 3 days, allow the goods to dry and store them until you are ready to apply the chalk bath and dye.

8. Dissolve the chalk in 20 cups (4.7 L) 90°F (32°C) water.

9. Dip the wet, mordanted goods into the chalk bath, making sure to wet them thoroughly.

10. Squeeze excess chalk bath from the goods and rinse with cool water. Proceed to dyeing the goods.

CELLULOSE-BASED GOODS WITH TANNIN AND ALUMINUM POTASSIUM SULFATE

Using aluminum acetate to mordant cellulose-based fibers (above) produces the clearest colors. That said, another way of mordanting cellulose-based fibers is to use a combination of tannin-rich plants and aluminum potassium sulfate—the same agent used in the mordanting of protein-based fibers. Just note that tannins generally impart a beige or coral hue, which can shift the colors normally achieved with aluminum acetate. You can use a different source of tannin, such as myrobalan or acorns (see page 172 for more information on tannins).

If you find yourself wanting to work with tannin instead of aluminum acetate, here are a couple of things to note:

• If you would like to work with a dye that is rich with tannin, you can use it as both the mordant and the dye. To achieve the deepest, most lightfast colors, first apply the tannin-rich dye, then the aluminum potassium sulfate, and then the tannin-rich dye again.

• If you would like to work with a dye that is not rich with tannin, such as madder, first apply a tannin-rich dye, then the aluminum potassium sulfate, and then the dye (in this case madder).

MATERIALS

Oak galls (15% WOG)

Aluminum potassium sulfate (14% WOG)

TOOLS

3-quart (2.8-L) or larger stainless steel pot with lid (size dependent on the amount of goods)

Measuring spoons

Liquid measuring cup

Stirrer, such as a whisk or spoon

Thermometer

Tongs

Rubber gloves

Mortar and pestle

Fine-mesh strainer

INSTRUCTIONS

1. Fill the pot with enough water so the goods are covered and can move freely once added to the pot.

2. Determine the amount of oak galls to use: Measure out an amount that is 15% of the weight of the goods. Grind the oak galls using a mortar and pestle. Add to the pot. Stir with a small whisk or spoon until mixed.

3. Heat to 180°F (82°C) and hold for 30 minutes.

4. Add the scoured, wet goods to the pot and cover. Increase the heat to 200°F (93°C) and hold at this temperature for 60 minutes, rotating the goods gently from the top to the bottom of the pot every 15 minutes. Make sure the goods remain submerged when rotating and during the heating process.

5. Turn off the heat. Allow the goods to cool in the water.

6. Squeeze excess water from the goods. Do not rinse. Set aside the goods—on the counter is fine. Dispose of the oak gall bath: Pour the bath through the strainer to separate the oak galls from the water. Pour the water down the drain. Compost the oak galls.

7. Fill the pot with enough water so the goods are covered and can move freely once added to the pot.

8. Add ¼ cup (60 ml) hot water to a measuring cup. Determine the amount of aluminum potassium sulfate to use: Measure out an amount that is 14% of the weight of the goods and add to the measuring cup. Stir with a small whisk or spoon until dissolved.

9. Add the dissolved aluminum potassium sulfate mixture to the pot of water and use tongs to stir to combine.

10. Add the goods that have had tannin applied to them to the pot and cover. Slowly, over 30 minutes, bring the water in the pot to 190°F (88°C), keeping the water just under a simmer. Hold at this temperature for 60 minutes, rotating the goods gently from the top to the bottom of the pot every 15 minutes. Make sure the goods remain submerged when rotating and during the mordanting process.

11. Turn off the heat. Allow the goods to rest in the mordant bath overnight.

12. Squeeze excess mordant water from the goods and rinse with cool water. You can either proceed to dyeing the goods or store them wet in a plastic bag or bucket; if left in a cool, dark place, they will be fine up to 3 days. If you need to wait longer than 3 days, allow the goods to dry and store them until you are ready to dye.

Oak galls (15% WOG)

Symplocos powder
(50% WOG)

TOOLS

3-quart (2.8 L) or larger
stainless-steel pot with
lid (size dependent on
the amount of goods)

Scale

Measuring spoons

Liquid measuring cup

Stirring spoon or whisk

Thermometer

Tongs

Rubber gloves

Mortar and pestle

Fine-mesh strainer

Nonreactive bowl

CELLULOSE-BASED GOODS WITH TANNIN AND SYMPLOCOS OR OTHER ALUMINUM BIOACCUMULATORS

This recipe follows the same procedure as Mordanting Cellulose-Based Goods with Tannin and Aluminum Potassium Sulfate (page 222), but in place of the mineral aluminum potassium sulfate, it uses a plant that has the ability to accumulate aluminum from the soil, such as *Symplocos*. This recipe was adapted from the Bebali Foundation. For more information on using *Symplocos*, including on other fiber types, see their website (www.plantmordant.org).

You can use a different source of tannin, such as myrobalan or acorns (see page 172 for more information on tannins). If you would like to use a mordant more local than *Symplocos*, you can use another bioaccumulator of aluminum, such as camellia leaves, hydrangea leaves, or heuchera leaves. Crush dried leaves gently before introducing them to the mordant bath. The ability of a plant to accumulate aluminum from the soil is dependent on many factors; the best scenario is for you to understand your soil and how the plant interacts with the aluminum in the soil. Your local nursery is a great resource to learn more.

NOTE: To save time, you can begin the process of heating the *Symplocos* (steps 6–8) while applying tannin to your goods.

INSTRUCTIONS

1. Fill the pot with enough water so the goods are covered and can move freely once added to the pot.

2. Determine the amount of oak galls to use: Measure out an amount that is 15% of the weight of the goods. Grind the oak galls into a powder using a mortar and pestle. Add to the pot. Stir with a small whisk or spoon until mixed.

3. Heat to 180°F (82°C) and hold for 30 minutes. Add the scoured, wet goods to the pot. Increase the heat to 200°F (93°C) and hold at this temperature for 60 minutes, rotating the goods gently from the top to the bottom of the pot every 15 minutes. Make sure the goods remain submerged when rotating and during the heating process.

4. Turn off the heat. Allow the goods to cool.

5. Squeeze excess water from the goods. Do not rinse. Set aside the goods—on the counter is fine. Dispose of the oak gall bath: Pour the bath through the strainer to separate the oak galls from the water. Pour the water down the drain. Compost the oak galls.

6. Fill the pot with enough water so the goods are covered and can move freely once added to the pot.

7. Determine the amount of *Symplocos* to use: Measure out an amount that is 50% of the weight of the goods and add to the pot. Stir with a small whisk or spoon until mixed.

8. Heat to 212°F (100°C) and hold at this temperature for 60 minutes. Turn off the heat and allow the mordant bath to cool to 140°F (60°C).

9. If you are working with yarn, pour the bath through the strainer into the bowl to separate the *Symplocos* from the water. Return the liquid to the pot. Compost the *Symplocos*. If you are working with fabric, you can skip this step.

10. Add the goods that have had tannin applied to them to the pot, and cover.

11. Allow the goods to rest in the mordant bath overnight. Squeeze excess mordant water from the goods and rinse with lukewarm water. You can either proceed to dyeing the goods or store them wet in a plastic bag or bucket; if left in a cool, dark place, they will be fine up to 3 days. If you need to wait longer than 3 days, allow the goods to dry and store them until you are ready to dye.

USING SOY MILK

Soybeans contain a tremendous amount of protein, and dyes are attracted to protein, so the application of soy milk to yarn and fabric makes a viable way to connect color to cloth. For best results, dye cloth treated with soy milk within a week of applying the soy milk to the cloth. Note: Unlike the other mordant recipes listed in this section, it can be difficult to re-dye goods treated with soy milk at a later date. Soy milk is perishable: Either use the soy milk immediately upon making it, or plan to keep it refrigerated in an airtight container, like a mason jar, for up to 1 week.

When applying soy milk to the goods, try to apply it as evenly as possible, and avoid leaving the goods for long periods of time in one position, as this can cause spotting and permanent lines to form. If treating yarn, using a bowl or bucket is helpful. When treating fabric, we prefer something flat that nicely accommodates the size of the goods we are planning to treat. Baking, lasagna, or roasting pans with at least 2-inch (5-cm) high sides work well.

When working with soy milk as your mordant, the key is to acknowledge the thickness of the textile you are working with and create a viscosity of soy milk that will alter the hand of the goods as little as possible. The recipe below is for a medium viscosity of soy milk and is good for light- to medium-weight linens, quilting cottons, wools, and silk. If you would like to use soy milk for a thinner fabric, add more water; for thicker fabric, add less water. If you would like to create a color requiring indigo and another natural dye, apply the indigo first, then apply the soy milk, and then apply the dye.

NOTE: For this recipe, make sure the goods are dry before mordanting them with soy milk.

YIELD

**This recipe makes 7
cups (1.7 L) soy milk.**

MATERIALS

**½ cup (95 g) dried
soybeans**

TOOLS

Nonreactive bowl

**16 × 16-inch (40.5 ×
40.5-cm) piece of
lightweight linen cloth
for straining**

**Strainer or fine-mesh
strainer**

**6-cup (1.5-L) blender,
mortar and pestle,
or suribachi set**

**Baking pan with 2-inch
(5-cm) high sides, size
dependent on the size
of goods you plan to
treat with soy milk
(recommended)**

INSTRUCTIONS

1. Rehydrate the beans: Place the dried soybeans in a bowl and cover with 4 cups (960 ml) lukewarm water. (Using warm water makes the rehydration process go faster.) Soak for 8 to 12 hours. The beans are ready to use when softened and enlarged. Drain and dispose of the water.

2. Wet the lightweight linen cloth until saturated.

3. In the jar of the blender, combine the soybeans and 3½ cups (840 ml) water. Puree the beans and water until chopped finely.

4. Line the strainer with the wet linen cloth. Place the strainer over the bowl. Pour the contents of the blender into the strainer, pressing on the solids to strain out the soy milk. Gather up the cloth and squeeze to extract as much soy milk as possible. Set the soy milk aside.

5. Place the chopped soybeans back in the blender and repeat steps 3 and 4 to create another batch.

6. Combine both batches. The liquid should be the consistency of non-fat milk. Either store the soy milk in an airtight container and refrigerate or proceed to treating your goods with it. Anytime you are not using the soy milk, keep it in an airtight container and refrigerate.

7. To treat the goods with the soy milk, pour the soy milk into the baking pan or vessel of your choice. Fully submerge the scoured, dry goods into the soy milk. Make sure the goods are fully coated by lifting the goods in and out of the soy milk, making sure if you are treating fabric that the soy milk covers the fabric in all directions and thoroughly coats all the threads. If you do not do this, the goods may dye unevenly. Once the goods are thoroughly coated, allow to rest for at least 3 hours but no longer than 24 hours, whatever is most convenient for you. Remove the goods, using your fingers to smooth and squeeze out excess soy milk into the baking pan. Hang on a clothesline or drying rack over a drop cloth and dry thoroughly.

8. Once dry, fully submerge in the soy milk again, making sure the goods are fully wet and well coated as you did in step 7. Though this time, once the goods are saturated with soy milk, immediately remove the goods and hang to dry.

9. Repeat step 8 one more time, completing the process. Your goods are now ready to dye.

two basic methods of dyeing

One-pot dyeing and mason-jar dyeing are two basic methods used throughout the book. The method you choose will be dependent upon the size of goods you want to dye. Refer to the shade cards to see examples of what kinds of dyestuffs can be used, as well as to understand the relationship between how much dye and water to use and the weight of goods you plan to dye and the color that can be achieved. Before dyeing, goods must be scoured (page 217) and mordanted (page 219) according to their fiber type.

MATERIALS

Dyestuff of your choosing, finely chopped

Scoured and mordanted goods

TOOLS

Kitchen scale

3-quart (2.8-L) or larger stainless steel pot with lid (size dependent on the amount of goods)

Liquid measuring cup

Measuring spoons

Sieve (optional)

Tongs

Timer

Thermometer

Rubber gloves

ONE-POT DYEING

One-pot dyeing can be used for small pieces of fabric and yarn but can also be used for large projects like clothing, and for everything in between. This style of dyeing is recommended when working with leathery leaves and barks, as the cooking time can be 2–3 hours to fully extract the color. During the longer dyeing process, the water may need to be replenished, and it is easier to do so with this method, especially when working with wool, which is prone to felting.

INSTRUCTIONS

1. Add the dyestuff and water to the pot. Simmer for 15 minutes.

2. Add the goods to the pot. Heat, covered, to 160°F (71°C) for silk, 190°F (88°C) for wool, and 200°F (93°C) for cellulose-based fibers. Adjust the heat to hold at this temperature for an additional 60 minutes, using the tongs to gently turn the goods every 15 minutes.

3. Turn off the heat. Let the goods cool in the water.

4. Wash the goods (page 236) and allow to dry.

MASON JAR DYEING (SMALL-BATCH DYEING)

This is a great way of dyeing, because you can create many colors at once and really build a beautiful palette to work with when making textiles. Place a different dyestuff in each jar. Or combines dyes in each jar! The possibilities are endless. This method of dyeing is a wonderful way to explore the color potential of the plants in your neighborhood and saves a tremendous amount of time over running one pot at a time.

This method can be used to dye small amounts of goods only. The quart (liter)-size mason jar can fit up to 50 g of yarn and approximately 25 g of dye. If you are working

with fabric and would like an even color, use small amounts of fabric and make sure they are not folded or creased when placed in the jar. If you are OK with uneven color, pack as much fabric and dye as you can fit into the jar. If you are sampling and using very tiny amounts of yarn or fabric, jam jars work well, too! If you would like to dye a larger amount of goods or use more dyestuff, the one-pot method of dyeing is your best choice. The pot we list below is what we use for our tests, but for this method you can use any size pot, as long as it is tall enough to accommodate the mason jars you are using.

MATERIALS

Dyestuff of your choosing, finely chopped

50 g or less yarn, scoured and mordanted

TOOLS

7 quart-size (liter-size) mason jars with lids

20-quart (18.9-L) stainless steel pot (12-inch/ 30.5-cm diameter, 10½ inches/26.5 cm tall) or enamel canning pot

Washcloth

Tongs

Thermometer

Liquid measuring cup

Painter's tape and Sharpie (recommended)

Rubber gloves

INSTRUCTIONS

1. Add 3½ cups (840 ml) water to each jar. If you would like more concentrated color and are dyeing very small amounts of yarn, use less water.

2. Add dyestuff to each jar. Record what is in each jar by using the Sharpie to write on the painter's tape. Adhere the label to each jar of dye.

3. Place the washcloth on the bottom of the pot. (This helps the jars from rattling too much when heating, which can lead to the jars breaking.)

4. Add the jars to the pot in a single layer, placing them on top of the washcloth.

5. Add 8 cups (2 L) water to the pot. The water in the pot should come three-quarters of the way up the jars. Cover the jars with the flat mason jar lids (lids only, not the threaded part).

6. Heat, covered, until the dyebaths in the jars reach 160°F (71°C) for silk, 190°F (88°C) for wool, and 200°F (93°C) for cellulose-based fibers. Hold at this temperature for 10 minutes.

7. Carefully add skeins of yarn to each jar (wear rubber gloves and use tongs), then replace the lids.

8. After 15 minutes, wearing rubber gloves and a pair of tongs to protect your hands and arms from hot steam, carefully rotate the skeins in the jars. Replace the lids and heat for an additional 60 minutes. Keep an eye on the water in the jars, making sure the level of the water stays similar to what you began with and does not evaporate completely. Keeping the jars covered with the lids will avoid this from happening. If the water level in the jar drops significantly, remove the goods from the jar, add more water, return the goods to the jar, and continue heating.

9. Turn off the heat and allow the goods to cool in the jars in the pot.

10. Once cooled, lift out the jars. Squeeze excess dye from the yarn, then wash the skeins (page 236).

recipes for widening the spectrum

SHIFTING PH

About pH

pH is a scale used to measure how acidic or alkaline a water-based solution is: 0–6 is acidic (also described as low pH), 7 is neutral, and 8–14 is alkaline (also described as a high pH or basic).

Color

Some natural dyes can be especially responsive to pH, affecting the resulting color. It is common practice in natural dyeing to raise and lower pH in order to achieve a wider range of color. Moreover, when dyeing with indigo, in order for the dye to adhere to the fiber, it is necessary in almost every case to raise the pH of the dyebath. So understanding how pH works and how it affects fibers is an important part of being a natural dyer. Notating the pH used while processing your goods in your dye journal, and recording all agents used to alter the pH (page 231), will help you understand your color results and allow you to create the widest range of color from locally sourced dyes.

Measuring pH

To measure pH, you can use either pH strips or a pH meter. To use a pH strip, submerge the strip in the liquid you wish to test. When testing the pH of a dyebath, submerge only the very tip of the strip, and allow the liquid to wick up the strip; this will make it easier to accurately identify the strip's color. Watch the strip change color, and compare it to the scale found on the packaging. To use a pH meter, make sure it is properly calibrated by following the manufacturer's instructions. Lower the tip of the meter into your solution, stir gently, and wait for the reading to stabilize. Always store your pH meter in the proper storage solution, and recalibrate often to get accurate readings.

Note that pH is temperature dependent, so make sure to record your temperature as well as pH. When you want to compare results with a previous test, make sure to take your pH reading at the same temperature.

How pH Affects Fiber Types

Animal-based fibers are easily impacted by pH. In alkaline environments, protein-based fibers can be damaged when encountering pH 10 and above, especially in combination with heat. However, animal-based fibers respond positively to acidic environments; for example, the addition of cream of tartar during the mordanting process can make them feel softer and allows the fiber to take up more of the dye, resulting in more saturated, colorfast hues.

Cellulose-based fibers can be damaged by highly acidic conditions. Unlike animal-based fibers, they are less sensitive to, and in fact can sometimes benefit from, alkaline environments. For example, cellulose-based fibers are scoured in with soda ash; the alkalinity helps removes excess wax in the fibers, allowing the fibers to connect more thoroughly with mordant and dye.

Silk falls in between animal- and cellulose-based fibers; process silk fibers within the pH range of 6–8 for the best results—with the exception of indigo, where there is a required pH of 10–10.8.

When working within conditions that can negatively impact the fibers, keep fibers in such conditions only as long as necessary to achieve the effect you are looking for.

Testing Dye to See If It Is Impacted by Shifts in pH

The relationship between pH and natural dyes can be quite complex and varied, but here is a simple and quick way to approach this topic to determine if a dyestuff may be affected by pH. We recommend using wool to test dyes, as it is very responsive to shifts in pH, making it the easiest medium to see if and how the color has changed.

1. Scour (page 217), mordant with aluminum potassium sulfate (page 219), and dye a skein of yarn or small piece of fabric in pH-neutral water using either the one-pot or mason jar method of dyeing (page 227).

2. Create a small acidic bath by squeezing lemon or lime juice into a cup and a small basic bath by making a heated bath with limestone solution (page 232).

3. Cut two small swatches from your dyed yarn or fabric, and dip one in the acidic bath and one in the alkaline bath. Compare your results to the original sample. If you see a shift, then yes, the dye you are using is impacted by shifts in pH. If you do not see a shift, the dye is not responsive to shifts in pH or at least does not respond as readily. You can either keep going and try other dyes to see if they respond to shifts in pH or continue to experiment by trying the methods on the following pages, such as raising the pH during dye extraction (page 232).

NOTE: Sometimes colorfastness is affected by shifting the pH. Consider testing the colorfastness, as described on page 231.

Agents Affecting pH

Agents in this book used to shift pH include:
- Lime juice, lemon juice, cream of tartar, vinegar— to decrease pH/create an acidic environment
- Baking soda, chalk, limestone, hardwood ash— to increase pH/create an alkaline environment

Though pH is a scale, and reading that scale can seem simple enough, the actual properties of what causes color to change can be quite complex. While the agents may result in the same pH, their chemical properties may be different and may impact the color differently.

Sometimes agents can be exchanged with one another and sometimes not. Look to the recipes in this book to guide you. As you practice, experiment, and record your findings, you will continue to learn the nuances and relationships among pH, the agents used to raise and lower the pH, the temperature of the solution, the dyes, and the fiber.

METHODS OF RAISING AND LOWERING PH

The pH can be shifted in the mordanting process, the dyeing process, and after the dyeing process by wetting goods in solutions where the pH has been altered.

The step in which you shift the pH in combination with the agent, the dye, and the fiber will impact the final color.

Shifting the pH in the Mordanting Process

There are two recipes that especially affect the pH in the mordanting process:

1. Mordanting Wool with Aluminum Potassium Sulfate and Cream of Tartar (page 220)—using this method will impact colors made by any dye sensitive to acidic environments. This includes cochineal, purple turns to pink, and madder, red turns to orange.

2. Mordanting Cellulose-Based Goods with Aluminum Acetate and Chalk (page 221)—chalk is used to remove extra mordant from the cloth, to create a more even color, and chalk lends itself to creating richer colors. Chalk creates a more basic environment, so dyes that respond to alkalinity will shift due to the presence of chalk.

Lowering the pH in the Dyeing Process

The pH can be lowered in the dyebath to create more shades using cream of tartar or lemon or lime juice. There are two ways to do this:

1. Add ½ cup (120 ml) lemon or lime juice per 3 cups (720 ml) of water to the dyebath.   OR

2. Add 10% WOG cream of tartar to the dyebath. Continue to follow the instructions for dyeing following the One-Pot or Mason Jar method of dyeing (page 227).

Raising the pH During Dye Extraction and Lowering for Dyeing

Sometimes it is possible to extract more saturated, interesting colors (beyond yellow and brown) by raising the pH during the dye extraction process. However, especially if you are working with protein-based fibers, it is important to lower the pH before dyeing, because the combination of heat and high pH can make the fibers feel rough and can damage the fibers.

1. Extract color first: Add water, chopped dyestuff, and ⅛ teaspoon baking soda per 1 cup (240 ml) water to pot. Heat, covered, until the dyebath reaches 170°F (76°C). Adjust the heat to hold at this temperature for an additional 60 minutes.

2. Strain the dyestuff out. Lower the pH to 7 by adding ⅓ teaspoon lemon juice per 1 cup (240 ml) water.

3. Add the scoured and mordanted goods. Heat, covered, until the dyebath reaches 160°F (71°C) for silk, 190°F (88°C) for wool, and 200°F (93°C) for cellulose-based fibers. Adjust the heat, and hold at this temperature for an additional 60 minutes.

4. Turn off the heat, and allow the goods to cool in the pot.

5. Once cooled, squeeze excess dye from the yarn, then wash the skeins (page 236).

MATERIALS

16 g baking soda (for baking soda solution)
OR
6 g limestone (for limestone solution)

TOOLS

1-quart (1-L) mason jar with a lid

Kitchen scale

Measuring cup

Stirrer, such as a whisk or spoon

Raising the pH After Dyeing

Similar to iron water (page 234), the color of the goods can be shifted after the dyeing process. Creating high pH baths, and introducing goods to these baths after dyeing as a second step, gives you the greatest control over the final color and reduces the possibility of ruining the fibers. Baking soda is slightly less alkaline then limestone. If testing a dye to see if it is responsive to shifts in pH, it is worthwhile to try a small sample in each and compare the results. The solutions are made the same and can either be used at room temperature or heated.

INSTRUCTIONS TO CREATE SOLUTIONS

Fill the jar with 4 cups (960 ml) of 120°F (49°C) water and then add the applicable material in the quantity listed. Stir with a small whisk or spoon until dissolved. The solutions can be stored indefinitely at room temperature. Use the solutions as directed in the recipes throughout the book.

MATERIALS

Baking soda solution
(weaker) or limestone
solution (stronger)

TOOLS

Butcher tray
Drying rack

ROOM-TEMPERATURE BATH

Used during the batik process (page 174) and the persimmon dyeing process (page 145).

INSTRUCTIONS

1. Pour ½ cup (120 ml) of the solution into a butcher's tray. Place the dry goods into the solution for 5 minutes, making sure they are fully submerged and saturated.

2. Remove the goods from the solution, rinse immediately, and hang to dry.

MATERIALS

Baking soda solution
(weaker) or limestone
solution (stronger)

TOOLS

3-quart (2.8-L) or larger
stainless steel pot with
lid (size dependent on
the amount of goods)

Thermometer

Tongs

Rubber gloves

HEATED BATH

Used to shift color on wool on the Icelandic shade card (page 27) and the Mexico shade cards (pages 78–85).

INSTRUCTIONS

1. Fill the pot with enough solution so the dyed goods are covered and can move freely when they are added to the pot.

2. Bring the solution in the pot to 100°F (38°C), then turn off the heat.

3. Add the dyed goods, stir to wet thoroughly, then remove immediately.

4. If you want a darker color, dip again briefly for 1 minute (or less). Remove and wash (page 236).

PH AND ITS IMPACT ON FIBERS AND COLORS

These examples show the impact of pH upon color on various fiber types:

• The pH was raised during the extraction of the dyes, and lowered to dye the goods for avocado pits, dock roots, and rhubarb roots in the Iceland chapter (pages 14–51).

• To create pinks, reds, and purples using cochineal in the Mexico chapter, the pH was lowered during the mordanting process and the dyeing process, and raised after dyeing (pages 232–233).

• When making concentrates to create rich colors upon cellulose-based fibers in the Indonesia chapter, the pH is raised using baking soda during the dye extraction process (page 232).

• To shift persimmon-dyed goods from rust-colored to brown, after the goods have been dyed, they are submerged in a baking soda solution.

• The pH is raised in the indigo recipes listed in Chapters 2, 3, and 4.

IRON WATER

Iron water is the combination of either scrap metal or granular iron (ferrous sulfate) and water. It is an optional step in the dyeing process. Goods, once dyed, are dipped into the bath to create darker, moodier shades: pinks shift to purples; yellows shift to green; tannin-rich dyes shift to dark brown, gray, and black. This is an easy way to widen your palette using local plants and to increase colorfastness. Refer to the shade cards featuring iron to understand how iron impacts dyed color.

A note of caution: Iron will leave a permanent mark anytime it comes into contact with naturally dyed goods (or goods that are going to be naturally dyed). To avoid unintended dark spots on your dyed goods, thoroughly wash the tools used in the process of applying iron water. If using iron often, it is worthwhile to have a set of tools used only for the application of it.

Iron—especially in combination with heat—can have a negative effect on the texture and hand of the goods. When used in large amounts or over medium to high heat, iron can destroy both protein- and cellulose-based fibers. The key is to use as little iron as possible to achieve the desired color and to use low heat in the application of iron.

Protein-based fibers are especially prone to damage during the iron application process. Iron can make the texture feel rough and the fibers feel brittle. Submerge the goods in the iron solution only as long as needed to achieve the desired color, and keep the heat low.

We recommend dyeing your goods first, and then applying iron water as a second step to have the greatest control over the final color and to reduce the possibility of ruining the fibers. If you are looking to create iron water through found and foraged objects, use the recipe using scrap iron. If you desire having a firm grasp and understanding of how you achieve particular dyed color, use the recipes that call for ferrous sulfate, as it can easily be measured. All the iron solutions listed can keep indefinitely if stored in an airtight container at room temperature.

MATERIALS

Scrap iron, such as a railroad spike

Distilled white vinegar

TOOLS

Large container (big enough for scrap iron)

Bottle or jar to hold iron water mixture (a mason jar works nicely)

Measuring cup

3-quart (2.8-L) or larger stainless steel pot with lid (size dependent on amount of goods)

Scrap Iron Solution

OK to use with protein-based and cellulose-based fibers with heat.

INSTRUCTIONS

1. Collect rusty scrap iron. Add the iron to the container and pour enough vinegar in so the iron is covered.

2. Let it sit for a few weeks; the liquid will turn a rusty orange color. The stronger the color, the better.

3. To use the solution, combine equal parts water and scrap iron solution to fill the pot with enough liquid to let the goods float freely.

4. Bring the water in the pot to 130°F (54°C). Turn off the heat.

5. Add the goods and turn constantly. Leave in the bath for as little as 5 minutes; if a darker shade is desired, leave for 15 to 20 minutes. Pull the goods from the pot, squeeze excess iron water from the goods, and wash (page 236).

MATERIALS

Ferrous sulfate

Dyed goods

TOOLS

3-quart (2.8-L) or larger
stainless steel pot with
lid (size dependent on
the amount of goods)

Kitchen scale

Liquid measuring cup

Stirrer, such as a
whisk or spoon

Thermometer

Tongs

Rubber gloves

Light Iron Water Solution Using Ferrous Sulfate

OK to use with protein-based and cellulose-based fibers with heat.

INSTRUCTIONS

1. Fill the pot with enough water so the goods are covered and can move freely once added to the pot. Note the amount of water added to the pot.

2. Add 3 g of ferrous sulfate if using protein-based fibers or 5 g of ferrous sulfate if using cellulose-based fibers for every 4 cups (960 ml) water, and stir until dissolved completely.

3. Bring the water in the pot to 130°F (54°C). Turn off the heat.

4. Add the dyed goods and rotate constantly, keeping them submerged. After 15 minutes, pull the goods from the pot, squeeze excess iron water from the goods, and set aside until cooled. Proceed to washing (page 236).

MATERIALS

50 g ferrous sulfate

TOOLS

1-quart (1-L) mason
jar with a lid

Kitchen scale

Liquid measuring cup

Stirrer, such as a
whisk or spoon

Thermometer

Butcher tray, 7½ × 11
inches (19 × 28 cm); for
larger pieces a rimmed
baking sheet works well

Rubber gloves
(recommended)

Clothesline and
clothespins

Drop cloth if
dyeing indoors

Concentrated Iron Water Solution Using Ferrous Sulfate

When applying dye without heat, as done in the batik process (page 174) and the washes used for the Aerial View Pillow project (page 188), even if you have pre-mordanted the fabric, it is necessary to set the dye using either a solution of aluminum potassium sulfate (page 174) or concentrated iron water.

NOTE: Use this only with cellulose-based fibers without heat. Do not use this solution with protein-based fibers.

INSTRUCTIONS

1. Fill the jar with 4 cups (960 ml) 120°F (49°C) water and then add 50 g ferrous sulfate. Stir with a small whisk or spoon until dissolved.

2. To use, pour the iron solution into the butcher tray. Soak the dry goods in the solution for 5 minutes, making sure they are fully submerged and saturated by the solution.

3. Remove the goods from the solution, rinse immediately with cool water, and hang the goods to drip-dry over a drop cloth.

washing and cleanup

After your goods have been dyed, they need to be washed to remove any excess dye. If you have a laundry room with a utility sink, wonderful: It's a great place to wash out your newly dyed fabrics and projects. Use your utility sink to wash the dyed materials and use your washer to spin out extra water. If you don't have this option, wash your goods in your bathtub or sink. If you're washing different batches of color at the same time, start with lightest colors first and then move to darker colors to save water. You can use the graywater, the water left over from rinsing, from the lighter colors to wash the darker colors.

MATERIALS

pH-neutral soap—or a gentle, biodegradable dishwashing detergent like Ecover

TOOLS

11-quart (10.4-L) buckets

Large sink or bathtub

Drying rack or clothesline

Drop cloth

Washing Protein-Based Fibers

Because protein-based fibers are prone to felting, it is best to wash yarn and fabric by hand. If indigo was used, see page 237.

INSTRUCTIONS

1. Place the bucket in a bathtub or large sink. Fill it three-quarters full with lukewarm water. Add a dab of dishwashing detergent to each bucket; it will wash out during this process without any additional rinsing.

2. Work with one piece of dyed goods at a time. Immerse the room-temperature dyed goods into the water. Pull the material out, pressing it flat between your hands to squeeze out the water into the sink or tub—not back into the bucket. Avoid wringing or stretching the goods. If the water becomes too saturated with dye or you use all of the water in the bucket, replace it following the instructions in step 1.

3. Repeat step 2 until the water pressed out of the goods runs clear.

4. Dry the goods on a drying rack or clothesline over a drop cloth.

MATERIALS

pH-neutral, mild laundry detergent such as Seventh Generation

TOOLS

Washing machine

Dryer, drying rack, or clothesline

Drop cloth (optional)

Washing Cellulose-Based Fibers

Because cellulose-based fibers aren't prone to felting like protein-based fibers, a washing machine is an easy option for washing fabric. However, you should wash yarn by hand in the same fashion as described for protein-based fibers, because it will tangle in the washing machine.

INSTRUCTIONS

1. Wash fabric in cool water in the washing machine for a full wash cycle, using 1 teaspoon (4 g) mild detergent or soda ash per 100 g of goods. If the fabric has been dyed a dark shade, wash it on an extra-long cycle, with an extra rinse cycle if possible.

2. Dry the fabric in the dryer if you prefer, but air-drying it in a shaded place on a drying rack or clothesline over a drop cloth will extend the life of the color.

MATERIALS

Vinegar

TOOLS

Bucket large enough to hold the goods and allow them to move freely in water

Neutralizing and Washing Indigo-Dyed Goods

After dyeing goods in an indigo vat with a high pH, it is important to neutralize the goods by placing them in an acidic bath before washing them. This is especially important for protein-based fibers, because they are most sensitive to alkaline environments.

INSTRUCTIONS

1. When you are done indigo dyeing, place the goods in cold water immediately.

2. Rinse your goods in several changes of water to remove excess dye. Never allow the goods to dry or they can become stained.

3. Prepare a neutralization bath by adding cool water (110°F/43°C) to a bucket (enough to cover your goods and allow them to move freely). Add about 1 tablespoon (15 g) vinegar for every gallon (4 L) of water.

4. Add your goods to the neutralization bath and submerge. Allow to rest overnight.

5. If washing protein-based fibers or cellulose-based yarns, see the protein-based fiber-washing instructions on page 236. If washing cellulose-based fabric, see the cellulose-based fiber-washing instructions.

Caring for Naturally Dyed Goods

Naturally dyed cellulose-based goods are more prone to fading than protein-based goods. Only wash when necessary, using the smallest amount of detergent required. Never use detergent with bleach on any of your naturally dyed goods. Dry in the shade.

Cleanup Practices

All the scour, mordant, and dyebaths used in this book can be safely disposed of down the drain. They are nontoxic.

To dispose of a fresh indigo leaf dyebath, liquid siphoned off of an indigo extraction, or an indigo vat made with fructose and limestone, pour the vat down the drain. If you find yourself doing this frequently, be kind to your pipes and add lemon juice to the vat to neutralize it first. To dispose of an exhausted fermented indigo vat, neutralize it using vinegar, then with the water running, pour the dyebath down the drain. Add the composted indigo leaves sitting at the bottom of the vat to your compost.

bibliography

All That the Rain Promises and More by David Arora

The Art and Craft of Natural Dyeing: Traditional Recipes for Modern Use by J. N. Liles

The Art and Science of Natural Dyes: Principles, Experiments, and Results by Joy Boutrup and Catharine Ellis

Awa Natural Indigo by Miyoko Kawahito

Batik Yogya & Solo: Techniques, Motifs, & Patterns by Sri Soedewi Samsi

Botanical Colour at Your Fingertips by Rebecca Desnos

Braiding Sweetgrass by Robin Wall Kimmerer

The Chemistry of Plants: Perfumes, Pigments, and Poisons by Margareta Séquin

The Dye Plants of Awa: The Color of Tears by Seiko Akiyama

El Caracol Purpura: Una Tradición Milenaria en Oaxaca by Secretaría de Educación Pública

Farming While Black: Soul Fire Farm's Practical Guide to Liberation on the Land by Leah Penniman

The Illustrated Book of Dye Plants 1, 2, & 3 by Seiju Yamazaki

Indigo: From Seed to Dye by Dorothy Miller

Japanese Indigo by Bryan Whitehead (Maiwa Textile Symposium 2013)

Kakishibu: Traditional Persimmon Dye of Japan by Chris Conrad

Katazome Manual by Maiwa Handpaints

Katazome: Japanese Paste-Resist: Dyeing for Contemporary Use by Kumiko Murashima

The Modern Natural Dyer by Kristine Vejar

Mottainai: The Fabric of Life, Lessons in Frugality from Traditional Japan by Gallery Kei and Sri Threads

Mushrooms for Dyes, Paper, Pigments & Myco-Stix by Miriam C. Rice

Natural Color: Vibrant Plant Dye Projects for Your Home and Wardrobe by Sasha Duerr

Natural Dyes: Sources, Traditions, Technology and Science by Dominique Cardon

The Plant Mordant Project: Natural Dyes 100% from Plants, Using Symplocos as a Mordant on Protein and Cellulose Fibers by Sara Goodman, Michel Garcia, and William Ingram

Plants of Iceland: Traditional Uses and Folklore by Guðrún Bjarnadóttir (author) and Jóhann Óli Hilmarsson (photographs)

The Rainbow Beneath My Feet: A Mushroom Dyer's Field Guide by Alan E. Bessette and Arleen Rainis Bessette

Salvation through Soy by John Marshall

Singing the Blues by John Marshall

Tintes Naturales Mexicanos: Su Aplicación en Algodón, Henequen y Lana by Leticia Arroyo Ortiz

Tsugaru Indigo, general editor Kitahara Haruo

resources

Dyes, yarn, fabric, and blanks featured in this book can be found at:

A Verb for Keeping Warm
6328 San Pablo Avenue
Oakland, CA 94608
www.averbforkeepingwarm
.com

Most of the common tools and materials used in this book can be found at your hardware store or kitchen shop. For specific materials used throughout the book, contact the following companies:

Blue Sky Alpaca (Yarn in Zigzag Ikat Woven Bracelet)
www.blueskyfibers.com

Botanical Colors (Mordant and dyes)
www.botanicalcolors.com

Cocoknits (4-corner bag in Persimmon-Dyed Tote)
www.cocoknits.com

Dharma Trading Company (Batik supplies, mordant and natural dye supplier)
www.dharmatrading.com

Earth Hues (Mordant and natural dye supplier)
www.earthues.com

Fog Linen (Scarf used in Skyline Scarf)
www.shop-foglinen.com

John Marshall (Books and dyeing supplies)
www.johnmarshall.to

Lopi (Yarn used in Basalt Knit Hat)
www.istex.is

Maiwa (Mordant and natural dye supplier)
www.maiwa.com

Michel Garcia (Natural dye researcher and teacher)
www.michelgarcia.fr/
www.naturaldyeworkshop.com

Schacht Spindle Company (Weaving supplies)
www.schachtspindle.com

acknowledgments

We thank the Earth for the gifts we have received: beauty, food, textiles, and color.

We acknowledge that the place where we abide, and from where we have drawn color, named Oakland, is home to the Muwekma Ohlone, who have lived here since time immemorial, and continue to live and thrive here. We stand with the Muwekma Ohlone people and respect their indigenous sovereignty in this beloved, ancient place.

Thank you to those who are in this book and those who consulted, translated, and guided our journey:

ICELAND: Guðrún Bjarnadóttir, Hélène Magnússon, Jóhanna E. Pálmadóttir, and Caitlin Ffrench.

MEXICO: Demetrio Bautista Lazo and Maribel Alavez Vasquez, Cristina and Agustina Velasco, Manuel Loera Fernández, Moisés Martinez Velasco and Gladys Garcia Flores, Habacuc Avendaño Luis, Rafael Avendaño Lopez, Eric Mindling, and Josephine Rodriguez.

JAPAN: Kakuo Kaji, Ken Yuki, Yuya Miura, Takdashi Kozono, Kazuma Osuka, Kyoko Nishimoto, Gwen Chan Mi Min, Kei Kawasaki, Masaaki Aoki, Kazue Yasui, Meri Tanaka Jemison, Tokuko Ochiai, Mari Hirayama, Yuko Fujishima, Takako Ueki, Jody Alexander, and Akiko Tokoro.

INDONESIA: Bu Dalmini and the members of Batik Tulis Kebon Indah collective, Daniel Grundlach, Saiful Nurudin, I Made Maduarta (Pung), William Ingram, Jean Howe, Wayan Mudana, Ni Wayan Juniani, Ahmad Hafid Zain Efendi, Sayid and Faisal, Gatot Kartono, David Mendoza, and Natalie Miller.

Thank you to our natural dyeing community, mentors, and friends: Janine Bajus, Dorothy Beebee, Rebecca Burgess, Sasha Duerr, Shiree Dyson, Melanie Falick, Fibershed, India Flint, Aboubakar Fofana, Sally Fox, Michel Garcia, Aleishall Girard Maxon, Christopher Hall, Kori Hargreaves, Kathy Hattori, Jen Hewett, Stephen Houghton, Dustin Kahn, Lora Kinkade, Deepa Natarajan, New Family Farm, Samin Nosrat, Nancy Ottenstein, Clara Parkes, Mary Pettis-Sarley, Judi Pettite, Rowland Ricketts, Katrina Rodabaugh, Nikhil Rode, Zoe-hateehc Scheffy, Brooke Sinnes, Sonoma Mycological Association, Adele Stafford, Yoshiko Wada, Julie Weisenberger, Bryan Whitehead, Craig Wilkinson, Michele Wipplinger, and those who volunteered to sort *Persicaria tinctoria* used for the research in this book.

We thank Sarah, our co-author, for offering her gifts of support, math, science, curiosity, and love of natural dyeing. We thank Rachel Marcotte for her support of this book, of Verb, and for our many natural dyeing research projects. Thank you to the community at Verb, the team of people who work there and those who come to Verb to make, who allowed us the great privilege to travel, teach, and research.

We thank the incredible team of women who brought this book to life: Meredith A. Clark, Sara Remington, Alessandra Mortola, Brooke Reynolds, Elysa Weitala, Jane Grimley, and Callan Porter-Romero.

We would like to thank our families and friends for their continued love and support. Thank you to Gilbert Rodriguez for sharing your love of plants and gardening. Thank you to Michelle Brauner, who made the trip to California many times, for many days, to watch our two beloved doggies while we were gone. We love you very much.

And thank you, reader—with your support, you are keeping the practice of natural dyeing alive.